A HISTORY OF
GREEK AND ROMAN PHILOSOPHY

A HISTORY OF GREEK AND ROMAN PHILOSOPHY

by

JOHN HACKNEY

The King's Library

PHILOSOPHICAL LIBRARY

New York

CONTENTS

	Preface	vii
1.	Introduction	1
2.	Ionian Beginnings	5
3.	Thales, Anaximander, Anaximenes, Pythagorean Thought	9
4.	Heraclitus	16
5.	The First Eleatics	20
6.	Zeno	24
7.	Empedocles	27
8.	Anaxagoras	29
9.	Atoms and Philosophy	32
10.	Before Socrates	35
11.	Sophism	38
12.	Protagoras	41
13.	Other Sophists	44
14.	The Entrance of Socrates	47
15.	Other Followers of Socrates	56
16.	Democritus	61
17.	Plato	63
18.	Plato and Knowledge	70
19.	Plato and Ideas	78
20.	Plato's Psychology	93
21.	Plato and Morals	98
22.	State and Statesmanship	102
23.	Physics	112
24.	Plato and Artistry	116
25.	The Academy After Plato	121
26.	Life and Works of Aristotle	123
27.	Logic	130
28.	Aristotle and Metaphysics	136
29.	Aristotle and Psychology	157
30.	Ethics	164
31.	Aristotle and Politics	175
32.	Aesthetics	181

33.	A Comparison	188
34.	Advance	193
35.	The Stoics	197
36.	Epicurus and His School	204
37.	The Sceptics and Others	210
38.	The Later Stoics	215
39.	Stoics (Continued)	219
40.	Cynicism and Other Developments	224
41.	A Pythagorean Revival	229
42.	Renewed Platonism	232
43.	Philosophy, Greeks and Jews	236
44.	Plotinus, Porphyry and Others	240
45.	Neo-Platonism	248
46.	Recollection	254

PREFACE

This history of ancient philosophy is intended to give average people of average education an idea of how the principles of thought which dominate our civilization today came to be. It is not intended for the scholar, and it is certain that any student of philosophy or history would find many things lacking in this work. Of them we ask indulgence.

Various notes of thanks are due in the preparation of this book. First of all to Almighty God who has given me everything of value I possess. Then my dear parents, my father an avid reader, and my mother who at great cost to herself equipped me with the sort of education that makes a mind turn to such things as philosophy and history. Next to the Very Reverend Father Casimir Walsh, O. F. M. who directed and encouraged me to put my findings into writing. To Miss Bernadette Nagly (now Mrs. Cyril Bates) who typed out a lengthy manuscript from atrocious handwriting, with unparalleled devotion and patience. Also that vast body of scholars, past and present, to whom I owe much. Without them this book could not have been written.

Even if one person puts this volume down better informed at the end than he was at the beginning, the task of writing will have been well worth while.

An attempt has been made to keep Greek and Latin phrases to a minimum, for it is generally irritating to the person unversed in these languages to be faced with long tracts of wisdom in an unintelligible tongue.

Finally, I accept all responsibility for all imperfections to be found in the following pages.

A HISTORY OF
GREEK AND ROMAN PHILOSOPHY

CHAPTER 1

INTRODUCTION

If we look at a fine building, one thing that impresses itself upon us is the dependence of one part of the structure upon the part beneath or beside it. The parts give a strength, meaning and unity to the edifice which otherwise would be lacking. Let us carry this hypothesis a step further. The thoughts I possess today did not come from just anywhere, however imperfect they really are now. No, they depend for their existence upon what has gone before in my mind. So it is with every person in a greater or lesser degree, according to their natural capacity. If then, there are a number or society of people thinking, then their thought will depend upon what that society has thought in years gone by. Now, if man thinks it will be upon lines which, he assumes, will answer his never ending question of "why?" so the particular data to answer this question is then dependent upon what has gone before.

It is necessary in the light of this to consider philosophy. But there are in philosophy various thinkers propounding various views. Plato and Aristotle, for example, two of the world's greatest thinkers, did not think alike, and even then, they cannot be understood without reference to Heraclitus, Parmenides and the Pythagoreans. So to see each thinker in his true perspective, it is necessary to study the philosophical background against which he worked. This will lead us to the History of Philosophy. The result of this would seem to be merely a collection of different points of view. But it does not take this form; neither does it take the form of a spiral, or of continued progress. Hegel said in speculation there are three stages, viz. viewpoint, objections or opposites and synthesis. But an historian cannot be expected to take a set scheme, and fit the pieces of his history within that framework. Hegel understood the various philosophical systems as a natural succession of progress in development. Such a position could only occur if the thinking of man is universal in spirit. But it is not. A limit must be set upon the capacity of each thinker, and this will depend upon his

1

education, mental outfit, temperament, and so forth. Not only this, but it will depend on the philosophical systems that have gone before. An example can be taken from practically our own times. Fichte thought he was following on where Kant left off; certainly there is a common likeness, but Fichte was in no way obliged to follow Kant. Anybody following Kant could quite easily revise this thinker's ideas, and so the newcomer would have to deny the conclusions Kant accepted unconditionally from Hume.

Again, Hegel says that a final philosophy is the result of development and is truth in its highest form.

But this leads to difficulties. For how is one to assert that the body of truth being dealt with at a particular time represents a final phase of development? Could one say, for example, when studying the ninth century, that John Scotus Erigena represents the truth in its highest form? Modern scholars have pointed out that the progress of philosophy is really more a curve than a straight line.

What then does the History of Philosophy reveal? It shows what was said at the beginning. Man wants to know "why?" And when he knows this, he has Truth; the Absolute Truth, Absolute Being, the term "absolute" is most important here. In a word then, it reveals man's search for God. The fabric which is gradually unfolded in this search will draw the veil aside of doctrines far removed from the truth; yet sympathy and understanding must be exercised towards these thinkers for, as St. Thomas Aquinas reminded us, even a mistake is useful to throw the truth up in relief.

The philosophy of St. Thomas represents the highest pinnacle man has climbed in his efforts to arrive at Absolute Truth. But this statement *can* be misunderstood. The philosophy of St. Thomas is not something hidden in the recesses of the thirteenth century, unable to be developed, because it is an epic of bygone days and bygone people, in short, a dead thing. It is alive and capable of development for scholars are studying it today, and are being taught it, and you cannot teach a dead thing. Neither is it set aside from other philosophies, but advancing through modern thinking; in the case of a philosophy of error, as St. Thomas said, these errors are useful. Now Spinoza is not understood by reading St. Thomas; but conclusions held by the former, if true, are also formed in the latter as a system.

How is the History of Philosophy to be studied? Firstly, by looking at the problem as a whole as far as possible, and this will mean to see the inter-dependence of one philosophy upon another, and in their own particular historical settings. Then, to be able to recognise a philosopher's' point of departure from the material upon which he has hitherto been working. The biology taught by Henri Bergson can be understood in far greater measure, if one also considers mechanical theories, and the general trend of French Philosophy in Bergson's time.

A viewpoint from the field of psychology is always helpful; it brings with it an understanding and sympathy that is always desirable. So the student then has a view of philosophy from within. This will prevent him finding (as many Catholics would do) other philosophies as grotesque and unreal.

But, of course, a sense of balance must be maintained, that is to say, in the History of Philosophy, we are *historians* first and foremost. The man is being examined for his philosophy; the psychological approach is very important but it depends in this case upon the philosophical, as the effect depends upon its cause.

To thoroughly understand a thinker then, it is necessary to saturate oneself in his system. But this is a slow process, and not only that, but the understanding of Aristotle, for example, requires a knowledge of Greek History and Religion, the Greek language and Greek science. So to be perfect historians, great equipment is required. But in spite of these needs of scholarship, it is unnecessary to overburden oneself with over erudition. What is needed is penetration to the very core of the philosophy.

In the light of what has been said, a whole lifetime could be spent in the study of one thinker. What will follow here is of little value to the specialist, but only to the general reader. If, however, the scope of the general reader becomes wider and more informed, and a degree of understanding of the effort of man to grasp the Truth be obtained, the effort expended here will be more than worthwhile. A further point for the study of the History of Philosophy is made in the name of a balanced education. For, in most history books, the student is introduced to great soldiers, sailors, statesmen, and politicians. If then, we are to have first hand knowledge of Julius Caesar, Hannibal, William the Conqueror, Drake, Nelson, Napoleon, and the like for the sake of balance should we not also be introduced to Thales, Heraclitus, Socrates, Plato and Aristotle?

Thus we are led to a consideration of Greek philosophy. Firstly,

3

because the most satisfactory way to study anything is to start at the beginning, and secondly, because Greek Philosophy has so much to offer the later Christians, besides being in itself a creation of unrivalled splendour. It should be of interest to anybody who studies philosophy. Perhaps in certain explanations, there is an air of over confidence, but this did not prevent Plato and Aristotle in particular, from bequeathing to the West, the Scholastic framework, within which was placed the thought of the Christian Church.

A certain point of view is rife amongst historians of philosophy. It is to the effect that every thought is borrowed from the thinker who has gone before. But under the circumstances, one can think quite logically of a Master Mind of philosophy from whence comes all thought. But the human mind can think on lines alike to its next door neighbour, without that sameness of thought being conclusive evidence of borrowing. The point of these remarks may be thus summarised: historical criticism should be dependent upon proofs as are found in philosophy, not upon the assumption that it is some notion merely borrowed — a priori. As far as the Greeks are concerned, their originality remains intact.

But not the same observations could be made about Roman philosophy, for it was largely dependent upon the Greek structure, and the same can be said for Roman literature. The Romans excelled in Law and Government, but not in philosophy. At the same time, it would be foolhardy to ignore the thought of the Romans in the field of speculation, because it represents the thinking of a higher milieu of the race who were then masters of the civilised world. The thought of Stoa, the deliberations of Seneca, Marcus Aurelius and others present a fine array of speculative consideration, even though it is necessary to add that there are many holes in this speculative fabric. It is highly desirable that the best of the pagan world should be known for it was into this world that Revealed Religion as we know it came and developed from these sources.

We have mentioned those who would know Julius Caesar. To his name, we would add Trajan, Caligula, and Nero. Why should we not also know Marcus Aurelius and Plotinus the latter who, despite the fact that he was not a Christian, was very deeply religious, and not only that, but his name and teaching were invaluable to St. Augustine of Hippo, who stands in the form of a bridge as it were, linking the old philosophy with the new.

4

CHAPTER 2

IONIAN BEGINNINGS

The birth of Greek philosophy took place on the seaboard of Asia Minor, where the first thinkers came from Ionia. As a result of Dorian invasions in the eleventh century B. C., Greece was in a turmoil, the older culture having been lost, whilst Ionia kept the tradition of the former times. It is quite certain that Homer came from Ionia, despite the fact that his poems enjoyed popularity in other parts of Greece. Homer cannot be considered true philosophy, the value of his work showing the Greek attitude and ways of life. His philosophical ideas are few and without order, which cannot be said of the mainland Greek writer Hesiod, who took a depressing view of history, his belief being that law existed amongst animals, and this combined with a great desire for justice among men. Both of these men belong to Ionia, but they did not follow necessarily upon each other. Homer's poems reveal an earlier stage, while Hesiod contributed to a breakdown of aristocratic life that made free development possible. The setting of Homer's best known works is not the setting in which the beginnings of Greek philosophy are found and although it was the work of a different person, it also owed a lot to the City, and reflected the law that was held throughout the State by these ancients.

With the settling down of social communities, it was then possible to concentrate upon matters of reflection, and in order that he might acquire knowledge through this act, man turned to the object of nature to provide him with his subjects.

It is a safe assumption that Greek philosophy went back beyond prehistoric times; but in precise terminology, it was early only in a relative sense, that is, to the development of philosophical culture upon the mainland. This later philosophy was more mature, marking as it did, the closing of one epoch, that of Ionian philosophy, and the beginning of another centered in Athens.

The meeting place for East and West was in Greece. Therefore, could it not be said that the early Greek philosophers were not

5

entirely ignorant of Eastern influences? Some have indeed held this view, but the Greeks were completely ignorant of any influence other than their own native one. The writing of Herodotus, who indicates Egyptian influences upon Greek thought, is in the main, due to writers from Alexandria, and then its adoption by early Christian writers. In the early Greek times, the Egyptians gave a meaning to their myths according to Greek philosophy. But at the most, it can be called an allegory in the same way as Plato is supposed to have obtained his wisdom from the Old Testament. A problem may arise when it is considered how the Greeks acquired Egyptian knowledge, for traders are not of the type who discuss profound philosophy, and scholars have remarked that it is a useless quest in any case until it is decided beyond doubt that the country possessed a philosophy. No record can be found showing the Egyptians as possessing a distinctive philosophy. Neither is it plausible to suppose its originating in India or China.

However, the problem may be approached from another angle. Greek philosophy and mathematics were related. It has been suggested that the Greek knowledge of mathematical science was influenced by Egypt and probably also their astronomy by Babylon. But Egyptian mathematics, to say the most, was a crude science. Again, being influenced by a science is not the same as to derive it. As regards Babylonian astronomy, it developed into astrology, whilst in Greece it was made a science. So the most that can be said is that a certain influence had been obtained, but this in no way robs the Greek speculative effort of its originality, for it bore science and thought.

So the Greeks remain as the unrivalled exponents of the art of thinking, and the art of Science. Two further points are noteworthy. Firstly, knowledge was pursued for itself, and secondly, this pursuit was unhampered by any priestly class who may have held restricted views on some subjects.

It was this basis of restriction that prompted Hegel to identify philosophy with religion in India. He makes a distinction between notions which he says are never thought, remaining in a poetical and symbolic form. Poetry has the purpose to release man from unhappiness, but in this way, knowledge can never be followed for itself. Whether this view is right or wrong will not be discussed here, but the part that will be emphasised will be the fact that Greek philosophy was the first to be *thought*. Probably, in some respects, it took the place of religion in the fields of assent and behaviour for example. The reason for this is due to the weakness of the Greek Religion, not to exaggerated claims on the part of Greek philosophy. Plotinus will edify the myth, and indeed there is no desire to deprecate it here.

The Greeks adopted an impartial outlook to the world around them, surveying it with two main forces, that is, a sense of reality and abstraction. Thus they were enabled to see the paucity of their religious ideas, though probably this is a too sweeping statement for the whole Greek nation. From the story of the Wise Men the myths of the poets were followed by semi-religious and scientific speculations culminating with the thought of Plato and Aristotle, and after them, Plotinus, with whom philosophy reaches a mystical state. The myth gave way, but slowly to reason however, and is discernible later than Socrates.

The beginnings of Greek philosophy are located in Ionia. In the state of Ionia, the town of Miletus was the central spot from which speculation as we know it today sprang. The first of these philosophers is Thales. Ionian thought generally was impressed with change, and the general flux of things particular to the seasons. This progress, the coming into being, development and eventual death were indelible marks upon the created universe. Sometimes, the Greeks are regarded as sheer sport lovers, but this was far from the case. They realized fully that there was a more serious side to life as can be seen by study of their early writers.

But the early Greek, despite the fact that he strove for a medium in all things, very often succumbed to the temptation of power. This was brought about by conflict between Greek towns and cities, whoever they were led by, and under what circumstances. It seems the man most admired was he who knew what he wanted, and possessed the power to obtain it. Thucydides, an early writer, gives examples of this almost national craving for power. He did not even protest against the forced slavery of women and children, whilst Athens was at the height of her fame.

To the Greek philosophical mind, it was obvious that power could easily be linked to excess. Anyone who went to excess in anything would incur the disfavor of the gods. Nothing faces such a person except failure. Unbridled passion leads to confidence in self, which in turn brings a man to desolation.

These factors contribute then to the ancient Greek character. In view of this, the consideration of Plato who opposed the power of the mighty, is outstanding.

Nietzsche saw in the Greek culture a two-sided figure, that is to say, the Greek culture itself and the craving for power. Always when dealing with Greek philosophy there is this two sided figure, one of a middle path, the other of unbridled excess. The latter may be observed in the Bacchae of Euripides, the former is seen in the idea that the gods watch over mankind with a jealous eye, which forbids them to go further than it is possible for a human being to go. These extremes are then danger points to the Greek mentality.

The Ionian philosophers were impressed by change. Very well, if there is change, something must underlie it or support it. This must be so, for what was not before, now is. It possesses something it did not have before, so a prime element must be acquired somewhere to support this particular change. These phenomena could not be explained by opposites, as the notion of opposites did not provide sufficient explanation in depth, for the ever recurring change. So gradually, these thinkers looked for the primary stuff of the universe. What is important here is their unanimous search for unity. Motion expressed this unity though it did not explain the unity itself.

One thing can be remarked upon with certainty with regard to these Ionians. They were all materialists. For Thales regarded water as a prime element, Anaximenes regards air, and Heraclitus fire. The distinction between matter and spirit did not, at this stage, exist.

It is a mistake to consider these men as purely scientists. Why? Because they did not leave their observations at a sense level only, but transposed them into thought. Their conclusions were not arrived at by appearance, but because they found it necessary to enter — albeit unwittingly — the spiritual sphere in their calculations. Thirdly, they made use of the power of abstraction; consequently, they became abstract thinkers, abstracting from sense and matter. Law also played a dominant role, for as we have said, through excess, man was brought to ruin. This concept obviously involved law.

It is possible to take another view, and say that at this stage, the distinction between science and philosophy had yet to come. These men hold the position of being wise, and the fact that geographical or other observations were made use of in their quest for what they considered the true, does not rob them of their place, which is of primary importance in Greek pagan philosophy.

CHAPTER 3

THALES

Science and philosophy were personified in Thales of Miletus whose date of birth is not known, but who died some time before the fall of Sardis, 546|5 B. C. This would mean that he was living at a time when it was possible to note an eclipse of the sun which took place on May 28th, 585 B. C. This eclipse could be seen in Asia Minor, and if the date we possess concerning Thales' observation of this phenomenon is correct, then the period of his activities is fixed in the sixth century B. C. Other scientific exploits are attributed to him, viz. the compiling of an almanac, and a system to aid the steering of ships. Tradition says he fell into a well whilst looking at the stars, but stories of this description easily follow a wise man.

Aristotle understood Thales to say the earth was supported by water, and from this, Thales arrived at the conclusion that the primary element in earth is water. Aristotle goes on to note that possibly Thales had noticed food coming from moisture which was also sustained by it. Again, we arrive at the conclusion of the principle of moisture as the prevalent one. Continuing, Aristotle suggests that Thales had thought of water as an object of veneration against the gods. It seemed that mist or drops of moisture could eventually become solid ground. But the importance of Thales lies in the fact that he enquired about the nature of the world, rather than in the rectitude of his theories. Other view points which Aristotle attributes to Thales are the fact that all things contain gods, and a magnet contains a soul, on account of its movable powers. But it is doubtful if absolute certitude can be given to these statements. To prove such propositions, it would be necessary to over-reach the bounds of interpretations at this stage.

The really salient point about the doctrine of Thales is that he thought of individual objects and thought of them as being composed mainly of water. By this thought, we assign him the first place in Greek philosophy, but this is not all. He also observed

9

a difference in things, whilst noticing that at the same time, these things were unified in some way.

Now this will be one of the important questions philosophy will try to determine. The reason for the one, and at the same time, the many, all existing in a certain unity. No appreciable advance can be made, however, until matter and spirit are considered as distinct. Even then, there will be denials of both. Sometimes material explanations will be given as in the case of Thales, or in the idea as put forward by certain modern philosophies. This problem is very rich in its scope, which can be lost in going to either of these extremes.

Probably the question as to whether the magnet contains a soul is an offshoot of former ideas, which conceived of man as almost a phantasm in a dream world. This watered down version of motion and life was transposed to material things, hence organic life seemed to possess the power to move.

ANAXIMANDER

The next philosopher of Ionia is Anaximander, and accurate details of his birth and death are not available. Younger than Thales, it appears that he was a student of the older man. Again there is the pre-occupation with science, and to Anaximander goes the credit of map drawing for use on the Black Sea. He was also active politically. Anaximander wrote down his doings, and these are available to us through Theophrastus. Thales had pointed the way to look for the ultimate reason for things, and Anaximander followed in this search. He considered it was impossible to give just one element as a universal cause, since water was not everywhere, and it seemed that an explanation was needed for this. Again, all other change, i.e. birth, death, growth, decay, etc. are due to opposition of opposites or conflict. One element was always disappearing to be replaced by another. Now, if everything was water, why had not all things returned to their source and become water? From Anaximander, we get the idea that this primary force is indeterminate. This force is more elemental than opposites, since they come from it and return to it.

Theophrastus says Anaximander was the first to use the phrase "material cause" to explain away this force. It is substance that appears boundless.

The ideals of the conflict of elements is well shown in the heat of summer, and the cold of winter, both passing into that which Anaximander called indeterminate.

There is more than one world; each passing away on account of the eternity of motion, from which also the Heavens came. This motion appears as a sievelike process if we accept the Timaeus of Plato. Naturally, the heavier elements fall, viz. earth, water, whilst the lighter remain suspended above. The sea gives life and our philosopher attempts to explain the beginning of man. He says that man was born from other species, and since other animals are able to nourish themselves quickly, and man is not, and if he had been left as he is at present, no survival would be possible. No explanation is given — indeed none is given to this day amongst those supporting evolution — how man *did* pass from lower life to the higher state.

Whereas Thales had said there was one element only in the world, now there are many elements, and in this has the doctrine been made more perfect. Also, an explanation is given to show how that change from primary to perfect form was accomplished.

ANAXIMENES

We pass now to a consideration of our next philosopher of Ionia. His name was Anaximenes, and it seems that Anaximander was not only his senior, but also his teacher. There is to be found a book written by Anaximenes, unfortunately, it has survived only in part.

A certain backward step seems to be taken by Anaximenes for he forsakes the idea of indetermination. Once again, we have one element as the prime stuff of the earth, as we had with Thales. However, the element is now a new one, for it is air. It seems a natural consequence to suppose that Anaximenes derived this principle from the fact that living things breathe. But once again, we are faced with difficulties, for it could not be said that minerals breathe, yet they exist. This problem was realized by Anaximenes, and great credit is due to him for his effort to supply an explanation of it. He says that air condenses and rarefies, and because of this process, it is capable of being seen. Then examples are given. Fire is the result of rarefaction of air; wind, earth, cloud, stones, etc. the result of condensation. Anaximenes further thought that when air becomes rare, it also becomes warm, and thus eventually becomes fire. Conversely, as it condenses, it becomes heavier, and

11

more prone to become solid. Thus air itself stands midway between two extremes, it being capable of transformation to either of these extremes. Further, Anaximenes pointed out that when breath is taken with the mouth it is warm, but with the nose it is cold. He used this example to prove his point.

He believed the earth was flat, being supported by air. Professor Burnet says that "Ionia was not able to accept a scientific view of the earth."

According to Anaximenes, the rainbow is due to cloud obstructing the sun's rays.

When Miletus fell in 494 B. C. the progress of philosophy was temporarily retarded. Summing up, its main representative was Anaximenes, who achieved this position in the eyes of those who followed for two reasons. Firstly, he was last in this particular school, and secondly because of his theory of condensation and rarefaction. This theory would give an insight into the nature of concrete objects.

So it can be observed that these philosophers were more notable for the fact that they enquired, than for the results of their enquiry. They did not conceive of matter not existing always, for them it had always existed. They can be called materialists in the sense that they attempted to explain things materially; but they were not materialists through ignoring the distinction of matter and spirit. In many ways, they were as children delighted with a new find, and the enjoyment that that find brought them.

PYTHAGOREAN THOUGHT

The Pythagoreans were a group or community of people who believed in the principles of Pythagoras; it is this group that we have now to consider. A common mistake is to regard them purely as followers of Pythagoras, but the distinction went deeper than this. It involved asceticism and religious observances. Its beginnings are extremely obscure, but Pythagoras himself was a Samian, and a society was founded at Kroton in South Italy in the latter half of the sixth century, B. C. We are indebted to Iamblichus for our information concerning Pythagoras and the society he founded. However, in the main, the facts are not reliable, tending as they do to imaginative flights of fancy.

It is obvious that the founding of a new school, or sect, was not new, for the early Ionians had experienced several already. But the one in question, because of its strong ascetic and religious

12

leanings struck a new note. It was contrary to the current myths and cosmologies. And as the Romans in their period of decadence tended towards the bizarre, so here again is the same tendency towards the new and startling. Religion was reborn with the Pythagoreans, and in addition, they provided a strong combination of religion and scientific thought as it then was. There was another sect known as the Orphics, where the doctrine of transmigration of souls was taught. This doctrine was passed on to the Pythagoreans, so it is reasonable to assume that the Orphics had influenced the Pythagoreans in this teaching.

The sect founded by Pythagoras was not a political venture, but some writers had maintained this view. Pythagoras was forced to leave Kroton by Cylon; this however, is insufficient to maintain his sect as purely political. Control was obtained by then at Kroton, but in later times, some of the reformers ruled where they were domiciled, but this does not again point to a purely political career, either by the Pythagoreans or the Protestant reformers.

After Kroton, the society revived at Tarentum in Italy. In the first half of the fourth century B. C., Archytas was a prominent figure among them. After him, also were Philolaus, and Eurytras, all operating at Tarentum.

The doctrine of transmigration naturally led to care of the soul. Music, silence and mathematics were considered of great help in this direction. If the sources available are accurate, the Pythagoreans went to great lengths in their external observances, some of which border on the foolish, such as to abstain from beans, and not to walk in the main street.

It is not clear in discussing this society how much of their doctrine was due to the founder, and how much to those who came after such as Philolaus. Aristotle prefers to speak of the Pythagoreans as a group, rather in the person of Pythagoras.

Xenophanes wrote a poem describing how Pythagoras saw someone he knew beating a dog. Pythagoras told the person to stop, for he recognised the sound of a friend's voice in the dog's cries. It is doubtful if the story is true, but it gives emphasis to the doctrine of metem-psychosis as held by the Pythagoreans. This idea gave new impetus to the idea of a life after death in pessimistic vein.

Later on in Plato's Timaeus, we have the soul described as the "harmony" of the body. Now, this could not be the Pythagorean view, unless the word "harmony" was understood to mean life in the body as a principle. This is how Dr. Praechter regards it. He says it would not necessarily interfere with the idea of the soul's immortality.

Thus the Orphics and the Pythagoreans have many points upon which they agree; but it would be difficult to determine actually how far this influence extended.

This Orphic doctrine was connected with the worship of Dionysus; a cult that arrived in Greece from Scythia or Thrace. It became popular because of it being "enthusiastic" and nature of ecstasy which found a niche in the Greek heart.

Neither of these attributes explain the linking of Orphic and Pythagorean doctrine. The transmigration of souls explains this, consequently the soul becomes the important factor in man, and not the body.

It is probably true that the Orphics were a religion, albeit, pantheistic in outlook. Therefore, philosophy was a manner of living, and not speculation, thus from this it is clear why the Pythagoreans adopted so many of the Orphic views.

The name of Pythagorean society has often been associated with mathematics. This mathematical outlook is overloaded with metaphysical philosophy, and it is necessary now to discuss it as far as possible. According to Aristotle, they devoted themselves to mathematics believing that in this discipline they would find the principle of all things. Firstly, number was important. All things then could be numbered. Relationships of any kind could be expressed numerically. Sounds of different pitch could be explained in this way. These various ratios of sound could then account for conflict in the world, according to the numerical full tones or half tones as we know them today; all submitting to the kingship of number.

We know that Anaximander said everything was indeterminate. So Pythagoras asserts that there is a notion of Limit, which formed the Unlimited. Examples of this are in music and in health. Going on with their speculations in the visible world, they claimed that all things are numbered.

Naturally this statement is difficult. What was meant by it? Did it mean the way in which numbers were thought? In this lies the clue to why the Pythagoreans said all things are numbers. According to Aristotle they said numbers were odd and even, the first being limited and the second unlimited. One comes from both, number is from one, therefore heaven is numbered. From this it seems that the Pythagoreans regarded number in relation to space. One then is a point, two a line, three a surface, four represents a

14

solid. In their view, to say all things are numbers would mean "bodies consist of points or units in space taken together to make a number." This view is given substance by the "tetrakyts", a Pythagorean sacred triangular figure, thus:

$$\cdot$$
$$\cdot \; \cdot$$
$$\cdot \; \cdot \; \cdot$$
$$\cdot \; \cdot \; \cdot \; \cdot$$

The visible purpose of this is to show that one is the sum of one, two, three and four, the first integers.

The trend then of Pythagorean doctrine, united with mathematics, would seem to be a transposition of number into material reality. To them, points, lines and surfaces are real units of reality which make up all natural things, and this again is the meaning of the expression "all things are numbers". But the Pythagoreans went further than this. Now, if all things are made up of points, lines and surfaces, the unification of these three elements gives a fourth element. Therefore, every material thing is an expression of the number four. Obviously, such teaching would lead to difficulties, and it is not clear how far this outlook influenced Pythagorean geometry, in representing a number of things in geometrical figures. However, if things are looked on as so many points forming quantity, and if again these points are regarded collectively in geometrical form, a step towards distinction of things is made.

But we have heard that the basis of number is odd and even. Again, this does not explain Limit and Unlimited. To these thinkers, the world was limited, being surrounded by a limitless barrier of air. Because numbers are composed of odd and even, they must be produced by limit and unlimited. This applies in a geometrical sense. Thus things are connected or identified with the odd and even. A figure was called a gnomon. Limited gnomons were geometrically represented as fixed, but unlimited gnomons were shown in the same manner in a changing rectangle.

The Pythagoreans did mathematics a great service. They dealt with most of Euclid's works, and they are of interest for other reasons also. They were a religious society; they discussed transmigration, and they had influence on Plato. They impressed him with their ideas on the soul, and the tenets of the soul, and with its proven tendencies. Also Plato became interested in the mathematics of the Pythagoreans. They were a great force behind Plato's thought; thus their importance in the history of philosophy.

CHAPTER 4

HERACLITUS

Ephesus was the birth place of Heraclitus, and he ranked as a noble in that city. His mature years were in the 69th Olympiad, roughly from 504-501 B. C. These dates given by Diogenes cannot be verified.

Heraclitus, of an aloof and lonely temperament, discarded his high rank in favour of his brother. He professed comtempt for the common man and also for those who had gone before. Examples of his forthright views can be seen from the following — "the Ephesians would do well to hang themselves, every grown man of them, and leave the city to beardless lads, for they have cast out Hermodorus." "In Priene lived Bias, son of Teutamas, who is of more account than the rest." This person had remarked that all men are evil. Scathing remarks were also levelled at Homer, Hesiod and Pythagoras.

The remarks of Heraclitus are sometimes shot through with humour, the overlay of this, and other sentiments making the real meaning obscure. Indeed, Heraclitus became known as the "Obscure," a title which is still recognized.

Heraclitus is suposed to have said "all things in the world are in a state of flux". There appears some doubt however, if this statement originated with Heraclitus. Be that as it may, it represents the sum total of information about him with many people. But it is not the central core of his teaching. We also will find the following: "you cannot step twice into the same river; for fresh waters are always flowing upon you." Both Plato and Aristotle will refer to this. The former asserted that he (Heraclitus) had said that all passes and nothing is stable; citing the ever-flowing stream as a sign of ceaseless change. Aristotle had quoted Heraclitus as saying that nothing is steadfast. As a result of this, what then is the true position of Heraclitus at this stage? He becomes the precursor of the doctrine nothing is stable, which, when reduced to its simplest, becomes the statement that reality is unreal.

16

However, Heraclitus realised that things do change, and yet we are stable in a relative sense. He gave what he called his "word" to the world, and he could have hardly done this if he visualised everything as changing.

Again, it may be asked what did Heraclitus contribute to philosophy? In a word, he observed a unity, whilst noting that things were at the same time diverse. This was hinted at by Anaximander in his doctrine of opposites. The tension which Anaximander had contributed to disunity, with Heraclitus becomes the principle of the One.

If a study is made of the sayings of Heraclitus, there is no possible doubt that he considered reality and the One as a single entity. But as this statement stands, it requires some clarification; for the things in reality are many, whilst One of its nature is single. According to Heraclitus, it is necessary for the One to be many in order to preserve its existence; it becomes Identity in Difference. The One then exists in many.

It is a mistake to align the philosophy of Heraclitus with becoming for One does not become one; it already is. Hegel made this mistake, overlooking the fact that besides positing the One in Many, Heraclitus had also described the stuff of all things as Fire. Now, this new principle of fire may seem just a variation on what had been said previously. Thales said the primary stuff was water, and Anaximenes air. It almost seems as if Heraclitus merely wished to find a new principle. Be this as it may, the Stoics of later times will borrow the idea from him. But let us examine the fact a little more deeply.

Heraclitus saw that fire consumed things; the result of this overall consumption is that fire becomes all things, and further, without an adequate supply of material to burn, the element of fire would die. The fire then needs replenishment. When it acquires this, it gorges itself upon that which it has acquired. Two elements evolve from this idea, although it is a sense impression only. It is of lighting up and extinguishing, described by him as "want and surfeit." Fire suggested to Heraclitus two things. These were an upward and a downward motion. To these upward and downward movements, he ascribed the world. Change is also due to this upward and downward trend. Upon condensation, fire turns to water which forms earth through being congealed. Now, everything on the earth is liquid, witness evaporation from the sea. This is due to the upward movement. So with Heraclitus, it was not a whim that caused him to teach fire as the stuff of all things. As he saw it, it was what he believed.

But how would he explain those things which are relatively stable in the world? The answer is by measurement. Fire takes only what it requires, and returns as much as was extracted. So a relative stability is attained. This leaves our Philosopher to explain why some matter is more in evidence at one time than another, for example, day over night, summer and winter, etc. Diogenes says Heraclitus explains this by different "exhalations." Thus a bright exhalation from the sun produced day. Warmth from this same exhalation produces summer, and lack of it produces a winter.

There is tension in the world, personified by the action of fire taking and giving in a way to ensure a balance. Heraclitus says that there is no way of knowing how that which disagrees could agree. The One is really the essence of these differences and these same disagreements are the One. The upward and downward motion will not stop; if it did, it would exterminate the One. Many sayings of Heraclitus go to prove this, such as "the way up and down are the same", also "good and ill are one", and many more. The element of relation is apparent in this last statement.

Heraclitus gives the name God to the One, whom he considers possesses wisdom. He is also Universal Reason and Law existing in all things. The intellect of man is the minutest fraction of this reason, but, because it is so minute, man should all the more copy that which is immeasurably above him. Two things are of value in man; first his reason, and secondly, his consciousness. Fire leaves the body; that which remains is not valuable, that is, the earth and water. So man must preserve his soul in a dry state, though moisture is a great attraction. Souls should not "sleep", but should enter the "waking" world of better things. This is the Thought of Heraclitus referred to before. Throughout, Heraclitus had emphasised Reason, and this undoubtedly would lay the foundations for his influence with the Stoics.

Reason appears in the Stoic doctrine, but possibly neither Thales, Anaximenes nor Heraclitus regarded their principles as a Personal God. They were materialists, and so were the Stoics. But the trend in Stoicism to treat a moral doctrine more than of a purely cosmic one, brought about a certain distinction between these two groups of thinkers. In the case of the Stoics, the notion of a Supreme Principle requiring an acceptance of day to day events, possibly led to this cleavage.

18

There is some doubt as to whether Heraclitus taught a doctrine of world wide conflagration at certain periods. It was taught by the Stoics, who borrowed from Heraclitus extensively. Should not everything resolve itself into fire.? But Heraclitus said "that the sun would not go beyond his measure." Again, Plato had compared Heraclitus and Empedocles saying that with the former the One is many, and with the latter the One is many and One in turn. But this involves a contradiction unnoticed by Heraclitus or Plato. Further, there is no direct evidence of Heraclitus having taught a doctrine of relapse into fire. This idea probably originated with the Stoics.

It remains to consider the notion of Heraclitus when he said many are contained in One. That there are many things is obvious, but the mind makes an attempt to synthesise all of these elements into one. This can be shown in many ways. Yet things as they stand are independent. Man is dependent upon the world for his food and his culture. Material things are unified in diversity, and this idea is exemplified in God, where Three Persons exist unified by a Common Nature. Furthermore, this unity in diversity in God would add to the Beatific Vision.

The question then is if it is possible to consider the world as a unity. It certainly is a substance; and there are other substances within it. It will appear to us as one, mainly because of the action of the mind to consider all things as one. The doctrine of opposites could even be accepted, and this, for a number of reasons. Firstly, there must be a change to explain composition of matter, and the explanation of light, etc. Secondly, if there must be finite life, then there must be change. The life of a finite thing also involves change. Thirdly, it is doubtful, given the first two points, if existence could survive on a finite universe without change. Nothing could move and so nothing could come to be.

Thus a material world without change is not practicable in any sense. Change itself involves two things. First the change actually, and secondly, the thing that changes. But the changing thing involves a certain stability.

Heraclitus then had a true deposit to give philosophy. Sensual and material as his concepts were, he did not approach purely substantial thought as Aristotle would do. Nevertheless, what he showed in some things led to a distinct advance upon his predecessors.

CHAPTER 5

THE FIRST ELEATICS

There was in Southern Italy at a place called Elea a philosophic school. This school became known as the Eleatic School, and Xenophanes was accepted as its founder. Xenophanes, however, had never visited Southern Italy, so it is improbable that he was the founder of this School. It is more likely that he became their patron who believed in the One. The reason for this would not be far to seek. Xenophanes had attacked the many Greek gods, and according to Aristotle in the Metaphysics, referring to the whole world said the One was God.

So the Eleatics could easily identify their teaching in this respect to that of Xenophanes. Nowadays, we are used to a single God; but in Ancient Greece it was a novelty.

If Xenophanes was the patron, Parmenides was the true founder of the Eleatic School. He was born toward the end of the sixth century, B. C. and at the age of 65 spoke with a young man named Socrates in Athens. According to Diogenes, Parmenides began by following the Pythagoreans, but relinquished this in favour of a system of his own.

Parmenides' writings are in verse, and in these he says that Being is One, and all Becoming is non-existent.

Being is, for if anything comes to be it must come from being already; whilst that which is non-existent comes from non-being. He goes on then to make a statement that is equally true today, for he asserts that, out of nothing, nothing comes. As for Becoming, it exists only in the mind of the deluded. Then equally as firmly, Parmenides proclaims a Way of Truth and a Way of Opinion. The latter is connected with his previous Pythagorean teaching. The point reached now is interesting, for someone could only reason in a sense manner if they followed the Pythagoreans. But the distinctions made by Parmenides will open the way for distinctions that would be made by Plato later on, viz. Knowledge, Opinion,

Thought and Sense. Actually, logically speaking Parmenides was bound to go against the Pythagoreans, for he would not admit of change, whilst on the other hand they accepted it. Now, we perceive change through the senses; so when he cast off the idea of change, Parmenides was also breaking with sense philosophy.

So now we have new distinctions, Knowledge, Opinion, Thought and Sense. Thales and Heraclitus, in their respective ways, had argued from sense knowledge, the latter introducing his Word; Parmenides made of it an accurate distinction. And so it became adopted by Plato as an important doctrine in his philosophy.

Although Plato's philosophy was idealistic, and Parmenides assisted it in this direction, it would be wrong to consider the latter as an idealist. His One or Being will remain material, for if he had thought of it in any other way, it is unlikely that it would have escaped both Plato and Aristotle. Neither would Socrates have found a balanced thinker in Anaxagoras with his idea of the Nous. Parmenides seems to say that Reason can apprehend Reality, but that same reality is material.

The world then "is". It is inconceivable that it might not be, for we can speak of it, and it can become the object of our thoughts. The question arises if it "is", then why? Because if it did not exist, it would be nothing. It is impossible to have nothing as the object of the mind. If it were only a probability, then it could never come into being, since as Parmenides had already said out of nothing comes nothing. So it is real, and was the first in realities, so it "is."

Parmenides considered that to mention the world as "existing" was a precise form of definition. Why? Because in this case, there was no real coming to be, as what was originated in being exists. It could not originate in non-being. If something originated from non-being, then we must conclude that non-being is something, which is absurd. So being is subsistent, simply because it exists. If it is asserted that something *does* come from non-being, then the conclusion must be a contradictory, resulting in the denial of change of any sort whatsoever. Why is this? Because in change something is acquired by the thing, which it lacked before. But if, according to Parmenides, that thing which "is" already, it cannot lack anything simply because it "is".

Division of being is inconceivable. For if it were possible then being would have to be divided by something outside itself, which is impossible. In like manner, it is impossible for additions to be made for these also would be being, which could not add to itself. This view of Being was a material one. It was also finite. For something infinite was indeterminate, and without definition, and Being must be determined and defined. Reality as being is spread equally in every direction. So Parmenides thought of being as a sphere, and it is difficult to see how he could do this without considering it solely from a material point of view. Authorities appear to be divided on this issue, some maintaining that Parmenides was an idealist.

From the point which this survey would take an historical view Parmenides was a materialist. His philosophy probably contains the point of departure of idealism, and this is what various critics have maintained as idealist. In one view, matter could not be destroyed, and in this, Parmenides was followed by Empedocles and Democritus. But Democritus wished to explain what was obviously a fact of every day life, i.e. the phenomena of change. Consequently, he explained it by saying that certain indestructible parts of matter were moved from place to place. Now, many years later, Plato will adopt Parmenides' idea of changeless being to give substance to his philosophy of Ideas. It is possibly this historical follow through that has made Parmenides an idealist. Again, Plato adopted the ruling between reason and sense contributing to the idea of Parmenides as the idealist in history. But it was a material point of view which prevailed upon his teaching, otherwise Democritus would not have felt so compelled to explain change.

So Heraclitus asserts all is Becoming; Parmenides a changeless Being, reason and thought are left to distinguish objects of sense. It will be left to Plato to compile a doctrine from the becoming of Heraclitus and the Being of Parmenides. He will take thought and reason from the latter, and say that some sense objects through sense perception do not give knowledge that is true, and in this, he will follow the flux of Heraclitus.

Stability exemplifies truth, as the doctrine of Parmenides would say. Stability however, is not material as the same doctrine would also say. To Plato, they will become immaterial forms which were the Good.

But Aristotle carried this doctrine a stage further. He said Being is ultimate reality and immaterial. God does not change, but is subsistent Thought. There is change, it is true, but Parmenides' position here is discounted. Also, Aristotle accounted for change better than did Heraclitus by giving to Plato's Forms, the principle of concretion in this world. The notion of potentiality resolved the difficulties presented by Parmenides. It is not incorrect to say a thing is A, but it could be B in potency. It exists as A now, but will become B in the future. So it is wrong to say that B comes from non-being, and equally so to say that it comes from being. It is made actual by the movement from potentiality to act, which makes a thing to be actually.

Melissus, a Samian, a follower of Parmenides, now claims our attention. Parmenides had said that the One was spatially finite, but Melissus refused to accept this view. He concluded that if being was finite, then outside it must be nothing. So nothing becomes the limit of being.

According to Aristotle, Melissus also conceived the One as material. But opinions differ about this, for Simplicius, repeated from a fragment, affirms that Melissus looked upon the One as incorporeal. The fragment referred to runs thus: "now if it were to exist, it must needs be one; but if it is one, it cannot have body: for if it had body, it would have parts, and no longer be one."

The authorities conclude that it was a hypothetical case. They also draw attention to the fact that Zeno had said that if all the Pythagorean doctrine had been considered together, it would appear that because of the various parts, its unity was impossible. The fragment mentioned is also considered as referring to the Pythagoreans, and not to Parmenides' doctrine.

CHAPTER 6

ZENO

Motion was not considered a possibility by all ancient Greek philosophers. Such a one was Zeno, born at Elea about 489 B. C. He also gave the world the riddle of Achilles and the Tortoise, and through such sayings he was credited as a wit.

Actually, he was a pupil of Parmenides, and it is from this viewpoint he will be considered here. His utterances were to show the superiority of the teacher.

We know that Parmenides said that change and motion were illusions. Zeno attempted to prove this point of view, for as teaching, it had had criticism levelled at it on many sides. Zeno's object is at least to prove that the theory is credible, and he employs the illustration that the Pythagorean society had surrounded itself with difficulties, and motion and change were not possible if it were to be based on their teachings. His aim in this campaign is to refute the Pythagorean opponents of Parmenides by showing them as foolish. This is Plato's opinion in the "Parmenides," when he refers to a book of Zeno's, no longer extant to us.

According to the Pythagoreans reality consists of units. These units contain mass, or on the other hand, do not. It is possible to divide a line because it is dividing infinitely, and each unit will possess mass or magnitude as it is called. The inference of this is that the line is of great proportion since its units are infinite. Now, things in the world must be immense if this principle is applied to them. But the problem can also be considered with the units deprived of mass in which case it is difficult to explain away things in the world, as they obviously exist and are possessed of magnitude.

From this problem, Zeno points out that the "unit idea" of the One could not lead into such an impasse. Again, if there are many objects, it is reasonable to ask their number. A problem is faced if there are a number of things and yet they cannot be counted. But it is not necessary for them to be counted, yet they exist into infinity. This is because between two given units, there are still other units. But it is not practicable to consider something on the one hand as finite and infinite at the same time.

An example follows where he says a bushel of corn makes a noise when it falls. But one grain would not make such a noise. Now, since the bushel is composed only of parts, why should it make a noise when a grain makes no noise?

When dealing with space, Zeno follows the same form of argument. He attempts, in defence of Parmenides, to reduce the contrary opinion to foolishness. The substance of this argument is as follows: if there is space which exists, things are existing in it. Very well. But space is itself a thing, consequently it will be in itself. This idea can be carried to infinity. Since it is impossible for things to exist in nothing, the teaching of Parmenides was correct in asserting that there was no such thing as nothing.

We come now to explanations where Zeno excels himself. These explanations concern motion, the point of the whole theory being that as motion was impossible in Parmenides' eyes, likewise was it impossible under Pythagorean teaching? Firstly, imagine a street that has to be crossed. To do this, it is necessary to cover an indefinite number of points according to the Pythagoreans. But you will do this in a finite time. Now, it is difficult to see how an infinite number of points will be crossed in finite time. The conclusion is that the street cannot be crossed, and no object can pass from place to place. Therefore, motion is impossible.

Secondly, there is the celebrated example of Achilles and the tortoise. The latter is given a start by Achilles. The tortoise goes forward from its starting point, and when Achilles has reached the point from where the tortoise started, it has already advanced a further stage. Now, Achilles can never — again on the supposition of the Pythagoreans — catch up with the tortoise, for a line is of infinite points, and to cover this distance, Achilles would have to travel an infinite time. The conclusion here is that the slowest is as quick as the fastest which is absurd.

Thirdly, an arrow moves through the air. The Pythagoreans say that the arrow could occupy a particular position in space. But for this to come about, space itself must be immobile. So it seems that the arrow is in flight and rest at the same time — again this is absurd.

Other examples are given by Zeno which are not as clear as those given above, but in any case, the question arises what weight can a thoughtful person give to such statements? In the first place,

Zeno was no sophist. He did not set out to be one. In his efforts to show the Pythagorean argument as absurd, he unwittingly showed that reality is a continuum. But his conscious aim was to uphold Parmenides' doctrine of the One, and refute Pythagorean pluralism.

It is now possible to assess the position of the philosophers who belong to the Eleatic School. They do not admit of number, but there is one principle, that of Being. Certainly, motion is felt as a sense perception, and this applies to multiplicity also. But they are both illusions, as something that simply *appears* to be so. There is grave difficulty among the Eleatics when they attempt to find one principle in the world, for many things abound in the world, contrary to their basic teaching. How then to equate the One and the Many? That is the vital question. Heraclitus had given the idea of unity in Diversity. The Pythagoreans insisted on pluralism to the exclusion of the One. But the Eleatics agreed there was, in a sense, change. But if this is agreed upon, you must also agree upon a linking element, under which as it were all will change. If the doctrine of the One is adopted, other things must develop from the One unless it is to be a lop-sided viewpoint. On this count of onesidedness, we can evaluate both the Pythagoreans and Parmenides. Heraclitus, too, could not be accepted on account of his material notion, and he completely failed to give a satisfactory explanation of stability. In consequence of all this, other systems were beginning which would seek to knit together the best in the deposit these philosophers had left behind.

The question could arise at this point, what is the relation between philosophy and religion in the minds of these early thinkers? Did it constitute a material element? In no sense can they be said to *worship* Being, Fire, the One, or any philosophical principle we have encountered so far. Heraclitus referred to Zeus as the One, but this is inconclusive evidence of worship. In any case, as has been mentioned before, they *thought* on the problem of the universe, which a materialist nowadays can be said to do.

Neither can the world, as envisaged by these men, be connected with the Greek gods. Schelling says there was no supernatural element in Homer, and this is endorsed by the modern writers. They say that the god of Homer was a natural god, or part of nature. The Greek idea of a god was a finite idea, and although the name could be associated or given to the One, it is impossible to take the meaning literally. An appropriate approach to these early thinkers is to consider them as monists, thinkers with little trend towards materialism.

26

CHAPTER 7

EMPEDOCLES

Our next philosopher is Empedocles who lived at Akragas in Sicily. There is uncertainty about the years of his birth and death, but it can be established that he visited a city called Thurii about 443-444 B.C. He was active politically at Akragas, and would appear to have been a prominent member of the democratic party in this city. He also gave the reputation for magic, and he contributed also to the advance of the study of medicine. Many stories are told about his death; one of the best known recounted by Diogenes is that he jumped into the volcano at Mt. Etna, in order that people should think that he was a god and had gone to Heaven. This, however, can be discounted from the fact that a slipper was found on the edge of the volcano with highly coloured soles. Empedocles wore such slippers. It is more probable that he went to Peloponnesus, and the manner of his actual death is not known. This philosopher expressed his ideas in poetical form in the manner of Parmenides. Empedocles became one of those thinkers who sought to unify the pieces of philosophy others had left. He thought that Being exists and as such it is material.

Previously, he undertook the view of Parmenides that being is One, resulting in the absence of change. It has not come from Being, neither from non-being, in short, it cannot be destroyed. Empedocles was forcefully insistent upon this part of his doctrine.

At this stage, there is little difference between the teachings of Parmenides and Empedocles. Now, the problem of change caused the latter some concern, as it is obvious that things do change from day to day, or even hour by hour, but this position was hard to reconcile with Parmenides who spoke of Being as neither forming or passing. However, Empedocles sought to solve this difficulty, and equate the doctrine of Parmenides by suggesting that things ceased to exist completely; this means that things come to be completely, and pass away in their completeness; only a part is left. Change then, he says, is due to the movement of particles which he asserts are indestructible. This gives rise to the notion of substance as conceived by Empedocles.

The older philosophers such as Thales, and Anaximenes had

27

thought that one type of matter can never become another type. Empedocles had taken Parmenides' doctrine of unchangeableness of matter, and had, in his specific manner, made a distinct advance towards the notion of substance. The result then of this is there is earth, fire, water, air, as fundamental bodies, neither of which can become the other. But this notion is, at this stage, but vague. Perhaps it would be very true to consider it as an advance on the doctrine of substance in sense relation only.

Because the world's seasons repeat themselves in circular fashion, Empedocles thought that this world process was in the form of a circle. As we see, Love brings the particles together, and apparently the same idea is valid for the seasons of the year. The object of Hate is to break up the compact circle as formed by Love, and when this is done, the particles are separated and Love is conquered. However, Love begins the work of bringing together of Love, and the breaking in of Hate.

With respect to the world as it stands now, it is in a middle position so to speak. That is to say, half way between a primary state and complete destruction of the particles or elements. This is due to the actions of Love and Hate already referred to. Air was the first element formed, followed by fire and earth in that order. Water is derived from the rate of rotation of the earth. Empedocles explains all this in terms that to a world blunted by the battering it receives from endless scientific formulae must appear if not naive, a little amusing.

Empedocles believed in the doctrine of transmigration of souls which he explains in a book called "Purifications". He also states that thought is "the blood around the heart of men." But this teaching is inconsistent with that of eternal life. So then, there is a decided gap between the philosophy of Empedocles and his religious thinking.

Thought and perception were one entity to Empedocles; at least this is the view of Aristotle. Plato adopts his theory of vision in the Timaeus, where vision was held to be the effect of objects upon the eye.

Empedocles had tried to reconcile Parmenides' theory of the One and the four elements. He introduced particles to explain change. Actually, he did not give an adequate explanation of nature, and deep examination will show that his data came from Greek myths. However, a great step forward is made by our next philosopher, Anaxagoras, in giving a spiritual concept to his explanations.

CHAPTER 8

ANAXAGORAS

A town called Clazomenae in Asia Minor was to become the birthplace of the next philosopher Anaxagoras. It is evident that, whilst remaining a Greek, he became a Persian citizen; for Clazomenae had been taken over, after an Ionian uprising. It is possible that Anaxagoras came to Athens in the force of troops from Persia. This is the explanation why he was in Athens in the year 480-79 B. C. which was the year of Salamis. He is notable as the first philosopher to settle in Athens, which to this day bears about it the glory of a bygone philosophical era.

Plato says that Pericles became a student under Anaxagoras. Eventually, after thirty years, Anaxagoras was brought to trial by those opposed to Pericles. This would be approximately in 450 B. C. Among other charges one was impiety, which, according to Plato, was based upon the fact that Anaxagoras had taught that the sun is a red hot stone, and the moon was made of earth. These charges were false, and it was an effort to discredit Pericles through his master. However, Anaxagoras did not remain in prison, but was released. He then went to Ionia and lived at Lampsacus, a part of Miletus. Here he founded a school, and the locals erected a monument to him. Long after his death, school children in the area were granted a holiday on the anniversary of his demise.

A book is existent, but only in part, where Anaxagoras wrote down his philosophy. It would seem that he accepted Parmenides' doctrine of the One. It is interesting to note that the parts of Anaxagoras' book which we still have, are due to the effects of Simplicius in the sixth century A. D. Both Parmenides and Anaxagoras thought that matter was indestructible. Also, both explain change by the local movement of particles. But the point of departure for Anaxagoras is that he will not agree with Parmenides in that these particles correspond to the four elements, viz. water, fire, earth, air. Those things which in quality resemble the whole

29

are not derived in any way. Aristotle called these "wholes", the notion being that if an inorganic body were cut in two, two halves would result, but both would be the same in quality. If, however, an animal were cut in two, two animals would not result. In the first case, qualitative parts are similar. Aristotle goes on to say that Anaxagoras did not consider the four elements as final, but there could be a series of mixtures. Anaxagoras continues, that at the outset, there is no difference between the particles; all things at the beginning had an infinite nature. He infers too, that there is a "wholeness" about this arrangement. Material objects arise from the facts that certain particles are brought together in a specific way. Thus a group, so to speak, of particles is formed which in turn emphasises the object to our experience. In this manner, if copper particles were predominant in an object, then experience would be of a copper thing. He next has to explain how an object changes, for example, when it is eaten. Anaxagoras does this by explaining that there were particles of flesh in the edible thing before it was eaten. Nevertheless, there is always a dominant particle formation in all things. What this philosopher is trying to do is evidently two things at once. He maintains Parmenides' doctrine of being, and at the same time, says there is change. So he adapts his doctrine accordingly. Many years later, Aristotle will be faced with the same problem. He will apply his famous doctrine of potency and act for the solution, possibly the best conceived by anybody.

Various modern scholars have thought that Anaxagoras considered a notion of opposites, that is, in everything hot there is a particle of cold, and so on. This view is considered as the most authentic, since Anaxagoras himself says that particles cannot be divided, and since this is so, there can be no final particles. Again, he remarks how can hair come from anything that is not hair? He is very insistent upon his doctrine of mixtures, which leads to the assumption that everything is contained within the whole.

Nothing really original has as yet developed in the philosophy of Anaxagoras. But a point is now reached where he has to provide a mover for the particles he has consistently referred to. In this, he differs greatly from his predecessors. Empedocles had said it was due to the movement of Love and Hate, but Anaxagoras says it is the Nous or Mind.

This is then, the main contribution by Anaxagoras to philosophy. The Mind has powers of everything. And the Nous was operating at the start of everything. It also brought a direction and order to life, and this includes not only life on earth, but the stars and heavens generally. The Nous or Mind is not finite, and is not subject to law as we know it. It is by itself and so rules itself. The idea of Nous was brought about by Anaxagoras thinking of the purest and finest elements in all things. It is "where everything else is."

There is some doubt among modern scholars if it is correct to assume that Anaxagoras was a materialist, since he spoke of the Nous as the "thinnest of all things". Opinions are divided, but probably it would be a fair point of view to consider Anaxagoras as not *fully* aware of the difference between matter and the spiritual element.

Nous therefore is present in all things; the difference in bodies is due not to difference of soul, but to an actual physical difference which prevents the move complete action of Nous. It must be remembered here that Anaxagoras did not explain consciousness of separate persons in his idea of Nous.

Neither does Nous create matter for this is eternal. The task of Nous is to set in motion. Aristotle considered that since Anaxagoras posited Mind as the first mover, he also invoked it when he was in difficulties to explain other philosophical problems. If this is so, Aristotle still spoke of Anaxagoras as "a sober man standing out against random talkers who had gone before him." Socrates was full of hope when he discovered the doctrine of the Nous of Anaxagoras, but he himself says that his hopes were dashed, for according to him, Anaxagoras did not use Nous to explain final causes.

At the same time, credit must be given to Anaxagoras for starting Greek philosophy upon an intellectual path, that was eventually, at the hands of others, to manifest its everlasting glory.

CHAPTER 9

ATOMS AND PHILOSOPHY

Mechanical philosophy is not new. Even in these early days of Greek speculation, we find a school called the Atomists, founded by Leucippus of Miletus. Some have doubted if Leucippus did actually exist, but both Theophrastus and Aristotle gave evidence to the fact of his actuality. It is doubtful if both could be mistaken. The founding of this particular school cannot be given accurately as regards dates, but it seems that Leucippus upheld the philosophy of Parmenides. Diogenes says he was a follower of Zeno, and again some doubt is shown over the probability of some of the works of Democritus being ascribed to Leucippus. It appears however, that Democritus belongs to a later period, consequently it would not be historical to consider him at this stage.

In effect, the philosophy of Empedocles gave rise to what can be described as Atomist philosophy. Why is this? Firstly, because Empedocles had tried to reconcile the doctrine of Parmenides and change, by instituting the various particles of matter. Now, Empedocles had left many loopholes in this philosophical structure, consequently it was an easy matter for some of those who came later to evoke a purely mechanical formula. This then was the path taken by the Atomists.

As it is described by Leucippus and Democritus, there are units incapable of division which are called atoms. They are very tiny, too small to be perceived by the naked eye. They are not the same in size or in shape, but their main characteristic is one of solidity. There exists a space in which they move — which by the way had not been admitted by Parmenides — whilst the Pythagorean school had admitted of space to keep their various units as not touching. But they said it was air, which Empedocles said was a body. But the atomists, as explained by Leucippus, would not agree to the reality of space or its existence. What was meant by this? For them, the term non-reality would correspond to a non-physical body. We can say on the one hand "that which is" and on the other "that which is not" in order to explain the same idea. Later philosophers believed atoms move downwards by their own weight, which was probably explained by Aristotle's' previous teaching of absolute weight and lightness. Some writers discussing Democritus have said he considered size and shape to atoms, but not weight. Others believed he included weight, and Cicero relates this view. According to this writer, there was no top, middle or bottom to an atom as held by Democritus. If this view was held by the latter, he was correct, but on the other hand, it is difficult how, under the circumstances, he could argue to the motion of these atoms. A likeness of the atoms of the soul to those of the rainbow is made by Aristotle in De Anima. The latter moves rapidly without the aid of wind.

It is clear that some atoms move in a space; they become intermixed, and so collections or groups are formed. The idea of Anaxagoras is once again met with in the formation of the world. Leucippus thought that the heaviest bodies would gravitate towards the centre; this was a mistake. He implied that this movement was due to wind currents. Further a sievelike action is responsible for the elements earth, fire, air and water in much the same way as round stones with round and square stones with square.

The outstanding points we have met with so far in philosophy are absent from this doctrine. The main point here is that atoms exist, and in a space. It is from this that our sensation arises, and to this idea, no further outside force is required. In the concept of atoms, the atoms themselves were thought to be self supporting. If this idea is examined further, we will also find on the one side Leucippus gives the impression of atoms as a single entity; on the other he says the "togetherness" of these atoms is imperative. The latter idea came about by the movement of atoms themselves. Change would appear to play a great role in the Atomist philosophy.

In Aristotle's opinion, they were at fault in not explaining motion and the source of motion. We have just referred to the fact that change *"appeared"* to play a great role in this philosophy, but no one is forced to accept that notion as an absolute opinion. From a modern point of view, however, there seems no alternative, since Leucippus considered that motion did not need to be explained. He was content to accept the movers as he found them and made no attempt to arrive at a beginning in this aspect. Now how can this atomist philosophy be summed up? Firstly, it is based on the idea of single Pythagorean number, shot through with the properties of being according to Parmenides. This is how Aristotle will view it when he says that the Atomists "make all things number too, and produce them from numbers."

It could be said that there is a reaction in not accepting the world as a sphere, but considering it something like a balloon floating in mid-air. This idea would be more like Anaxagoras and Anaximenes, returning in this way to the early cosmology.

But really there is nothing that has not been before, but several particular tendencies are worked out, such as the mechanical notions held by Leucippus and Democritus. Greek philosophy was to struggle towards the conclusion that the depth in the created universe cannot be expressed in atoms. But there will be other philosophies of a modern era which will not abandon mechanical ideas or notions.

CHAPTER 10

BEFORE SOCRATES

At this stage, it is possible to make a resume of the progress which actually appears to have been made by the Greek philosophers. Firstly, it would be accurate to say that they considered a unity as possible, that is, some primary element which bound all the universe together. So we have Thales with water as principle, Anaximenes air, and Heraclitus with fire. But there was more than this. These philosophers have been called Cosmologists. It is necessary to decide if this term is justified. Since they all regarded the Cosmos as it stood, that is, as we know it, it is understandable that their answers to its unity would be a material one. But all of them looked at the universe, and not at man, so for this reason the name of cosmologists seems fitting.

It is interesting to notice the nature of this operation. A material element was cited in every case. Now, this would appear on the face of it, as a purely scientific explanation. Quite unwittingly Thales had remarked that "every thing" is One. Unwittingly in the sense that he did not consider the viewpoint of a metaphysician when he made that statement, yet such a statement did in fact put him in that class. Some may not take the idea of water as fundamental seriously. But if philosophical history is to be followed through properly, this view must be accepted, and for three reasons. Firstly, because it strives to point to the origin of all things, secondly, because it does this with truth, and thirdly, because it contained in germ the supreme idea that everything is one. Thus Thales makes a contribution to religion on the first reason, natural philosophy on the second, and on the third he became the first Greek philosopher. This metaphysical aspect can also be applied to Anaximenes and Heraclitus, who in a way, share with Thales the crown of the first European thinkers, because they submitted data to reason, and were not content to leave it on a purely imaginary level.

Nevertheless, the probem of One and the Many proved a difficult one for these early Cosmologists. This involved explaining how things were diverse, yet contained as one in an overall and universal principle. We have Anaximenes with condensation, Parmenides with his theory of being as One, Empedocles with Love and Strife, and Anaxagoras showing that quantity had a place in explaining differences in quality.

Despite all these efforts the problem remained. It was more satisfactorily dealt with by Plato and Aristotle. But a danger lies here, if there is a tendency to consider Greek philosophy from Socrates, or Plato, or Aristotle alone. The latter are scarcely intelligible without the study of these early thinkers, and although the problem of the One and Many remain, its identification with these present Ionian philosophers is not possible. They sought the Object, the World. Man was yet to consider himself as a subject. Again, anybody who looks for a first cause — however confusedly — that person's researches are philosophical. The Ionians proceeded in this way. Because their findings were purely material, the modern physicist would claim them as his own.

What emerges from all this is that we distinguish Ionian philosophy by its interest in the World. What marks the philosophy to follow is its interest in man himself.

To every action there is an equal and opposite re-action. This formula may be applied to these Ionians, for we have the Becoming of Heraclitus, and the unchanging Being of Parmenides. In what was taught here were the beginnings of other philosophers. The latter, when intermixed with the idea of the supremacy of reason, becomes idealism. Anaxagoras and the Nous provide the beginnings of theism, and it has already been hinted that Leucippus and Democritus laid the foundations of mechanical philosophy.

It is evident that this era of philosophy before Socrates sometimes receives but scant treatment from some historians, the tendency being to consider Greek philosophy from the time of Socrates and Plato. We have tried to show before in preceding sections, that present thought exists only in its present state because of the thought held by the individual or society previously. This means that there is a state of development in the individual or society which depends upon a number of aspects. Greek philosophy is no exception to this rule, and firstly is found in it a preservation of type throughout. This means an essential idea of philosophy is maintained. Secondly, its principles are continued, involving two main elements, the principles themselves, and degree of influence in philosophy. With these is brought in a power of assimilation, which almost unconsciously as far as the participants are concerned — absorbs other ideas into itself. The development of philosophy illustrates this in many cases. In an absolute consideration, the power of absorption will facilitate the first point, i.e., preservation of type. This fact may, on the face of it, be obscure, but in virtue of this assimilation the original idea borrows and accepts as its own elements which are infused by the passing of time. Thus Plato and Aristotle borrowed and made their own doctrines ideas which had gone before them. In all cases, however, it is the main idea which gives the unity. These borrowed elements follow in logical sequence. This would follow through from the process of reason to the natural growth of ideas and notions. There is next an anticipation of the future, which comes about by the inflexibility of logic, and the bond between ideas thus formed. Thales had a metaphysical view of the world; men today take a metaphysical view of the same world. There is then a preservative action on the past. This is because the new idea added to the old will help strengthen the older concept. The philosophical example of change illustrates this, for the purpose of change is perfection; thus the more perfect added to what is imperfect will make the whole organism perfect. Lastly comes the idea of chronic vigour in something alive and its consequent continued advance, for something cannot live and not move. Decay by itself can never endure. The points enumerated above must be considered as a whole. It is useless to consider one point alone, or a number of points alone. We are now, however, in a position to apply these points to Greek philosophy, and it is these different actions which contributed to the ultimate glory of such a philosophy. Probably, at times, it was not a pure philosophy, but the explanation for this rests in the very gradual workings of the aspects noted above. Nor was this philosophy isolated, for if it were, the above plan would be inappropriate. But concepts from it, as stated before, will recur from time to time.

CHAPTER 11

SOPHISM

It has been said that up to this point the Greeks studied the exterior world. But their replies to the question of how it was formed were diverse in the extreme. Now, diversity can never make for unity. Consequently, no trust could be found in Greek philosophy at this stage, and this led inevitably to scepticism. It was felt that the study of pure Cosmology led to many differences in the light of past teachings, and so now we come to a change in outlook. If an objective approach failed in its quest for truth, then a subjective one may do better. Thus it is we perceive the change from objectivism to subjectivism in Greek thinking. It was the Sophists who first appeared with this change, and since the dialectic of Zeno had made teaching on Cosmology very difficult, this new development was timely.

As philosophy had advanced, so had the Greeks acquired knowledge of other peoples, and it is probable that this position led also to a study of man as subject. Contact with peoples such as the Babylonians, Egyptians, Scythians and Thracians, the two latter being particularly backward, led all the more to this view. The Greeks felt they had, in consequence, to know something of man in himself. One of the first questions they ask in this respect was are religious customs everywhere the same? Are they conventions of laws, particularly in respect of morals? Other questions that suggested themselves were developed upon lines which would show nature as having a ruling hand. But could this be changed? We shall see in due course too, how some of the most gifted Sophists came not from Greece itself, but from Thrace.

The direction of Greek philosophy therefore, changed. No longer was it a question of the Cosmos, but it became a question of man; which could be said too, to arise from the fact that man suddenly found himself self-conscious. But in discussing Sophism, we must also consider the method philosophy was now to adopt. Prior to this period, a deductive method had sufficed; but now there

38

was to be a compilation of facts from which it was hoped to draw conclusions. These conclusions were to be in part theory, and in part practice. Now, if there was a store house of conclusions in this manner, so could there be numerous opinions and beliefs. Knowledge could, itself, become doubtful. Viewing this position from another angle, it is possible to arrive at some form of idea of the civilizations and languages of others. Again, organizations, good or bad, would be evaluated. This appeared to be the path upon which Sophism would lead philosophy. But neither objectivity as such, or necessary truth was paramount to the Sophist. Until now, these two points had been of the utmost importance, but in heralding in this new era, a new end in view is also demonstrated. If we consider for a moment what has gone before, we see that everyone was concerned with the object, and consequently the objective. But Sophism tended to practicality more than speculation. They undertook to train and to teach for the role of life. The previous philosophers had found out the truth; the Sophists were prepared to teach it. It is interesting to see how this position became integral with politics in Athens at this time. As a consequence of the Persian Wars, most Greek citizens adopted some form of political activity. Certain training was required to accomplish these political ventures, particularly in public speaking for example, and also in debate. It was upon these lines that the Sophist instruction fashioned itself, their teachers travelling from place to place in their role of instructors. Grammar, Mythology and Religion, and above all Rhetoric became favourite subjects. Various pitfalls present themselves at once with this approach. Obviously Rhetoric or the art of powerful speaking would be open to misuse for spurious political ends. This did not help the Sophist cause.

However, at this particular time, Athens was so constituted that if anyone wished to make easy money, he would do so by means of bringing a lawsuit against someone else for some particular offence. The Sophists claimed that, trained as they were in Rhetoric, they could assist in their clients' success in the winning of these lawsuits by persuasive speaking. Again, this leads to pitfalls, for the obvious outcome, however clever and eloquent, was often to make the false appear true. In this manner they wandered far from the bent of the true philosopher and it makes it clear why Plato, with his utmost sincerity, did not spare them in his writings.

It is true that the Sophist movement was reactionary; they made an appeal to the young as is often the way with novel movements. But the fact that they were fluent and lucid speakers, did not prevent them from being mistrusted by the general populace. With the backing of youth, it was mainly their sceptical views that appeared to the fore, particularly so, since they did not put back any solid thought into the framework that they had disturbed. Neither were they opposed to payment for their labours in teaching, which was quite in order legally, but was bitterly attacked by Plato and Xenophon who said they speak and write to deceive for gain.

Sophism was merely another stage of development. But it is not worthy to be condemned out of hand as a system. For, by directing man to himself, they laid a tradition which would be used by Aristotle. They certainly assisted the political life of the Greeks. If there was a poverty of actual doctrine, it was due to two reasons. Firstly, the break-up of the old Cosmology. Secondly, the contact with foreign peoples. It influenced Greek dramatic art in Sophocles' hymn to the Antigone, and in plays such as the Melian dialogue found in the writings of Thucydides.

The more mature members of Sophism were looked upon and respected as historians. In certain instances, they could lay claim to represent their particular cities or city. A fraud would not be called upon to do this. It was in the light of this latter term, that we find them in an unfavourable light, particularly in Plato. But a balanced view is necessary, and it would be impossible to discharge them from the counts of relativism, their unstable teaching, acceptance of payment, and tedious arguments. Plato will say they are "shopkeepers with spiritual wares". But there was a reason for Plato's attitude. It was because Socrates always was before his mind, who had extolled these Sophists, and their acts appearing to be superior to those who performed them.

CHAPTER 12

PROTAGORAS

It was mentioned in the preceding section that one of the foremost Sophists was a native of Thrace. His name was Protagoras, and he was born at Abdera, as far as can be ascertained about 481 B. C. He held important political positions under Pericles, and was responsible for drawing up a constitution for the colony of Thurii under the direction of Pericles. He was living at Athens at the start of the Peloponnesian War of 431, and again in 430, a year which was tragic for Pericles, for during the plague raging in the city at that time, he lost two of his sons. A traditional story related by Diogenes Laertius says that Protagoras was condemned for blasphemy because of a book he wrote on the gods; the book itself being burnt in the market square. This story also says that Protagoras escaped by fleeing to Sicily. However, there is disagreement amongst eminent scholars upon the veracity of the story, and there appears some doubt too, upon the date of Protagoras' actual birth. According to one of Plato's dialogues, Protagoras appears as an elderly man in the year 435. It is generally concluded that Plato could not possibly have an ulterior motive in depicting Protagoras in this fashion.

Protagoras is famous for saying that "man is a measure of all things, of those that are, that they are, of those that are not, that they are not". There are various interpretations as to what Protagoras actually meant by this statement. Some maintain that it did not refer to man, but men in general, in which case the conclusion is that what would stand for one man's thinking would not necessarily stand for the next man's line of thought. Again, are values to be included in the conception of things as considered by the senses?

A dilemma of no mean proportion is presented here; the answer seems fraught with difficulty. Seeking a way out however, we would appeal to Plato in the Theaetetus where an individualistic stamp is definitely established, and this conclusion is arrived at taking

41

the senses into consideration. Thus it must be clearly said that Protagoras meant something personal and individual when he made this famous remark. Now, when the Protagoras of Plato is considered, it is found that in this work, the former does not apply the individual concept to values. But it is hard to see that what is true of the senses, could at one and the same time be true of values also, as applied to ethics. A secondary view shows that Protagoras said that man is the measure of all things. If words are to represent a reality or realities, then it is claimed that statement does in fact include all things. Nothing is excluded. This leaves the way open for a clear acceptance of an individualistic mode for ethical values. Really a choice must be made between the Theaetetus and Protagoras, both by Plato. The decision of choice is made more pressing by the fact that sense knowledge cannot become universal, whilst ethical values can. This was Plato's teaching. Another point from the Theaetetus shows Protagoras as saying that ethical values are relative, in the sense that one can be better than another.

The ultimate meaning of these divergent views are that whilst values of ethics are implanted in all men, in various places, they may be better or stronger in some than in others. The Law would, in this case, be upheld in that particular plan by the State. Education and the need of the citizen to work with the community are stressed by Protagoras. It is wrong to entertain your private judgement against that of the State, and in Protagoras is found also a glimmer of teaching on the natural law, which was so much to the advantage of later thinkers. An interesting feature of these different views which we have so far witnessed, is that the thought as a separate movement cuts across the existing line of argument thus widening and deepening it; for any idea will hold its ground by its force and depth.

Protagoras was uncertain as to the existence of the gods; a fact which could lead to his being sceptical. At the same time, if a sceptical attitude were adopted, that in itself was no reason for discarding the religious views handed down by others.

This was the position Protagoras adopted, and it has lent weight to the verbal portraits of him drawn by Plato. This point may also be viewed from another angle when the Greek idea of religion is considered. They were not interested in affirming complicated theological formula. In their case, it was worship pure and simple, nothing more. Some have thought that the overall tendency among the Sophists was to reduce the faith in tradition, but in Protagoras' personal case, he seems to present a very balanced outlook, indeed he did what he could to encourage social tradition at least among the people.

It seems that if a relativistic theory be adopted, this will develop into many opinions. But there would be, and indeed are, probabilities although quite independent, served to give strength to the conclusion of the perfection of philosophy as an idea. All callings will subscribe to this idea, the better and the worse among them. Certainly at times, the worst would appear to prosper, but taken as a whole, the idea itself can only prosper.

Protagoras was also interested in grammar. He seems one of the first to make a scientific study of it starting with the sentence. Later, he advanced to giving the genders of various nouns.

CHAPTER 13

OTHER SOPHISTS

There are other Sophists whom it is necessary to consider historically. The next is Prodicus who came from Ceos, which is an island in the Aegean Sea. The occupants of this island were extremely pessimistic in outlook, and Prodicus appears no exception to the rule. He believed death preferable to life in order that one may escape the evil of life. He looked with scorn upon those afraid to die, since he considered this view as irrational.

Prodicus is included here chiefly because of his view of religion and his attempt to explain it. According to this view, man first worshipped the sun, moon and stars, etc. Fruits and foods were also included in this group. They were worshipped because they benefitted man in some way, and he consequently felt obliged to them. The worship of the Egyptians of the Nile is a good example of this. Later, there developed a second phase during which man worshipped those things he fashioned or worked on with his hands. Prodicus considered that at this stage, there was no need of prayer, and this view lead him into difficulties with the authorities at Athens. Like his precedessor Protagoras, Prodicus was interested in grammar, and he examined synonyms. His overall work is characterised by somewhat forceful mode of expression.

It appears that while Plato treated him in an offhand manner, Socrates was prepared to send pupils to him. It also would seem from the written evidence that the pupils who were sent, were so, because of their failure to understand or respond to Socrates. The latter considered they might do better with Prodicus.

If anyone could be considered a master of many subjects such a person was Hippias of Elis. He had knowledge of mathematics, astronomy, grammar, rhetoric, rhythmics and harmony, history, literature, and mythology. He was the junior of Protagoras, and when visiting the Olympiad, claimed he had made all his own clothing. He paved the way for the Greek system for dating the Olympiads, the virtual founder of which was Timaeus. According to Plato, Hippias considered that law was a tyrant of men, making them do many things contrary to nature. This would presumably mean that the law of the state is often unjust, thereby forcing men to do that which they would not otherwise have done, thus compelling them to be at odds with their natural inclinations.

Next, in 483 to 375 B. C. in Sicily, lived Georgias of Leontini, and in the year 427 he arrived in Athens as Ambassador of Leontini. His diplomatic mission was to seek assistance from Syracuse. At first, Georgias seems to have been a pupil of Empedocles; but it would appear he was lead astray into scepticism by the philosophy of Zeno. There is some mention among scholars of Georgias having written the book on Optics. However, under Zeno's influence, he produced a work called "On not-being or Nature". Sextus Empiricus tells of the content of this work, and it would appear that whilst Protagoras would say that everything is true, Georgias would hold the absolute contrary. Georgias claimed there is nothing, for if there was something it could be either (a) eternal, or (b) have come into being. It has not come from an eternal source, because if it had, it would either be in itself or in another. As it is, it is neither of these things, and further, if it were, it would not be known. If it is neither in another or in itself, it is nowhere. What does not exist in any place at all is nothing. Neither is it possible to come into being, for out of not-being can come nothing. If being be thought then it must be actual. This arises through knowledge of being. Thus, if being is thought, what is thought is actual and material, and not being which could not be thought of. This excluded error altogether, which is absurd. If knowledge were acquired, it could not be taught, since every word is different from what it signifies and thus it is not true knowledge. How can colours be demonstrated by words, as the ear hears sound waves and not colours? How could one and the same concept exist at the same time in two different people?

These certainly are startling views to say the least; but some have tried to read into it a subtlety on the part of Georgias, playing the part of rhetorician, speaking as it were with his tongue in his cheek.

But Isocrates compares Georgias' philosophy with that of Zeno and Melissus. It is difficult, however, to consider as true the fact that Georgias thought of nothing as existing. Gradually, it seems that he abandoned philosophy and studied rhetoric. Now, rhetoric was defined by Georgias as the power of persuasion, and he practised the art of suggestion, which of course, could serve good or bad ends. He attempted to justify deception. He describes a tragedy as "better to cause than not to cause," and to succumb to it, "shows greater artistic appreciation than not to." Plato adopts a might is right principle from Georgias; Lycophron says all men are equal, whilst a third follower of Georgias required slaves to be freed according to the natural law. Professor Zeller and other modern scholars ascribed Georgias' forsaking philosophy for rhetoric as being the real reason he failed to answer pressing questions concerning the truth.

Among other thinkers of this particular group was Thrasymachus of Chalcedon who is shown by Plato in the Republic as believing in the right of thought. Also, there is Antiphon of Athens who claimed all men are equal, thereby attempting to abandon the demarcation line between slaves and nobles. He was a great advocate of education, and gained a reputation by claiming that anyone could be made happy by use of proper language.

Some have claimed that the Sophist cause was one which sought the overthrow of religion and morality. But again and again their chief adherents — Protagoras and Georgias — referred to a natural law. Also they did a great deal for education, and this is a great advantage in any community. The average Greek mind was consequently broadened, but on the other hand, one must not overlook the fact that the Sophists made grievous mistakes. They said all opinions are right, and again, Georgias asserts that every opinion is false, which reasoning has a certain kind of outcome. It will lead men to be persuaded rather than convinced with respect to important problems. While it is no understatement to emphasise the Sophist trend toward education, it was mainly an education in Rhetoric which was attained, and it has already been pointed out that this can be used in a good way or a bad way. Rhetoric tended by virtue of its nature to raise problems it could not answer, which also laid the foundation of a relative attitude to questions which could only be successfully answered by concise propositions. The reactionary force to this position will be Socrates, and later Plato, both of whom aimed at just such a precise knowledge as would be contained in such propositions.

CHAPTER 14

THE ENTRANCE OF SOCRATES

The history of philosophy contains principles and doctrines. Now principles are general and abstract, and facts relate to doctrines. The latter grow and develop, whilst the principles appear permanent. Further, doctrines pertain to the intellect whilst principles are more practical, and are concerned with ethics. This explains the various systems encountered so far, which live in their principles, and are representative of doctrines. Doctrines are related to principles in somewhat the same way as fruitfulness is related to generation, although this likeness must not be used to excess. For doctrines are developed and enlarged by the operation of principles. Now, if a development must be consistent, it must maintain its contact with its principle. Without this principle, the doctrine produces nothing. This explains why systems of philosophy have fallen by the wayside through losing contact with their principle, whilst remaining a doctrine.

Socrates, who died in 399 B. C., will contribute according to the above remarks in his own particular way, as will other individual philosophers. Plato represents Socrates as seventy years old at the time of his death, which would fix his birth at approximately 470 B. C. His Father was Sophroniscus and his mother Phaenarete, both members of the Antiochid tribe. There is some doubt as to the calling of his father, some writers mentioning he was a stonemason. Present day historians see it as a playful error in the Euthyphro when Daedalus is spoken of as an ancestor of Socrates. It does not seem that Socrates followed his father's calling whatever it may have been, and there are further indications to show that Socrates could not come of poor parents. He served as a hoplite and must have had means to enable him to undertake such a service. His mother is referred to in the Theaetetus as a midwife, but it would be mistaken to consider this term in the light of its present day usage.

Athens was blossoming as a great city in Socrates' early years. The Greeks had won victory over the Persians at Plataea in 479, and Athens also was becoming a sea power.

Alcibiades and others represent Socrates as a possessor of above average physical strength; apparently he also had a habit of rolling his eyes. He did not change his clothing according to winter or summer, and preferred to go barefoot whenever possible. Normally very sparing in food and drink, it was possible for him to drink excessively without ill effects. Also he was subject to mental distractions of long duration, and some writers have considered these as ecstasies. But this is unlikely on account of the abnormal length of these abstractions.

The Ionians began, in Socrates' early manhood, to turn from cosmology to the study of man in himself. Socrates began following various philosophers such as Archelaus, Diogenes of Apollonia and Empedocles. Archelaus was the successor of Anaxagoras, and Socrates attended this school, only to suffer disillusion at its hands. Enhanced with Anaxagoras' concept of mind, Socrates began assiduously to study this idea. But he found that Anaxagoras had not developed this major concept in any way, when it was quite obvious it was so capable of development.

To offset this disappointment, Socrates decided to start investigations on his own account. Some have considered that he was Archelaus' successor, but no real proof can be found for this; although this possibility seems to play an abnormally big part in the minds of those who so speculate.

The occasion of the Delphic Oracle changed Socrates into a moral philosopher. Chaerephon asked the Oracle if there was a wiser man living than Socrates. The answer was no. This led Socrates to think that in seeking true and stable truth, he must first acknowledge his own ignorance. This most likely is a true story, since once again Plato could have no other motive that put the truth in Socrates' mouth in a work which also recounts the death of the philosopher.

Socrates was married to Xanthippe of whom stories abound in the Phaedo concerning her feminine wiles. They may or may not be true. The marriage took place within the first ten years of the Peloponnesian War, during which Socrates distinguished himself at Potidaea 431/430, and again in 424, and also at the action of Amphipolis in the year 422 B. C.

There are three different points of view concerning Socrates, which makes an accurate assessment of his philosophical views very difficult. The first of these views is that of Xenophon who was not particularly interested in philosophy, or had no particular bent for it, and consequently he portrays Socrates as the citizen but not as the metaphysician. An absolutely contrary viewpoint is taken in the dialogues of Plato, where Socrates is shown as the supreme metaphysician. Lastly, there is the view of Aristotle who says that Plato is in the habit of expressing his own view through the mouth of Socrates. Of these three views, the last, that of Aristotle, is most reliable. In it, neither Xenophon nor Plato appear as opposed, and this position is given strength by the fact that Aristotle himself maintains a balanced perspective throughout.

But this opinion is not universal. The view has been expressed that the most apt view is that of the Platonic dialogues. Prof. Burnet and Taylor say they think it is not likely that Plato put his own words in the mouth of Socrates when the latter did not hold such views, particularly because people were still living who knew what Socrates himself had taught. This opinion states that in the Timaeus, Plato is making statements which he himself does not believe, and a consequence of this position would be if Socrates does not stand for these statements, it is difficult to see why Timaeus should do so.

In other cases in Aristotle, it seems that Plato's actual discourses are ignored sometimes. The probability here is that Aristotle only considered true Plato the theories developed in the Academy in which he worked with Plato for twenty years. It is not true to assume, however, that there is a split between Aristotle's actual views, and those developing in the Academy. That there is development at all in these views is proof of a reflective mind on the part of Plato. However, the general consensus of opinion is that Plato introduced a lot of his own thought into this work.

There is a letter written by Plato in which he described Socrates in glowing terms. It is apparently upon this letter that Prof. Burnet and Taylor base their opinions in favour of the Platonic dialogues being the most authentic. However, whatever may be said by these eminent scholars and others, it seems neither would deny that historically speaking, Socrates is found in this document. Notwithstanding certain views as to the latter being genuine, it is significant that Socrates did not in Aristotle separate Forms from things, and surely this would be a mark of Plato himself, Aristotle knew Plato's teaching extremely well, and it is unlikely that he would be mistaken over the doctrine of Forms. There are other dialogues which do no violence to Aristotle's views, therefore, this latter appears as most trustworthy. Great controversy is possible over this question; but it seems a matter of justice to render to each what is his own. Plato can present Socrates in an historical aspect, Aristotle can present him with a direct bearing on philosophy itself. But it almost seems as if Socrates historically speaking has been assimilated to such a degree that absolute knowledge is impossible. But this is but a stage in the overall development of philosophy.

On a purely philosophical level, Socrates did two things. Firstly, he employed inductive argument, and secondly propounded universal definitions. For him, these were not separate; but Plato coming after him gave each of them separate existences, and this is the doctrine of Ideas.

To the truth developing at the moment, Socrates attaches great importance to these universal or fixed concepts. This was in opposition to the Sophists who had taught their theory of relativity. Now, something of a relative nature, necessarily excludes the universal. But Socrates saw that universal concepts were unchanged, despite the changeableness of contingent things. Aristotle had defined man as a rational animal. This would mean, presumably, an unhampered use of reason. Things to hamper the exercise of this faculty would be sleep or mental defectiveness. Again, because the reason is free, there are many ways in which the individual follows a problem with his reason. Some are good, and some are defective, but all owe allegiance to the faculty of reason.

It is definitely a mistaken view to consider universal concepts as subjective, since they must have foundation in objective reality. The significance of the universal concept at this stage is that it is a firm foundation against ever changing accidents. This stability was very welcome purely through its very lack of change.

Universal concepts also affect justice and ethics again showing a clear basis for building a firm structure. It is obvious why Socrates held it in such esteem, for when we come to consider justice, it is found that this varied from state to state in Greece. But this universal idea provided a norm that was acceptable to all.

At this stage, it is necessary to make two observations. First, when Socrates speaks of the universal, it is not the universals that so intrigued the philosophers of the Middle Ages, i.e. in a metaphysical sense. Secondly, when Aristotle speaks of Socrates' "inductive argument" this does not refer to logic. It is a pointer to method.

This approach of Socrates was to get into a discussion with someone, and slowly gather, in the course of this same discussion, what the person really held as regards the truth of things. Socrates would profess ignorance concerning a certain virtue for example. Then he would enquire the other person's views on it. When his ignorance had been transformed into knowledge, which would mean that Socrates, according to the laws of thought, would then possess some idea at least in germ of the concepts held by the other, he would express gratitude and thanks for what he had learnt. Socrates always asked most of the questions: this process being known as dialectic.

This dialectic was really a process from the less perfect form of knowledge to a more perfect form; it had as its end a universal definition acceptable to all. It was possible for no satisfactory result to emerge from this type of discussion; one on Ethics that Socrates is shown as having in the dialogues of Plato, is an example of this. Injustice was dealt with at length. Occasions of deceit, injury, slavery and so on. It is shown that if a weapon is stolen from a friend who wishes to do himself injury with it, this is no crime. Nor is a father's action wrong in deceiving his son to take medicine if that medicine will restore the son's health.

It is possible that this form of reasoning was objectionable to those who were proved in their lack of knowledge. If it was so to a misdirected few, it does not detract in the least from Socrates' main aim which was to discover the truth. He was quite sincere in his profession of ignorance; he wishes to learn from others, and wherever he could. Mainly ethical in his approach, he wished others to think rightly, with a view to right action. By such an operation, he too, would benefit intellectually.

He was also very interested in the nature of the soul, as thinking and willing. Definition led to an ethical outlook, if used for practical ends, and this is one reason Socrates was insistent on accurate definitions, and their application of ethics.

A very interesting light on Socrates' main aim in this life is given by Plato in the Apology. In his profession during the course of his trial, Socrates says that it is his intention to assist everyone to virtue and wisdom before they look to their own individual interests. Also a man should look to the state, before considering the interests of the State; this was what Socrates regarded as his

51

end in life to assist everyone to care for their souls. This, he considered, was imposed upon him by the god Delphi. If he was subtle in his dialectic with others, it was out of no desire to appear superior, but merely to assist them to a higher level of thought, and to acquire knowledge on their own account. In the Community of Athens, or any Greek city, a manner of behaviour was inseparable from good citizenship. To become a good member of society, one had to live properly. Socrates is shown already as saying the State itself is prior to its interests. But, of course, the question arises, how does one behave properly? The answer is by the acquirement of knowledge. Good behaviour and knowledge then are inseparable, and assist each other to a proper end.

By means of this approach, Socrates concluded that no-one did wrong things because they were in themselves wrong. Knowledge guides the action to what *appears* to be right. This amounts to knowledge and virtue considered as one.

But let us go along the lines proposed by Socrates for a moment. At once we come face to face with all kinds of degrees of human depravity as well as virtue. Bad acts in a greater or lesser degree of evil are happening every day. How then are we to reconcile the facts of knowledge and virtue as one, when it is quite obvious that many people act with full knowledge of what they are doing is evil? Thus is human responsibility for human acts. The answer lies in Aristotle's comments on Socrates, when he says that in his assessment of virtue, Socrates did not take into account those parts of the soul not completely subject to reason. So far, so good. But from here, various points arise. Firstly, Socrates himself appears able to control his passions remarkably well, whilst this is not the case with the masses. Hence, he ascribed moral failures as due to ignorance only. Certainly, where there is sin there is ignorance, but also there are irrational parts of the soul in act. Socrates overlooked this latter consideration. One concludes that it was a personal conviction at stake in his view. Secondly, when Socrates speaks of "right" what does he mean? Apparently, if the act serves man's true happiness is the rightful answer. But various distinctions must be made. At the outset, everyone wishes for his own happiness, but not everything he does serves him well in the end, for some acts only have the appearance of good. These latter often tend to rob a man of his freedom by forming bad habits which in themselves are contrary to what man really wishes, i.e. happiness. In following an unreasonable or bad habit, there is no difference between man and a brute, for the man has lost his reason in so far as he acts unreasonably.

If a person drinks to excess, thinking his goodness lies solely in that direction, that person is a victim of ignorance. He is blind to his real good. If, however, he knew his goodness did not rest in drink, then according to Socrates, he would not drink. But Aristotle will tell us that it is possible for a man to detest drink, and yet through weakness, fall a victim to it. This point has been examined deeply, and it appears that although Aristotle is right in his assumption, if it were a case of a deep conviction against drink, then that person would not indulge in the habit. The strongest argument for Socrates's case is in the psychological field; when possible, a man considers his unhappy life, and looks for diversion in drinking to excess.

It would be a mistake to think of Socrates advocating the following of whatever is pleasurable only. Control is needed to decide what is good and what is not good, and in this way the advantage of control is realised. It is obvious that although pleasure is very attractive, moderation and subsequently happiness will follow the moral man rather than the immoral. This is because material things do not make for happiness, for the immoral man must tend toward the material.

It is perhaps true that Socrates laid a too great emphasis on pure intellection. Nevertheless, his teaching in ethics is very strong. For example, Hippias had remarked that sexual relations between members of a family were not wrong. Socrates replies that under such circumstances, social deterioration would quickly follow. So here we have a first glimpse of what today we would know as the Natural Law. But this Law does not bind in conscience unless it is considered under the concept of obligation and duty to binding forms of conscience. But the ethical system laid out now by Socrates was the beginning of one of the first phases in Greek philosophy. It is a fact that human nature does not change, consequently, values in ethics do not change either. Socrates realised this, and with the aid of definitions, attempted to arrive at a degree of stability in human behaviour.

If wisdom and virtue is considered as one entity then a unity must ensue. Through this unity, it is possible to teach virtue more easily. This still remains true despite the fact that the Sophists also sought to teach virtue. But the methods employed are quite diverse. The Sophist was always in the role of instructor. Socrates by professing ignorance, became a great teacher. He taught then these two disciplines, knowledge, and from it, virtue. He also considered that virtue *itself* could be taught in this way, but he overlooked the fact that a man can possess knowledge of a thing, and yet that knowledge is not necessarily operative all the time. On the other hand, when Socrates deals with knowledge and virtue, we must not overlook the fact that they can be united to a personal conviction. On this account, i.e. the personal element, it may be possible for virtue to be taught. However, it seems that Socrates aimed at giving his pupils an inner knowledge and with this attribute came virtue. The real fault of this doctrine lies in an over emphasis of intellect, and overlooking man as a person.

This approach would not help to endear Socrates' teaching to the general populace of Athens as it then was. For if a man who has knowledge is purely a specialist, then the idea of electing public officers from the so-called intellectual mob, would seem to be out of place. It is necessary to possess knowledge in order to rule, and Socrates insisted on this attribute.

There is a tendency in Socrates' teaching to a single god, although he does not discard the idea of multiplicity of gods whom he says are present in all places.

In the main, there is no particular distinction between monotheism and polytheism, and this trend is maintained both in Plato and in Aristotle. It was Socrates' belief that the human body was made up of materials from the world, and this theory was to be developed by those who came after him. Socrates can be regarded as the founder of teleology in the world sense, but strictly he was neither a theologian nor cosmologist. His main interest was in human behaviour.

Aristophanes draws a picture of Socrates in the Clouds. But in this portrayal, Aristophanes does not seem to realise fully the difference between the Sophists and Socrates. Consequently, the doings of Socrates in this account have a dash of Sophist in them, which is to distort the true picture.

Moral usage was not lacking in Socrates. At the conflict of Arginusae, light commanders had been reprimanded for neglect of duty. Socrates, at this time a member of the Committee of the senate, refused to agree to try them together on the grounds that a too hasty decision would involve injustice. He repeated his action in 404/3 when Leon of Salamis was arrested and an oligarchy intended to murder this person.

In 400/399. Socrates himself was arrested and brought to trial. A politician named Anytus was largely responsible for the trial being continued. The charges were that Socrates did not worship the State's gods; introducing unfamiliar religious customs; and of corrupting young people. The death sentence was remanded. The first charge was never really clearly formulated, and when we look at the second, it probably was nullified by an amnesty of 404/3 of which Anytus had been responsible. The third charge — that of corrupting the young — referred to leading youth in a spirit of criticism. Socrates had been responsible for the education of Alcibiades and Critias; the former had gone to Sparta, and had caused much trouble in Athens; whilst the latter was a prominent member of the Oligarchs.

It was presumed that Socrates would go into exile, but he did not do this. He stayed until 399 for his trial, and was his own defender. He aligned himself with absolute facts and may have mentioned his military service. But the verdict went against him, for he was condemned to death by a majority to 60 to 6 on a jury of 500 or 501.

It was possible for Socrates to tender an alternative penalty, and if he had done so, it would have been accepted. Actually, the jury were angered by Socrates' gallant manner, and his death sentence majority was increased in consequence. The sentence was due to be carried out in a month's time, during which time a ship from Delos would arrive (in memory of the city's deliverance). During this time, an attempt at escape was moved by Socrates' friend (Theseus) but he refused this offer on the grounds that it was contrary to his principles. Plato records his last earthly day in the Phaedo. He spent the morning talking with friends. He drank the poison of hemlock, his last words being "Crito, we owe a cock to Aesculapius, pay it, and therefore we do not neglect it." Shortly after the poison reached his heart and his death took place. Thus ended the life of a great early philosopher.

CHAPTER 15

OTHER FOLLOWERS OF SOCRATES

Mention has been made in previous sections with regard to the different ways an idea can develop. These notions apply to the history of philosophy since it is an intellectual discipline, and ideas grow in the human mind. Further, if new ideas form from previous ones it is neither possible to discredit the former without injustice to the latter and vice versa. The power of reason in the case of philosophy is the fulfilling force behind the formation of ideas. In philosophy there is a progress of the mind from the judgement made by one act of reason to the judgement made by another which follows. Accordingly, this is the position with those who followed Socrates. This is particularly evident at this stage, since Socrates did not found any specific philosophical school.

There are two Euclids known to ancient history. One was a celebrated mathematician, and he does not concern us here. However, one of Socrates' followers was called by that name and he came from Megara. In 432/2, citizens of Megara were forbidden to enter Athens, yet Euclid defied this order for the purpose of his philosophical researches. The story is told that he entered the city under female disguise during the night. He sought Socrates out, and was with the philosopher when he died. After this, however, Euclid and other followers were compelled to return to Megara. Well versed as he was with the teachings of the Eleatics, Euclid subjected Eleatic teaching to certain changes. This consisted of considering the One as Good, and also in a repetition of virtue as a unity. Diogenes Laertius wrote that Euclid thought of the One under many names such as God and also Reason. But he would not admit of a contrary of the Good, since, according to the Eleatics this would mean many things or multiplicity. Consequently, these philosophers did not accept this. In short, Euclid was an Eleatic despite Socratic leanings.

A thinker by the name of Eubulides developed the philosophy of Megara, in such a way that it endeavoured to reduce to absurdity, any theory with which it was not in agreement. One such argument said there was one grain of corn and that could not be considered a heap; very well, add another grain, still there is no heap, so where does the heap begin?

In this particular group of philosophers, there is Diodorus Cronus. He only believed in the actual. He said that if a thing is possible, it cannot be impossible. Of two contradictory notions, if one takes place, it is not possible for the other to occur. On these grounds, if the impossible were possible at all, it would be contained in the possible. This shows that the impossible *is* actually impossible, consequently only the actual can exist. It is clear the world exists. It is equally clear that it is not nonexistent. But if it were to be considered that the world did in fact not exist, then the possible would become impossible. This is absurd. Involved though this theory may sound, it has found adherents in modern times, who maintained that given a complete set of conditions, and only these, nothing else could happen. Professor Nicolai Hartmann has developed this idea in Berlin.

Another member of the school of philosophy of Megara was Stilpo. This thinker was a teacher in Athens about 320, but was forced to leave the city later. He was a teacher of ethics, and upon Megara being burnt and pillaged, he was asked what he himself had lost. He replied no one had carried wisdom and knowledge away from the city.

Phaedo of Elis and Menedemus of Eritrea both shared the honour of giving their names to yet another school of philosophy. The former is mentioned in Plato's dialogue in the Phaedo. The name by which this school is known is the Elean-Eritrean School. Dialectic and Ethics were its two main points of teaching. The influence of Megara is known in Phaedo's handling of dialectics, Menedemus continued the idea of knowledge and virtue considered as one.

Antisthenes (c. 445-c. 365) whose male parent was a native of Athens and his female a Thracian, taught in what was known as the kynosarges. This procedure was followed by those of not pure Athenian stock. The Kynosarges was an exercise hall or gymnasium which was dedicated to Heracles. It was the teaching of Antisthenes which founded the Cynic School, which was also known as the followers of the dog, possibly because of their manner of life, and also the gymnasium teaching already referred to above.

Antisthenes had been a pupil of Georgias but later he admired Socrates to whom he gave great adulation. The latter's moral independent nature impressed Antisthenes, and it seems that he followed this aspect of Socrates without preserving a medium mode of behaviour. This is illustrated in the fact that independence with Antisthenes became an end in itself. Under these conditions what was virtue? It was simply freedom from everything earthly — possessions, etc. — which is looked upon as a negative idea. Socrates, while he possessed it, did not seek to make it a positive issue in itself, while Antisthenes took it as something positive. Now this position led to other difficulties. The emphasis on ethics led to the idea that nothing else was wanting, such as learning. Virtue we understand is sufficient, which means freedom from all desire of any thought.

Now, it was the principles that Socrates held that were responsible for his independent views. This must always be so, since doctrine of any sort rests on its principles. In this case, we have a distortion of the original idea because the principles held by the Cynics were not as sound in an overall sense as those held by Socrates. Thus, Socrates could defy public opinion; but when he did so, he did not treat the defiance for its own sake. When the Cynics followed the same path, it simply led to a defiance of convention for its own sake. This shows very well the relationship between principles and doctrines.

The doctrine of Ideas did not find favour with Antisthenes. Nothing according to him can be attributed to the subject except the subject itself. Thus, it remains in isolation. With this form of reasoning, it is impossible to consider a class of any kind; so for Antisthenes only individuals are possible.

Antisthenes had taught that wisdom and virtue are as one. In what did this really consist? It meant primarily being able to ascertain man's values at a glance. Passions of every kind are not true goods; neither is affluence. The true good is independence, though it is not won easily. This knowledge is a great advantage when dealing with the State, for the State does not recognize true virtue.

This view is a development of what Antisthenes thought Socrates would have meant by independence. Actually, the latter had great respect for the State's laws, whilst Antisthenes' inability to find an average mode of behavior, led him to despise these same laws. He believed, however, in one God; and virtue which he had taught was in the service of God. The Greek myths were to Antisthenes a source of morality. The vigor with which these various thinkers followed through their thought is a manifestation of how alive philosophy really was in these times. For only something alive can be vigorous.

One of these who came after Antisthenes, Diogenes of Sinope (d. 324 B.C.) considered that Antisthenes was false to his beliefs. Diogenes spent most of his life in Athens, but died in Corinth. He upheld animals as examples to men, and it was his purpose to set up new values in the Greek world.

Apparently, he concurred with the idea of many wives and general promiscuity. He advanced the idea of an asceticism in order to attain the concept of independence advocated by Antisthenes. He did not consider convention in any way, doing in public what is generally a private matter, and went so far as to perform acts which are morally privately forbidden.

Nevertheless, he had followers. They were Monimus, Onesicritus, Philiscus and Crates of Thebes. The latter gave up a large fortune to the city, and was followed in this by his wife Hipparchia. Thereafter, both lived a life of poverty.

A further school of philosophy known as the Cyrenaic owed its beginning to Aristippus of Cyrene who was born in 435 B.C. He was present in Athens in 416 B.C., and during the years 399-388 B.C., was in Aegina of the court of the elder Dionysius where he worked with Plato. Athens saw him again in 356. There appears to be some doubt as to the accuracy of these dates, and also to the accuracy of the fact that Aristippus was in actuality the founder of this particular school of philosophy. Despite this assertion, he can safely not be confused with his grandson, also named Aristippus. Again, it appears that Diogenes Sotion and Panaetius all agree that Aristippus did in fact leave his philosophical views in writing, while against this Socrates says he wrote nothing.

Whilst in Cyrene, Aristippus studied Protagoras, and when he arrived at Athens, he formed an association with Socrates. It is possible that the former was responsible for the idea that sensations provide knowledge. In any event this is what Aristippus taught. Further, we must rely according to Aristippus upon subjective sensation only, which led to the idea obviously that the only thing would be to seek pleasure for this purpose.

These sensations, when they were gentle, produced pleasure; when they were strong they were productive of pain. It is impossible to consider the notion of ethics and motion as compatible; on the other hand, the absence of motion would result in neither pleasure nor pain. Consequently, the path we follow would appear to be that which produces pleasure, and this then is regarded as the ethical end.

Now Socrates had said that virtue leads to happiness, and thus provided happiness as a motive for virtue. Aristippus took part of the truth that Socrates had taught, but only part. He ignored those facts not relating to pleasure. But assuming that pleasure is an end in itself, and taking into consideration the fact that there are many kinds of pleasure, what form should this pursuit follow? It could either be positive or negative. Epicurus taught that it was a negative aspect whilst for Aristippus it became decidedly positive. The position is then arrived at where the Cyrenaics say that physical pleasure is all important over intellectual pleasure. A position such as this would seem to lead to a lack of balance, where excess would seem to be found, but this school taught that if a person did go to excess, then he was not experiencing pleasure but pain. A limit is obviously necessary.

There is some confusion between pleasure looked at here and now, and the faculty of judgement in this reasoning. Aristippus does not appear to correlate these two particularly well. There naturally follows from this some indecision on the part of those who followed his doctrine.

One such follower Theodorus who was called the Atheist, said that judgement and justice are good, but he also maintained that the good of the intellect was the highest good, bodily pleasure being in his view incidental. But according to him, no one who was really wise would die for his country; furthermore, people would steal, commit adultery and so forth, quite willingly according to favourable circumstances. In his view, a God did not exist.

Another follower, Hegesias, took a pessimistic view of life in general. This resulted in a negative approach seeking only the elimination of pain and sorrow, even physical pleasure was of little avail. In later times, Cicero writes that this outlook resulted in many who heard Hegesias committing suicide. The story is told that for this reason, his talks were banned.

However, the positive side was not without its adherents either, and so we have Anniceris claiming that acts of pleasure were man's true end. He placed emphasis on friends and family life, which according to him, were a pleasure on account of the sacrifice they sometimes involve. In this, he differed from Theodorus who had maintained that man was sufficient unto himself.

60

CHAPTER 16

DEMOCRITUS

In a previous section, it has been necessary to mention the name of Democritus of Abdera. He properly belongs to the Atomist School of thought, but is included here because he examined various texts of knowledge of Protagoras, and was concerned in ethical problems which the Sophists by their teaching had not clarified. Throughout these apparent corruptions, it must be noted that the *idea* of philosophy remains intact, for it is possible for ideas to remain whilst they can be expressed in many different ways. In the same way, the corruptions that have been met with so far, outwardly at least do not seem to differ from the substantial idea of philosophy. If a discipline must advance in any way at all, then a certain type of advancement must be maintained. Possibly nowhere is this seen to greater advantage than in philosophy. For surface corruptions are different from alterations, since only the latter will corrupt.

In the case of Democritus, Plato ignores him, but we come across his name frequently in Aristotle. He was Principal in a school at Abdera, and when Plato founded his Academy, Democritus was still alive. None of his writings are extant, although it is believed that he left many works.

In an attempt to account for the faculty of sensation, Democritus employs a mechanical theory. It is possible he borrowed this from Empedocles who had spoken of influences reaching the eye from various objects. According to the Atomist teaching, this was due to atoms controlled by mechanical necessity. Apparently objects are always giving off these various influences. These so-called influences unite with the soul, which, being contained of atoms, unites at once to combine with these forces. Air will distort these effects which explains why things cannot be seen from a distance. Colour had its root in the texture, either rough or smooth, of these influences. In like manner, sound was caused in the same way. For Democritus, the gods live longer than the average man, and any knowledge of them is contained in the fashion above described. Now, the pure Atomist teaching would not admit of a god; consequently it illustrates the advancement made by Democritus in admitting one. Also, at this stage, it is useful to recall the Sophists who had said what was bitter for one could be equally so for another. Democritus said this was incorrect, for in his view, there is nothing of like nature outside the subject itself. Thus all sensation is an affair of the subject. The senses themselves are not reliable, and consequently two forms of knowledge are available. These are the true and the untrue, the latter being arrived at through the senses. Despite this, however, it is not altogether possible to separate sense and thought.

Human behaviour should be mainly concerned with the pursuit of happiness.

A work on cheerfulness is found among the works of Democritus. This work will be used by both Seneca and Plutarch in years to come. It is quite clear from what Democritus says here that the soul is the place where happiness is to be found. This in itself is the reason for any action, i.e., in order to be happy. Pleasure and pain give different degrees of happiness. Sense does not represent the summit of happiness; in like manner then, neither is sense pleasure true happiness. Apparently good and true as concepts have the same meaning for everyone, but what is pleasant varies from person to person. An overall summary of this work could consist in saying that if well being were achieved in a balanced fashion, then cheerfulness would ensue, and the soul would be in a state of happiness.

Democritus is also worthy of consideration on account of his contributions to the explanation of culture. He says that common need gave birth to civilization. Then man followed what would be most helpful to him; in addition to this, the art which has been cultivated down the years, owed its development to mankind studying nature in general.

His attitude toward the State was that the State itself is of paramount importance. Consequently, politics rated highly in Democritus' estimation. However, ethically Democritus advocated a free line of action, whilst from his atomist ideas he could not avoid a determined or fixed mode. He did not seem to realize that he was telling two different stories at the same time.

Possibly in his teaching on the world Democritus does not fit into the true Socratic picture. Furthermore, his observations on ethics showed he realized that certain problems were raised by Protagoras. Unfortunately, Democritus did not provide an adequate answer, and it is left to Plato to do this.

CHAPTER 17

PLATO

Thus we are led to a consideration of Plato, one of the greatest minds in the pagan philosophical world. His birthplace was Athens in the year 428/7 B. C. His father and mother were Ariston and Perictione. His mother was a sister to Charmides and was also a niece of Critus. Both these latter men are found in reference to the oligarchy of 404/3. Aristocles was the original name given to Plato; he acquired the latter on account of his strong appearance. Later, Ariston died, and Perictione then married Pyrilampes, and their son Antiphon (related to Plato as half brother) is mentioned in the Parmenides. His step father provided for Plato's upbringing. This was an advantage since Pyrilampes was friendly with Pericles, consequently it is likely that Plato obtained the opportunities that this regime provided. It cannot be denied that Plato was prejudiced against democracy, and at this stage, we may be able to provide the reasons for this. Firstly, his bringing up under Pericles and secondly the manner in which the democracy had dealt with Socrates. Also, it seems that Plato fought in the Peloponnesian War in 406 B.C., and it appeared to him then that democracy as a way of life seemed to lack a leader and cohesion.

Without doubt, Plato received a cultural education. He met Cratylus the Heraclitian thinker. From this philosopher, Plato learnt of sense perception, flux and its implications. He would also have learnt that they are unreliable as far as the truth is concerned. The best way to obtain knowledge was through conception, and this he would have learnt from Socrates.

A young man of Plato's birth in Athens at this time, would possibly embark upon a political career. Indeed his relations urged him to follow this calling, but the manner in which the people had dealth with Socrates seems to have made a lasting impression on him. Consequently, he gave up the idea of politics. Plato was one of those present during the trial of Socrates, and he was one of a group who persuaded Socrates to increase his fine from one to thirty minae. He even offered to stand security. He was not, however, present at Socrates' death, as he was sick at that particular time. After the event of Socrates' death, Plato went to Megara, and stayed with Euclid. Then he returned to Athens. Some historians have made of Plato a very travelled man, for example, by some he is supposed to have visited Cyrene, Italy and Egypt, but Plato himself gives little indication that he ever visited the latter country. In his works, he shows remarkable knowledge of Egyptian mathematics and games for children, and this may have given rise to the assumption. Euripides is supposed to have accompanied him, but this writer died in 406 B.C. It is possible that Plato if he did visit Egypt went there in 395 B. C., as a member of the Athenian forces sent there.

When he was about forty, Plato *did* visit Italy, and nearby Sicily. This much can be ascertained without doubt. He met many learned men, including Archytas the Pythagorean. An incident took place when Plato was invited to the court of Dionysius I of Syracuse where a friendship sprang up between Plato and Dion, the king's brother-in-law. Plato was not too tactful in his speech; this made Dionysius angry. He ordered Pollis to take Plato away and sell him into slavery. Pollis did sell Plato at Argina, but with the aid of a man named Anniceris who ransomed him, Plato eventually returned to Athens. This happened in 388 B.C.

The next step was for Plato to found his famous Academy in 388/7. It was founded near the Sanctuary of the hero Academus. Since no other school of this type hitherto existed, this would be looked upon as the first university Europe ever knew. Scholars came from far and wide to participate in it, including Eudoxus the mathematician who abandoned his own school and taught at the Academy. The educational program did not only include philosophy, but treated of this as a summit study. Mathematics, astronomy, and the study of science generally was diligently pursued. The aim was to produce a pupil with a balanced education, which would fit him for public life.

Plato acted as lecturer in the Academy, whilst his hearers could make notes. There is no record of these discourses, unlike the dialogues which were meant for every day reading. This throws light upon some radical differences between Plato and Aristotle, the latter entering the Academy in 367 B.C. Plato is present to us in his dialogues but not his lectures, whilst Aristotle is present in his lectures, but we have his dialogues only in very incomplete forms. It is clear from this that a true comparison cannot be made since each philosopher is present to us in a different aspect where obviously different things are dealt with, and different views stated. Aristotle did not appreciate, for example, a lecture on the Good being turned into a mathematical display. Of course, Plato defends this. In his second Epistle, Plato reveres once more the name of Socrates saying too, that he himself had never written a word.

Probably this means that Plato did not place his confidence purely in books; but it must be disregarded to some extent, for Plato in fact did write books. The point also has to be taken into consideration that Plato did not write those excerpts which point to this conclusion.

In 367 B.C. Plato paid a second visit to Syracuse. This time it was to act as a tutor to Dionysius II, a man of thirty. The invitation came from Plato's old friend Dion, and although Plato went to fulfil the task required of him, the results were not happy. Dionysius became jealous of the friendship of Plato and Dion, and eventually only after great hazards did the philosopher return to Athens. He continued to instruct Dionysius by correspondence. He attempted to bring about more friendly terms between the king and his uncle, but failed. Dion eventually undertook a journey to Athens to be in more direct contact with Plato. The philosopher spared no pains however, for in 361 B.C., he went for the third time to Syracuse to instruct Dionysius. His aim apparently was to unite the Greek cities against the menace of Carthage, but this venture, too, unfortunately was doomed to failure. In addition, Dion was left a pauper by an act of Dionysius, and Plato could not persuade the king to bring his uncle back. Plato was compelled therefore, to return to Athens and the Academy where he died in 348/7 B.C. As a postscript to the affairs to Syracuse in 367, Dion became master of the island; he was killed in 353, much to Plato's chagrin, as he nursed the idea of a king guided by philosophy and sound instruction.

THE WRITINGS OF PLATO

There can be no doubt that Plato's works are all authentic. Further, it can be said with equal certainty that most of these works have come down to us, the exception being the lectures already referred to. It is unwise to distinguish between what was contained in the dialogues and what was contained in the teachings of the Academy. Popularity cannot be attributed to all the dialogues, for in some of them, Plato seems to be feeling for what he really wishes to express. After the present lapse of time also allowance must be made for false copies of various manuscripts. The oldest Platonic manuscript known comes from early Christian times, and is an arrangement by Thrasyllus. These works were based on an arrangement by Aristophanes in the third century, B.C. Thus thirty-six dialogues, including the Epistles as one work — became recognized as the genuine works of Plato. Among scholars, the question is: how many of these are true copies, and how many false? It would seem that doubt has been thrown upon them from the earliest times. For example, that some were attributed to Xenophon by Athenaeus in 228 B. C. The Alcibiades is the work in question here. Proclus rejects the Epinomis, Epistles, Laws, and the Republic. These attacks reached their zenith in the nineteenth century in Germany, the main doubters being Ueberweg and Schaarschmidt. Latterly, however, criticism has been much more moderate, and a wide scope of agreement reached upon the authenticity or otherwise of various works.

The following dialogues are regarded as not Plato's true work; the Alcibiades II, Hipparchus, Amatores, Theages Clitophon and Minus. All but the first are possible fourth century; not meant deliberately to mislead, but of the same stamp as some of Plato's works. They lead to some idea of the knowledge of Socrates during the fourth century.

The Alcibiades II is probably of a still later vintage. There follow six works, the authenticity of which is doubtful. They are Alcibiades I, Ion, Menexenus, Hippias, Maior, Epinomis and Epistles. The first could be a work of someone who followed the Platonic school of thought; and second, the Ion, is thought to be the work of Plato himself. Again with regard to the Menexenus, Aristotle attributes this to Plato, and this is the opinion today. The Hippias Maior is also regarded by Aristotle to be authentic, and again modern opinion bows to his decision on this.

There is modern disagreement on the Epinomis. For whilst Professor Jaeger thinks it not be to be genuine Plato, Taylor and Praechter think it is. The Epistles are important, for they give us an insight into Plato's life, and it appears that 6, 7 and 8 of these can be regarded as true, among some scholars apparently, this would lead to accepting the others with the exception of nos. 1 and 2. Because a work gives information on the life of a thinker or writer, this is no reason to say that the work is truly that of its author.

It is conceivable that the other dialogues may be taken for Plato's true work. Of thirty-six in all, six are definitely in doubt while six others may be accepted until proved otherwise. We are left with a corpus of twenty-four works upon which to form our idea of Plato's true conception of reality.

At this stage, it is worthwhile to recall the seven stages of development which it is believed are very manifest in the study of the works of Plato, or any other eminent thinker. These stages can also be observed in a biological study of organic nature. They are: Preservation of type, continuity of principle, power of assimilation, logical sequence, early anticipation, preservable additions and chronic continuance. Also it is a question of experience which fulfils every present act of perception. Thus philosophy pursues its onward course becoming at once in sequence, and contextual, bearing more and more a study of the real, which merges into the world of experience. Only in this way too, can philosophy reflect and correct its previous errors. Let us see how Plato assists in this forward movement. The notes or stages referred to above must be considered as a whole; that is, as a complete working together. Otherwise, it is useless to consider them at all, since then they would not form an organic unity.

Firstly, language is a help in revealing Plato to us. It is an unconscious style, probably assimilated from those who had gone before, and shows that the Republic belongs to the philosopher's early years, whilst the Laws belong to his old age. Isocrates is the style which is assimilated here.

Diogenes Laertius is not a reliable source when he says that the Phaedrus is a late work by Plato. Because Plato wrote of love in his youth, is no certainty that these dialogues were written at that time.

The people referred to in the dialogues do not fix the time of writing for if, as in the Phaedo, the death of Socrates is mentioned, this fact does not say how long after the death of Socrates this work was written. However, some indication can be given in the case of Meno which was probably written on the occasion of the corrupting of Ismenias of Thebes, so that this episode remained in the mind of the people. But in general, it is not a good guide since a mature character might be introduced at the outset, then his early years represented in a later work.

If one dialogue is referred to before another, and in another, this would indicate that the work in which the reference was made was the latest. This is not always an easy task; for one must be satisfied that a reference is directly made. Examples of this, however, are when Plato mentioned the Republic in the Timaeus and the Politicus in the Sophists.

Something of the same thing pertains to the subject matter in these dialogues. For if in one case, a doctrine is treated in summary form, and in a latter, there is a long exposition, mistakes might easily occur as to which dialogue was written first, and which last, for it does not follow the long exposition would come last or vice versa.

But if the form of content is considered, then it is found that the Theaetetus, Parmenides, Sophists, Philebus, and Timaeus are distinctly related. Again, taking the same basis, the Parmenides, Sophists and Politicus are very much the same in content, being the Eleatic dialectic.

Sometimes, the general construction of these works, viz. the manner in which they are laid out, is helpful. The numerous sequences and light and shade generally portray artistic merit, this being the case with the Symposium. Again, in other works, philosophy is the absolute consideration; it is interesting to notice that as Plato's life advanced, the artistic effort lagged behind his pre-occupation with pure philosophy which retained its chronic vigour.

Bearing in mind what has been said, under the influence of Socrates, there is:—

1. the apology which concerns Socrates' trial.
2. Crito which takes its name from one of Socrates' friends who urged him to escape but Socrates refusing says he will obey the Laws of the State.
3. Euthyphron which concerns the charges against Socrates for impiety. Nothing conclusive came of this.

4. Laches concerning courage.
5. Ion concerning poets, etc.
6. Protagoras concerning virtue.
7. Charmides on temperance indefinite.
8. Lysis concerning friendship, with indefinite conclusion.
9. Republic, first book on justice.

All these were prior to the first journey to Sicily in 388/7.

Next, Plato is able to formulate his own ideas. Consequently there is: —

10. Georgias concerning politics and justice.
11. Meno, on virtue.
12. Euthydemus concerning views by Sophists.
13. Hippias I concerning beauty.
14. Hippias II on wrong doing.
15. Cratylus concerning language.
16. Menexenus concerning rhetoric.

Plato next consolidates his philosophical position with the following:—

17. Symposium contrasting earthly and true beauty.
18. Phaedo, on ideas and immortality.
19. The Republic, on the state, and introducing a metaphysical tone.
20. Phaedrus concerning love.

The latter works include:—

21. Theaetetus concerning knowledge.
22. Parmenides on ideals.
23. Sophists concerning ideas.
24. Politicus on the power of knowledge.
25. Philebus concerning pleasure and good.
26. Timaeus concerning science.
27. Critias concerning the ideal State.
28. Laws and Epinomis Law in relation to life.
29. Letters written after the death of Dion.

It has been hinted that the role Plato assumed in the forward march of philosophy must be examined. This then is the excuse for the catalogue of works that has just been given, for it is sincerely hoped that it will provide a sound basis for further investigation, which can be proceeded with once it is known what works can be attributed to a particular thinker. These particular works display clearly the seven phases of development, which can be applied to them as a whole.

CHAPTER 18

PLATO AND KNOWLEDGE

An approach to Plato's actual teaching contained in the works enumerated in the last section, will begin with his ideas on knowledge. The data is somewhat scattered through the Theaetetus, which it would seem is an advance on what has already been imperfectly expressed in the Republic. The explanation of this may lie in the fact that Plato was not as addicted to critical study as for example Kant was. This fact also will explain why it is a difficult task to split up epistemology and ontology in Platonic thought.

Socrates had been adamant that it was necessary to obtain fixed values of morality for all men, and these values must be universal. Plato continued this train of thought, and consequently in the Theaetetus, the first task is to separate truth from error. He does not agree with Protagoras who had said that knowledge and perception are the same. Also, this philosopher had concluded that what appeared true to a certain person, remains the truth for that individual. Plato lays down two rules which are (1) knowledge must be true, and (2) it is what is. Pure sense perception is neither of these, therefore knowledge is not sense perception.

Theaetetus as a mathematician starts talking to Socrates. The subject under discussion is knowledge, and Socrates asks Theaetetus his ideas on this matter. Theaetetus replies that geometry is a good example of knowledge, but Socrates points out that this discipline does not explain what knowledge is in its essence. This inquiry is sincerely an enquiry into Epistemology; that being so, ontology of its very nature, must come into consideration, for the moment I think of something that something has being, and so is related at once to ontology. Probably, this is further emphasized by the fact that the human mind cannot consider nothing as an entity.

Thus fortified, Theaetetus suggests to Socrates that knowledge is perception, which he would obviously consider as visual in this case. Socrates mentions that the idea is worthy of more profound study and discovers that Theaetetus has held Protagoras' views in this regard. A further advance is maintained when Theaetetus admits the *being* of knowledge and its consequent infallibility. Socrates next shows that perception is as Heraclitus would have said in a state of flux. It is not true to maintain that Plato held this view in respect of all things; in this case, it was only in the case of perception. It is obvious as I observe various objects they are changing before my eyes, but this is becoming something else. Certainly my perception is individually true, so in effect Theaetetus has been right in maintaining knowledge as perception.

But there is another point. Supposing that knowledge is perception, then it is impossible for one man to be wiser than another, since I surely am the best judge of what I perceive by sense. Where then can there be a reason for teaching others, and in addition to do so for financial gain? Is there not an ignorance that requires us to listen to a teacher? But we have said each is the judge of his own wisdom. The objection against perception and knowledge could be pushed further, when it is shown that as the proof stands, there is no difference between knowledge and perception, in fact they are as one. Memory tells us that though I remember a thing now, I in no way see it in the concrete here and now. In contrary manner, it is possible to remember something I have perceived, I maintain this knowledge without the aid of perception.

Protagoras said that man was the measure of all things. Now surely this is in reference to truth as a complete whole. Also most people will admit of knowledge and ignorance, and most in fact, hold various things to be true which are not true. Since, according to Protagoras then, anyone who believes something to be false, in effect, holds it to be true, if we take the individual man as the measure of everything.

Socrates then sums up his points thus: It is impossible to consider perception as the whole of knowledge. Also when considered by itself, it still does not amount to knowledge. Elaborating on this, Socrates says that perception is not knowledge because knowledge contains many truths which are not found in sensible data. Reflection on the latter gives much information not provided by the senses, existence and non-existence for example, or the truths of mathematics. Again, the assessment of a Man's character does not lie within the bounds of perception.

Further, it is impossible to know anything unless we know the truth about it, and this we cannot do through the senses. This is achieved by reflection and judgement only.

Therefore, some perception is not knowledge. It is interesting to note that even at this stage, Plato was reluctant to consider sense data as knowledge. The view is that there is nothing stable in what the senses tell us; the valuable data is what *is*. It was this unending search for perfection in what is that led him to adopt this theory of Forms. At this point, this development is discernible when he contends the "particular" of the senses with the "universals" of the mind.

As the dialogue proceeds, Theaetetus sees that judgement is not rightly considered as knowledge; for the reason that a person can make a false judgement. Theaetetus and Socrates agree then to make of judgement only a provisional definition until the matter can be examined further. The discussion next attempts to probe the reason of mistaken judgements. Why do they happen at all? The conclusion is that they are due to the confusion of object and memory, for example, if A sees B in the distance, the judgement could be formed by A that it is someone he knows. As B approaches, however, a mistaken judgement has to be admitted by A. This is because A had various objects in his memory, actually, none of which applied to B. At this point, Plato does not consider it profitable to continue the discussion on judgement; we find it again in the Sophists.

But there is a further angle to consider, for it is possible for someone to judge of something and it to be true, without knowledge on the part of that person. To illustrate, I could say "John Smith is in Brighton" which in actuality is a pure effort of guess work on my part, although it could be true. Obviously true judgement and knowledge are not the same, consequently Theaetetus is asked to give another opinion of what is knowledge.

Theaetetus responds that to explain certain phenomena would bring judgement and knowledge closer. But this could lead to difficulties as Socrates points out by saying that to explain certain parts, then these parts must be known. Otherwise, foolish conclusions could ensue which would really mean complex phenomena being changed to something that is unknown. No, this data must be irreducible, in addition, what is an explanation?

Firstly, it is not possible to take it in the same way as assent is given in words, otherwise, in this case, judgement and knowledge would be the same thing. Also there is a difference in what in effect is a supposition and true facts.

Secondly, the adding of the explanation of parts does not differ, for then anyone who could detail the simple parts of a piece of furniture, legs, doors, top, etc. would possess scientific knowledge of the words which go to make up those parts.

There is another point of view, which consists of being able to discern in one thing, a unique part, thus setting it off from all other things. This idea is perfectly right but not sufficient for the purpose of answering the question "what is knowledge?"

Nevertheless, if there is one, certain aspect whereby Theaetetus is understood, if I have to add notion after notion to this aspect of certainty, then the position reached is absurd. For in my certain aspect of him, I must have had a certain degree of certainty, otherwise my notion could not be certain. Where then is the sense of adding other certain aspects simply to arrive at a notion of certainty? Now if my concept of Theaetetus includes a singular distinguishing aspect, then I can know Theaetetus. Otherwise, the idea I have of him is but one of universality.

Again in my correct notion of him, if I have included all other additions, it is hard to see how I could gain knowledge by still further complements, for this amounts to additions by saying I am adding to my distinctions which I have made already as a set of distinguishing marks, apart from those already known.

The object pursued in this discussion as represented by Plato, is to show that individual sensible qualities are unable to provide true knowledge. The particular, therefore, is not true knowledge, the place to look for this being is in the realm of the universal, where more stability is obtained.

Therefore, if the search for true knowledge is continued, it is evident it must possess two outstanding qualities. They are firstly, infallibility, and secondly, it must be real. All data therefore must be submitted to these norms, and will stand or fall in the quest for truth by their relationship to them. Thus far has Plato advanced. The idea of a relationship between sense and sense perception stems from Protagoras. Plato however, refuses to go the whole way with Protagoras to include everything in a universal sense. It is certain absolute knowledge is obtainable, but for this to be done, it would need something more stable than mere sense perception. Plato further assimilates from Heraclitus the idea of flux with reference to objects. But again Plato draws a line with Heraclitus. He says that it is possible to gain true knowledge from objects despite their apparent flux and change. In effect here, Plato joins hands with Socrates in proclaiming that it was the universal concept that gave true knowledge. To illustrate, I can say a committee is good, I say it is good, because of a fixed concept of goodness I may have. Later, I may revise my opinion and say that committee is bad. But I still judge the body of men by a fixed concept as before. The universal concept will always be one of goodness. The fact that the particular committee in question may be an ecclesiastical one, or an empirical one does not matter. It is still good, because it bears relationship in a particular manner, to my concept of goodness.

Both Plato and Socrates laid great emphasis upon definition. Actually Plato followed Socrates in this. Thus goodness as described above, must be defined by a noun which indeed is the correct way to describe being of any description. This could, and does, involve the idea of universals, and so it is to the universal concept that we must look in order to attain that stability so desirable for true knowledge. It would follow then that universal would be superior, whilst particular knowledge would remain inferior.

This to some minds would create a discrepancy between superior knowledge and inferior. To answer this, it is best to bear in mind the actual teaching of Plato's Ideas or Forms. All universals have an objective in reality. So to each universal there is a corresponding object. Universal concepts do not float around aimlessly in space so to speak. They are all the perfect exemplars of something in concrete reality. Despite Aristotle's criticism of this doctrine, a meaning of it is not to be found in separate universals. However, Plato was faced with a definite problem when he tried to coalesce the universal and the particular.

The work in which Plato's ideas on true knowledge are laid out is the Republic. Knowledge is given as a Line which is identified at various stages by its objects. It is certain that in this work, Plato was only developing ideas which were later to mature, consequently there is great room for supposition in considering what is said.

The advancement of the mind from ignorance to knowledge depends firstly on opinion, and secondly on knowledge. These two operations, the last of which is true knowledge, is specified by their objects. Opinion is mainly concerned with images, whilst knowledge is concerned with the original. A particular act will always be referred to the universal which is its true prototype. Often a man will mistake images for the truth. If however, it is possible for a man to rise above the particular to a consideration of the universal, then he is in a state of knowledge. Further, it is possible to go from one intellectual state to another. This takes place when a man recognizes images for what they truly are, and in that case, he will dimly realize the presence of universals. If it be possible for a person to carry his thought beyond pure images to the Universal Form, as he would do in considering true justice for example, then that man has advanced to a state of true knowledge.

The Line in which Plato illustrates knowledge has various subdivisions. Apparently there are two degrees of ignorance and two of knowledge. The first corresponds to images or shadows, and this in Plato's view would cover the whole of reality. Thus if a man were misled by another, he would still be in ignorance of the truth, despite the fact that it would seem he has acquired knowledge or reality. This is because the concept held by the man in consequence of his informant's words would really be as a shadow of the real truth.

The next step in the advance of knowledge is to be informed by the material objects about it. To illustrate once more, if a person has a particular idea of a horse, for instance, then that concept is not a perfect one, since it is derived from an image of a horse, and is not a Pure Horse. According to Plato, this would constitute an opinion of a horse. In like manner, any knowledge of a purely material character is still taken by Plato as opinion. However, this is an improvement on somebody given entirely to phantasy.

In the tenth book of the Republic, there is a mysterious passage which says that an "artist is the third remove from truth." What does Plato mean by this? What has been said already will, it is hoped, throw a little light upon this statement. Firstly, there is the ideal concept or Form; secondly, there is its image which we see about us, and thirdly, the artist produces a third form from this secondary image. One doing this makes an image out of an image, and for this reason it is imperfect, and the person making this image is in a state of what could be called still an opinion. But anyone who has an ideal thing or form possesses knowledge.

The next consideration is the second division of Plato's line to knowledge. This division is purely non sensible, and can be thought of as representing the world of thought as a pure concept, and secondly that of mathematics. The latter is obvious, for in mathematics, one proceeds mentally from certain given data to a certain conclusion. Thus, upon reflection, it would seem that true knowledge is attained as a state of mind, whilst the other divisions refer to a distinction of things. Nowhere does Plato's epistemology fit this Line of knowledge, and if the previous statement is borne in mind, this should become clear. Pure reason, too, holds pride of place in the intellect; next comes understanding and lastly opinion.

It was Aristotle's idea that Plato held mathematical entities as half way between "forms and sensible things." He goes on to say that whilst mathematical formulae were capable of alteration, Forms do not in any way change. It is thus clear why both divisions of Plato's Line of Knowledge cannot be considered in the same way, i.e., as states of mind.

The actual place that Plato did assign to mathematics has been a celebrated topic for scholars. But although naturally allowance has to be made for human error, it seems that Aristotle's original idea of its place in Plato's thought is still valid.

Thus the highest state of mind attainable is left for consideration. This is a state where purely abstract reasoning holds sway; no images or phantasms are used at all. In this state, it is consequently possible to arrive at the Pure Idea or Form of a thing. It is also possible as one is on a high level of intellection to descend to a concept of knowledge in which images are involved. This idea of Plato's is at once epistemological and ontological.

In Book Seven of the Republic, Plato himself illustrates his ideas on epistemology.

If we imagine a large cave with its mouth opening towards the sun. Behind this there is a fire burning. Behind this again, there is a low wall. Then in a row are numbers of prisoners chained in such a way that they connot turn around, but only face the back of the cave. Figures constantly pass along the low wall. Their shadows are thrown by the light of the fire onto the rear wall of the cave. These shadows are constantly being seen by the prisoners. How is this to be interpreted?

The prisoners stand for the ordinary people, chained by their passions, so that they see only mental shadows of the real. Added to this, they have no desire to improve themselves, and are content with shadows. If, by some chance, they became free, their minds could not stand the brilliant light of true reality. They would still probably consider shadows as true on account of the blinding effect of the truth. It is possible, however, to become accustomed to the bright light (signified by the fire), in which case a person would be able to consider material things at their true worth. This person's mental state will have developed from ignorance to opinion. If, furthermore, he advanced into the sunlight at the mouth of the cave, he would then be in a position to see his companions as slaves of their own passions. But he will see good in its truest form, i.e., the Ideal Good. So, also, will he arrive at a state of true knowledge. If the man thus converted to true knowledge were to return to the cave and attempt to enlighten his former companions by freeing them from their mental slavery, the other prisoners would seek to kill the enlightened one if it were possible. Obviously here, Plato had in his mind the example of Socrates, who tried to enlighten and teach others, only to be put to death by those whose minds were darkened.

The progress along Plato's Line of Knowledge is not easy. It requires concentration and effort coupled with discipline. To achieve this very desirable end, however, Plato had always emphasized education as a principal means. In the Athens of the period under consideration, politics was a major calling. So Plato points out that to be a good politician, one must be well educated. Otherwise it is a case of blindness among the leaders, and blindness among those who are led, a state to be abhorred.

Plato's interest in life was not confined, he showed interest in the individual which he realized, many of whom go to make up the State. If the individual leads a good life, then the State will be sound.

Can religion be infused into these examples of the Line and the Cave? Certainly, the neo-Platonists will do this, and much later on in the Christian era, we will find the Pseudo-Dionysius teaching that God is to be found by negation. This concept he developed from Plato's idea of the cave where man becomes blinded to everything else as he stands at the mouth of the cave, bathed as it were, completely in light and oblivious to everything else. However, we cannot say if Plato as an individual, regarded his teachings in any light other than that in which he presented them.

CHAPTER 19

PLATO AND IDEAS

In the foregoing section, we have attempted to present Plato's teaching on knowledge. We are now in a position to take this viewpoint to higher ground and consider it from the standpoint of being itself. Thus it is hoped our concepts mature and develop with the assimilation of the main trends in his dialogues. Simultaneously, the type of teaching is preserved, for what we examine now, too, logically follows from what has gone before. Further, the principles are continued and various additions will preserve and strengthen that which we already have. Again, these developments were anticipated in the former section.

What then is the data at our disposal? Firstly, true knowledge involves universals and secondly these universals are not bereft of material objects. But what actually are these material objects? To answering that question, we must now turn.

Plato was engaged upon this doctrine of Form all his life; even Aristotle will not say that the doctrine was substantially changed in any way. Attention has already been called to the fact that we do not possess Plato's lectures in the Academy. It can only be repeated how much this fact is to be deplored.

Plato says in the Republic that where singular things have a common name, they possess an idea to correspond to them. This will be known as the universal, which we know as "truth" for example. Certainly, many things can be truthful, but one main idea of truth remains. It will be the Perfect Idea. The intellect takes hold of reality; it is not an intrusion or subjective movement. Again, to Plato, with his contact with Socrates, it could be argued that the latter engendered in Plato's mind this idea of absolute perfection. The weakness in Plato's doctrine will reveal itself when he considers things, i.e., wood or dog, etc. One can conceive of absolute Truth, but the same degree of perfection is not attainable in natural things. Left to themselves, there would be an essence here, and an essence there, without having apparently a unifying principle. Consequently, it was this principle for which Plato had to search.

In the Phaedo, we can see how Plato tackled this problem. He uses two words which are convertible. They are "Ideas" and "Forms"; when he spoke in these words he was referring to concrete reality. In the Symposium, these words are not always in use, but their meaning is unchanged. So it is, that Plato speaks of Absolute Truth or Love, as the case may be, that is what is meant by an essence contained by an object.

These essences thus formulated are of great importance in understanding Plato. What exactly is their status? Are they related to one another, and so on? These questions naturally present themselves and some attempt must be made to answer them. With respect to their state, either supernatural or otherwise, it is obvious that Plato often infers a state of heavenly bliss by virtue of the language he employs. But now, language is primarily meant to describe sensibles, so it is difficult to arrive at an accurate estimation of this medium. Human nature being what it is, is forced to use language in order to communicate its thoughts one to another. Therefore, it is not wise to attach too much attention to the use of language. But some attempt must be made to get to the core, if possible, of what is meant.

For the moment, we will have to resort to a somewhat unscientific approach. The perfect Ideal Types are "out in space" so to speak. They exist there in a heavenly state of their own; whilst things as we know them on earth are constantly changing, and because of this change, can never "be" completely. Further, in this Ideal power of types, each exists apart from its neighbour, that is to say, in an isolated state. Now, because of unnecessary duplication, an untoward split is made between essence and existence. According however, to St. Thomas, there is a distinction between essence and existence, but this distinction takes place intrinsically. St. Thomas goes on to say that only in God are these Absolute Values universal. Why then is the doctrine of Plato presented in this fashion? The answer involves three points. Firstly, Plato asserted that the Forms lived in a separated world quite apart from this present cosmos. This would involve considering essences by themselves. Secondly, Aristotle says in the Metaphysics that Plato separated the Ideas from things. Yet the Idea of a thing is its substance. How then could Ideas be divorced from things?

Thirdly, in the Timaeus is found the teaching that the things of this world are formed by the Demiurge who takes the models from the Forms, who in turn take their own exemplars from God. Thus it would seem the Forms occupy somewhat of a midway position between God and the created things.

Various objections are raised against this doctrine. These are as follows: Firstly, that reality becomes dual; secondly, innumerable separate essences are created without a sound metaphysics; thirdly, the relation between things and the Ideas is never absolutely clarified; fourthly, no indication is given of the relationship of the Forms to one another, i.e., there appears to be a lack of unity.

It is necessary to examine Plato's theory of Forms more deeply to discover its actual content of truth. But even at this stage, it can be definitely stated that Plato realized the need for a theory of unity, and indeed tried to find one. The method he adopted to do this was to adapt the Eleatic doctrine of the One. It is a debatable point as to whether this process was successful; in any case, however, Plato at this stage did not foresee the problems Aristotle was to raise in later times. Plato did see certain difficulties, but he solved them satisfactorily in his own mind. It is possible that Aristotle was right in the pursuance of his objection, but no further observations on this will be made at this stage.

Certain points suggest themselves in relation to Plato's ideas. They are: firstly, he really speaks as if Ideas are apart from the possible, secondly, as a consequence of this, they must possess reality in their own right. The idea of place, and Form in that place, are quite incompatible. Nevertheless, Plato was bound by human language, which in itself would suggest space. It is language then that is the barrier to understanding Plato's real intentions as he meant to imply that the Ideas and things were as one. The transcendent quality of the Ideas themselves would prevent any notion of decay in Forms themselves, even when they were unified with things. We today, think of God as the perfect Exemplar of all things. In like manner, did Plato regard his Ideas. We do not think of God as being contained completely in a corporal thing; neither did Plato consider his Ideas as completely contained. Consequently, giving any mathematical dimensions to the Ideas is quite mistaken.

It is found that occasionally Plato makes use of the myth; but he does not intend this to be used as one would use scientific evidence. The proof of this is found in the Phaedo. Here Socrates tells of the future life of the soul. Then he points out that this particular man is not a man of sense and these notions are purely as described. The probable inference is that the future life is not to be understood in its entirety, whilst maintaining the idea of immortality. He shows too, that a Form in a place really implies in a metaphysical sense only. Neither would it be logical to deduce from this the idea of separated essences. It is possible for them to be included in an overall idea of being.

Aristotle had referred in the Metaphysics to the fact that Plato separated Forms from things. The question as to the actual value of such a statement by a person as philosophically gifted as Aristotle obviously presents itself. Did Plato and Aristotle mean exactly the same thing when each referred to the Forms, and each in his own specific way? Was it that these two thinkers created a divergence over the actual meaning of the verb "to separate"? Aristotle's views could but have followed from Plato's teaching, consequently at this stage, it is most prudent to try and discover what was the meaning of this doctrine of Forms in its fullest sense from the point of view of Plato.

If the Timaeus is consulted, it will be noted that Plato speaks of the Demiurge making things, after the pattern prescribed by the Forms. Now this would indicate that the Demiurge was different from the Forms. Further, if the Demiurge is looked upon as divine, then the Forms are not included in a thing at all, even God. This would, however, probably be the outcome of the limitations of language. Again, Plato developed ideas which he incorporated in his lectures, that were only touched upon in the dialogues.

Considering then, the Phaedo, we find the central theme discussed is the notion of immortality. We cannot say this is obtainable in a corporal sense, but by reason which apprehends things actually. The question arises what is true being? It is that which makes a thing what it is. Some abstract examples are then given to illustrate that the essence of things does not change, despite external changes. In this book, this changelessness is shown as a proof of the immortal. It is true also that man can acquire a knowledge more or less of these essences. Thus we are able to set up standards. When we are born, we do not know of the Perfect standards of the essences. But we are still able to judge in reference to the universal later in life. Why is this? It would point to a stage of preexistence of the soul with the body after which knowledge and memory are inseparable. It seems a practical view that, after

81

having had to transcend thought above the body during life, man should see pure essences after death, when freed from the body.

The Phaedo says that Ideas are universals, reinforced as it were substantially. But this is presented purely as a mode which, upon contact with an Absolute, is either positive or negative. There is some hesitancy in the presentation of this theory. This is done on purpose by Plato, for at this stage, Socrates had not arrived at the level of metaphysics. Be that as it may, this work contains a good deal that is Plato himself. In some minds, what is said here in the Phaedo is associated with principles without demonstration which, later thinkers have identified with a neo-Kantian line of thought. But what is taught as Plato's own ideas on the Forms and further, in his view, were universal concepts apart from purely created things. According to Aristotle, Plato identified the One and the good; but as yet in their work, this particular line of reasoning is not apparent.

Diotma, a prophetess, is represented in the Symposium as attaining beauty under the influence of Eros. Beautiful in this sense will take on a purely physical aspect, and from here, man will ascend to purely spiritual beauty, until he reaches a state where perfect Beauty can be held in contemplation. This perfect beauty is not open to decay or corruption in any form whatsoever; it simply remains what it is, Perfect Beauty in every respect, impossible to be increased and impossible to be decreased. All other things are beautiful only because they share in a greater or lesser degree in this Supreme Beauty, which lives with itself in perfect harmony and rectitude. It is referred to again in the Hippias Maior in somewhat the same manner.

The discussion continues with Diotma telling Socrates to concentrate all his efforts to attain this Supreme Beauty; otherwise he may be unable to obtain it. This is thought by some to be an indication of Socrates' humility in attaining spiritual heights. It is discounted as anything personal on the part of Plato himself. There seems no valid reason however, why Plato should not have been able to attain equal spiritual heights with Socrates, without, as he has done in the eyes of a few, being guilty of arrogance.

The question now is whether the Beauty spoken of is absolute or objective in something. Is it an existence of its own separate from things? If this is so, then no category can be attributed to it. It is impossible to fix the place of a transcendental force of this kind. But it possesses being, and therefore is real. It is definitely not correct to think of these concepts of Plato's as without any anchorage whatsoever, as something indefinite as floating anywhere in space as it were. This concept of Beauty in absolute form is imminent, in a purely subjective manner.

What then does the Symposium illustrate at this stage? It gives a firm indication of unity in Beauty in absolute form. Now if this is so, we will find that absolute Good is referred to in the Republic. So we have Beauty and Good as convertible.

But the Republic says more than this. It shows the true bent of the philosopher. He delves into the nature of things; without concerning himself overmuch with particulars, but meditating over the properties which make a thing what it is at one and the same time, a mystical and religious setting. In it, Plato discusses the Forms from a mathematical standpoint. This is the way Aristotle sees it. Under such conditions judged on what he says, Socrates as presented here, cannot be authentic historically. But it shows too, that a mathematical mind can exist with a religious one, and even a mythical one; indeed this fact is borne out by history. It is further possible that a person given to philosophical research will find himself aided by mathematics. But as already indicated, it is impossible for one person alone, to reduce to reality, all the elements of the real.

Dialectic was presumably the route whereby one would discover the Ideas; but it is not clear if a mystical or religious approach was fitting to many of Plato's utterances on the One and the Good. Many have believed there are these elements in the works; in which case they would be satisfied with their findings. It would appear that this dialectic is applied in two ways. Firstly, to those spiritual properties such as beauty and goodness; and secondly, to merely physical goods. This method can lead to belief in the superiority of the soul over the body. In like fashion, beauty existing in the sciences can be appreciated. The ultimate in this path is the Ideal of beauty which it is possible to obtain once a person has gained control over his lower appetites. The ideal life then is the life of the wise man, or a life where speculative thought dominates.

Between the divine and human, there is Eros or Love as portrayed in the Symposium. Eros has nothing and is the child of two extremes. But the meaning of the word Eros has often been misunderstood. Generally, it is taken to mean love or possession in a physical sense. Certainly, it can be connoted with desire, but the fullness of its meaning is to "generate in the beautiful relation to both soul and body." It would appear too, that this desire is perpetual, which would lead to the idea of the immortal. By an inferior Eros or love men are compelled to find this immortality by the generation of children. But in contact with true Beauty only does the soul become immortal and thus virtuous also.

It seems that the approach to the Good, and the Idea of Beauty is a purely ontological one, nevertheless there appears to be no reason for these principles to be apprehended in other ways, such as the intuitive way.

In none of Plato's major works does he identify the One or the Good with any aspect of Greek religion. Only in the Laws is some modification suggested by the application of virtue to the will of religion itself. The inference is in this that the One is apart from such considerations, and it was left to the Neo-Platonists to infuse an ecstatic element into the following of religion. We are then left with two points; firstly, that dialectic is a sure path of this philosophy, and secondly, that of the uncertain nature of Plato's intention as to the employing of a religious or mystical element in his work or not.

The person who does not philosophise is not concerned with essences of things at all; theirs is not the concern of the general nature of a thing; it is only the appearance of the object that attracts. Things that are now, and will not be later on. But this outlook will not lead to knowledge as is the case with the philosopher, who acquires this attribute because his main concern is that of Being. Thus is the difference between shadows and knowledge.

There has been little indication as yet as to what Aristotle meant when he said Plato separated the Forms. However, it may now be discerned in Plato's concept of the Good, which seems to be almost the foundation stone of the Republic. An analogy of Good is made to the sun which enlightens all around it. This is but an effort of illustration however, consequently one should not think of it purely in a material way, or in any *particular* way at all, since the force of Good is evident in everything to a greater or lesser degree, and consequently the only adequate definition of Good is surely to be found only in ontology.

Considering the workings of the intellect, it seems clear that Beauty of the Symposium and the Good of the Republic are as one. They would almost form a synthesis at the peak of intellectual activity. In all these discussions Plato was converging on one central idea, that of the absolute. Some writers have attempted to deal with the doctrine of Forms only logically. The result of this procedure is a reduction of the Platonic metaphysics, thus doing violence to the whole thought of Plato.

Now, Aristotle had said that Plato identified the Good and the One. Arestoxenus recalled that those who had gone to this lecture were surprised to hear a discourse of mathematics, astronomy, etc., when they had expected a discourse on worldly things such as wealth, power and so on. Now, later in the Metaphysics without calling Plato by name, Aristotle went on to assert that the Good and the One were as one, and their substances were due to the unity thereby created. In the lecture referred to by Arestoxenus above, Plato had said the same thing. In the Republic, Plato speaks of the Ideas as the source of truth and reason in this world and light in the next. Thus Truth and Beauty are One, owing their being to the One. It is not an easy task to decide how Plato conceived of the Forms having the One as their Principle. But that this is Plato's idea is certain. Two elements can be ascribed to the One, that of transcendence, and secondly with the individual Forms. It would seem that Good can be thought of as above being, because it is above everything visible; whilst the Real acts as principle in all things.

Plato considered that it would be difficult to find the "father of the universe". Even if he had been found, communication with him would be hard. The Timaeus reveals this quite emphatically. Nevertheless, this statement can throw a light on the Demiurge as it is called, and which appears in this work. The Demiurge will fascinate Christian thinkers also, but it simply is shown to signify Reason working in the world. In addition, Plato had also remarked that he could not write about everything. We could assume with certainty this bore reference to the teaching of the One.

The Demiurge is shown in the following from a letter of Plato. "God is the captain of all things present and to come, and the Father of that captain and cause." Both of these references are not to the Demiurge alone; considering the "captain" as the Demiurge, then the "Father" as God. This was the opinion of Plotinus.

We are now in a position to see the One as absolute in Plato's mind, and also he had so stressed that the One transcended all human experience, that this idea became the foundation for the finding of God by negation, dear to the hearts of some brilliant Christian thinkers. Even before this period, Plotinus will conceive the approach to the One as almost heavenly. But in this, Plotinus was mistaken, for the Republic states that this approach is to be made by dialectics.

But what of sensibles? We have been told by Plato that the Forms are derived from the One, although the precise fashion of this procedure is not stated. An obvious rift would seem to appear between knowledge and sensible things. In the two works, the Republic and Timaeus, in the former, Plato showed his disdain for science; in the latter, he modified his views. In respect of being one can only judge a sensible by its prototype to some Idea or Form; in itself it is vague and is not capable of being known, Plato mentioned this position of separation all his life, and it is not surprising to find that this was the point upon which Aristotle disagreed. It was Aristotle's contention that both matter and form belonged to the thing, and to the real world; whereas Plato insisted on parting these two elements. If one looks for a universal aspect then it must be found in a determined manner. It is, as it were, enveloped in matter. It would appear to the mind of some, that this criticism of Aristotle's is due to Plato ignoring the genus, while noting the species.

The absolute way of the spiritual apprehension of things is shown in the Phaedrus. These absolute qualities stem from the One. Possibly the actual text will appear naive, but the point is the intention behind these figures. In the Parmenides, the question is raised as to what Socrates considers valid as Ideas. To which he replies that there can be many ideas or likenesses, but eventually comes to the conclusion that there is no substance without the Idea. But assuming one were to accept the doctrine of many ideas, what would be the outcome? If we are to be consistent with Plato's teaching, this will lead to endless duplication, which seems to threaten the very concept of unity. There would be many worlds like this one, and the Idea of man could be, and probably would be, repeated into infinite regress. Again, this was a point of difference between Plato and Aristotle.

The arguments in this work concern the relation of the object to the Idea; and Socrates' explanation is not let go unquestioned. In respect of relation he asserts that two points of view are possible; firstly, by participation, and secondly, by invitation. Both of these concepts appear in the Parmenides and the Symposium. What is the reason for the objections raised against Socrates' teaching in these dialogues? Mainly, it was an attempt by Plato to develop his theories to meet criticism to which he laid himself open.

When the Idea is considered, is it fully contained in the thing, or merely in part? Parmenides asks this question as the result of the teaching on participation. The answer is that in the first way, the Idea would be completely contained, and in the second, it would be the Form which is capable of division, whilst the Idea remains one. In either case, there is a contradiction. Now, the attribute which makes two things equal is equality. Take away that equality and they cease to be equal. So as regards participation in size, if something is large, it is so by something which is less than largeness which is not reasonable.

In respect of an imitation, Socrates says they are but copies; Parmenides replies that white things being white, whiteness is then like the thing that is white. From this is obtained a Perfect Form whiteness. Aristotle followed this line, and the net result is to show that the Idea and the particular object are not identical. Two other points also emerge. They are that it is desirable to study relations further, and as yet, Plato's Ideal types have not been shown as invalid.

According to Socrates, it would not be possible to know Ideas. This is because human knowledge is rooted in the particular thing. Any relationship on this basis can be understood; but it does not follow from this that an absolute value of these aspects can be attained. Consequently, it seems pointless to argue to the Ideal World from the data of this world.

The Parmenides does not answer these questions; one reason it does not do so is that the procedure adopted does not furnish the reason for Plato's having written it. The point of the whole discussion is to urge Plato on to a deeper examination of his Ideal World and the objective world of experience. The dialogue goes to the point of admitting the need for a principle of unity. That is as far as it goes. The One and the many will be explained only by the discovering of a unifying principle.

The second part of the discussion is tedious. It starts with Parmenides talking of the development of various hypotheses. But it does not prove against the One, any more than the first part did against the Ideal theory. In any case, such an assertion would be foreign to Parmenides. The conclusion is that the One exists, even if both men are not too sure of its present nature.

What is a Sophist? This in a word expresses the object of the book of that name. It simply tries to anwer that question. The Sophist must, in effect, be defined. The discussion turns on class concepts to do this by means of genus and difference. The method is one of analysis from a large group, containing smaller groups, and finally to particulars. This produces the observation that Ideas can be one and many at the same time. Animal is one of these, which is a large group, contains many smaller ones. All forms are subservient to the One, the highest of all Forms. For Plato, the more abstract a Form was the purer it was. For Aristotle, the real was contained in all its richness in the particular.

But division cannot be continued indefinitely. The Form of man for example, is divided many times, and so one discovers individuals. Thus, for Plato, the individual was the lowest Form. So too, the chasm existing between the individual and the infinite was not satisfactorily answered by Plato.

There is certain unity amongst the Forms. What does this imply? Well, if I say "It is daylight", I am also asserting that it is not dark here and now, and for it to be light and dark here and now, would be impossible since the terms are opposite. Therefore, there is no unity between these two terms. On the other hand, if I said "Light is darkness", I would at once express a false judgement. In this manner may be elucidated many of these problems of falsehood which Socrates found it difficult to explain in the Theaetetus. An example of unity among Forms is "Socrates is walking" since it is quite legitimate to conceive of Socrates doing this. In short, a true statement is supported by being and is something; a false statement has no being to support it, and is about nothing.

In the process of answering what is a Sophist, this work also presents an ascending scale of Forms. Plato says that there are non-existent things; but he takes great pains to show the all enveloping power of something that is real. Forms do not change, but the spiritual element must also be included in the concept of reality. Now, if reality does not admit of change, there seems no place for spiritual qualities such as understanding, intelligence, and so on. Consequently, change must be accepted, and further, we must assert what changes are the real thing. But pushing this argument a step further, we will find a whole host of things that are becoming something else. How are these related to Supreme Reality? One will look in vain for an answer to this.

What the Sophist does further show is that all grades of being are contained in a Supreme Being, and in following this idea, Plato was quite sincere in his belief that he was demonstrating the Structure of Being. The Philebus also demonstrates where an end should be set in the non-limited, and considering sense objects at the lowest level. Therefore, it seems that the division of genera and species was not of great assistance in answering the question of the gap between Reality and sense objects. Plato thought of sense objects as not limited, and not determined; they became limited and determined only by the fact of their existence. Outside this existence, they did not possess the power of apprehension.

The next problem that faced Plato was how did the sensibles come to be? We can demonstrate by influence the grandeur of the One to some extent, and Real and Absolute qualities, but the things that are seen cannot be classified as non-being, so it becomes necessary to explain their presence. If they do not come from the One, where do they come from? Plato gives his answer to this in the Timaeus. The Demiurge is represented as providing shapes for existent material things within Space, thus creating an order where before there was no order. The Forms contained all these requisite shapes. When Plato talks of creation, he does not necessarily mean creation out of nothing; what is implied is more by nature of analysis of order from disorder. The Greek mind did not consider creation out of nothing at all. The non-existent entities were purely logical ones. No explanation consequently is given for reason entering the world. It is possible that Plato considered that this fact defied exploration. It simply is there.

Thus Forms brought order in the world through the power of the Demiurge. But were the Ideas those of God apart from Him? According to the Neo-Platonists, the Ideas and God were identical. But how did Plato consider this problem? Again, the inference would seem to point to the fact that the Ideal World is at the same time One and Many contained in the Divine Mind.

Passing on to the Republic in this work, Plato clearly says that God is creator of all things. This would simply mean the essences of created objects. Also He is spoken of as a King, and also as Truth. It could conceivably follow from this that He is the author of Being and Essence of things.

But what would such an interpretation of Plato's work reveal?

Firstly, it would show that Plato left many untidy ends, and even unexplainable ends. Such an explanation would be acceptable to those who would wish to defend Plato in some of the aspects where his doctrine seems thinnest. But such a path would be strewn with difficulty. Why? Because Plato represents the Demiurge as purely a symbol of Reason. Now, in the Laws, he suggests a council to punish atheists. But to Plato, an atheist means one who flouted Reason. Further, in the sixth letter of Plato already referred to, the Demiurge is identified with Reason. But this leaves no niche of identification for the Father.

A possible line to adopt would be that the Demiurge does not represent the final and ultimate in causes. It proceeds from the One. The Good is not indicated as possessing a soul, so it is never clear if it must be considered as more or less than this. In the Sophist, Plato asserts that "reality is the sum of all things". This includes naturally intelligence and life. The sixth letter emphasis on the One as total Reality is noteworthy. We are further led to understand that Ideas and mind are included in this conception. But in the Timaeus, mind was shown as in relation to the World-Soul. How can this be explained? They are separate in this work, the mind creating the World Soul. In many of Plato's utterances in such cases, it is not certain if what he actually says is to be taken literally. It is possible he did not mean them in that sense.

The Ideal theory is said to have a mathematical aspect. This is because according to Aristotle, Plato concluded that Forms are numbers; Existence is therefore by sharing in these numbers; the numbers themselves are composed of the One and limited, and unlimited elements; in between elements are midway between Forms and thing. Obviously, these assertions of Plato gave rise to a number of questions. For example, why does he associate Forms and number? Also how is it that Forms share in being of numbers? How do things come from the One in great and small numbers?

In answer to the first question, it may be said that Plato's intention was to make Forms intelligible. This was done by attempting to find an order among principles. Secondly, it is clear that all objects participate in order. For this reason then did Plato suggest Forms sharing in numbers. Thirdly, things are built up by arrangement of their composites. A greater or lesser arrangement can obviously lead to greater or smaller things. Now, if natural things employ order to either a greater or lesser degree, they can be thought of in conjunction with nature, to share in the principle of numbers, since number would appear to provide the individual element.

The question which seems to present itself from what has been said is formed in the following way: Is a mathematical approach to Plato justified? The answer given here is that it is not, for the following reasons. Mathematics is only operable if the material it works upon is made rational, and consequently abstracted in some way from matter. But it cannot be proved that *all* data can be made rational by the individual. Therefore, mathematics are inadequate to deal with all reality.

From this survey of Forms, it must be argued that Plato had improved upon what had gone before him. The pre-Socrates philosophers were materialistic, and Plato showed clearly the immaterial and material world. He joined hands with Heraclitus to assert that there is flux in things; but he saw as Heraclitus did not that this was one aspect only, that there did exist a full immaterial Reality. Credit must be given to Plato that he did not follow Parmenides into the error of One Being, which would automatically do away with change of any kind. Reality possesses life, soul and a mind where Plato shows force of the real as being many and One, the things of this world taking their essences from the Forms. Mind operates in the world; it is not something practically automatic as Anaxagoras taught.

Plato also developed beyond the Sophists and Socrates. Science and morality are not related as the Sophists had maintained, and Socrates although advancing many cogent arguments, never arrived at the concept of unity. Plato is always pointing to the peak of speculation — the One — which contains the unified of all other things. In short, Plato sought to make a synthesis of what had gone before him, maintaining the best, and discarding the bad.

On the other hand, it must be claimed that the theory of Forms was not adequate by any means. If one and good represent all intelligibility, there still remains a gap between the intelligible and sensible worlds. The endeavour to solve this would evolve a particular element which Plato did not explain. The views of Plato and Aristotle are far apart on this issue, but this does not mean that Aristotle had the right solutions all the way through. Reality was, in effect, between two great minds. Each saw it in his own way, and in his own aspect, neither leaving a complete picture.

Throughout his philosophy, Plato was relentless in his search for the truth; though as has been shown here, these efforts were not without grave imperfections. Despite this, it is most necessary to emphasise his main objective. There are minds who will make of Plato a sublime poet, but this was not the aim of the philosopher. The reason for this point of view probably lies in the flight from reality indulged in by some persons whenever the supernatural is encountered. There is nothing more real than the supernatural, consequently this viewpoint represents an intellectual error.

Another mistaken view of Plato that is sometimes adopted is to link him with Kant's doctrine. The reason for this is the supposed subjective approach to reality. But Plato was objective. The real can be known because it is rational, he says. But to *know* some object it must be objective. Further, what cannot be known is not in accord with reason. In other words, there is nothing exterior for the reason to work on. In this case, the phenomena remain unknown.

It is true we make up a world for ourselves by our interior life, and by our own acts, for example, my acts belong to me whether they are good or bad, they will always be attributed to me, and not to any other person. In like manner, other people's acts can never legitimately be credited to me. Plato, accordingly, built up a world for himself that was coloured in some respects by disappointment in the State and in Sicily. Some have argued that this would affect his philosophy, and would in effect constitute escapism. But this was not the intention of a man who set out to become a philosopher.

Again he has been accused of setting up a heavenly world in comparison to the material world, on a somewhere-else-is-preferable-to-now principle. But looking with reason at his work, there is no possible reason to assume his dislike of this world was complete. Only where ideas expressed were unstable or incomplete did he voice his dissatisfaction.

It is a fair estimation to say that Plato made great advances in his search for truth; he also demonstrated that what he said was true. Obviously, the Absolute Concepts are impossible with purely material means; but great advances were made as to what is truth, and what is demonstrated is true.

CHAPTER 20

PLATO'S PSYCHOLOGY

The relationship between soul and body was not neglected by Plato. Previous philosophers had reduced the soul to a purely material element, or else as purely separate from the body. Plato took neither of these extreme views, maintaining that the soul was that part of man most like to God, and therefore of great value. This drift is shown in many works. Socrates prays in the Phaedrus that the inner man might be beautiful. In the Laws we find it described as a self mover, and its superiority to the body is demonstrated. Again, in the Timaeus, Plato clearly says that anything intelligent is the soul, and it is not possible to see this invisible power in the same manner as it is earth, fire or water, for example. An objection is raised that could not the soul be but a harmony of the body, which dies with the body? Socrates to whom this question is directed replies that the soul rules the body, and further as a consequence of this, desires should be subdued. It is foolish to think that a harmony rules something of which it is supposed to be the harmony. Another view, too, says Socrates, is that if the soul is a harmony, then it is no more than any other soul — which is again a foolish conclusion.

By astute observation in which the Greeks excelled, Plato also noticed that the soul and body could radically influence one another, while remaining perfectly distinct. According to the Republic, Plato maintains that certain types of music can make the soul prone to bad influences. This course of reasoning is interesting if we follow it through to the Timaeus where he says that damage can come about by bad physical training, and by habits of vice which can so influence the soul so as to make it a slave. Hereditary aspects cannot be ignored, and a poor constitution inherited from the parents, and bad surroundings all make for a warped character. Man will always desire the good; in the main, most people become bad by a bad bodily habit and poor instruction, and often the misfortunes befall a person whether he chooses them or not.

A point against Plato made by the Scholastics of Christian times, notably St. Thomas Aquinas, was that the philosopher often speaks as if the soul were as a motor to the body, the latter being used and not co-operating with the former. It would be foolish to deny that this is the impression that Plato has left, but he was consistent with the idea of the soul and the body acting on one another. Certainly, he did not say how this came about; he merely accepted the fact as a condition of a living person.

We find in the Republic that there are three aspects of the soul, viz. rational, courageous and appetitive. This plan Plato developed from the Pythagoreans and he never altered his ideas on this matter. Actually in the original Greek text the word used by Plato is part, but this is used as a metaphor, and does not indicate material extension of any kind.

Animals do not operate on the same level as man, they do not possess an immortal element in their soul, whilst man does. Normally the spiritual and rational parts should be co-eval as is the case with animals. There are two kinds of desire, physical desire and spiritual desire. Spiritual desire seeks after the truth, and physical desire craves the appeasement of the appetites. Referring once again to the Timaeus, Plato fixes the rational soul in the head, the spiritual in the breast, and the appetitive below the waist. Homer had mentioned the locale of the spiritual element in the chest many centuries before. Now did Plato intend these distinctions literally, or just to indicate the interaction of soul and body? When he mentioned these differences, he was possibly not consciously aiming at a specific order.

Without doubt, it was Plato's firm belief that the soul is immortal. In fact, he says so in the Timaeus. Now, in the passage in this work which refers to this, it is the rational part that is immortal. Presumably, the spiritual and appetitive parts die, the only other solution being the explanation of more than one soul to a person. But in the Republic and the Phaedrus, we have equally clear implications that the soul as a whole survives death. In the light of this evidence, it seems that Plato was not, as stated above, laying down a rigidly specific order for the parts of the soul.

On the face of it, there seems no particular reason why Plato taught the soul as having three parts. Again, it was a matter of observation of the internal struggle going on in all men. This led to an illustration which is very famous, and is contained in the Phaedrus. Reason is like a man drawing a chariot, trying to control two horses. One is a good horse which loves all good things, and the other is a bad horse which strives after all immoderate indulgence of the passions. Obviously the good horse is the spiritual element and the bad horse the appetitive, which must be controlled by force, if its clamourings become too strong. Plato shows all men have experience of this, and constantly this experience is one of conflict within the person. Nowhere does he say how these two forces can be reconciled. If anything it lays emphasis upon Plato adopting the three-parts-of-the-soul explanation.

The principal aim in this is an ethical one. That is how to behave properly as the charioteer must drive properly in the illustration. It is clear that the rational part of the soul is born to rule, and its affinity with higher and divine things is most marked. Other parts of the soul tend toward the material world, and really only have indirect contact with reason. It is noteworthy that this view is held today very widely and has been passed to modern Christians by St. Augustine and others. This is all the more remarkable, since St. Thomas Aquinas adopted Aristotle's teaching on the soul. It persists because of the inward battle everyone experiences, and everyone feels this conflict as an internal experience. This internal experience, however, requires a fuller explanation than Plato gave. For if, as he asserted, there were two souls in man, that is to say, rational and non-rational, then consciousness of this inward struggle would not be possible. In addition the unity of the soul was definitely taught by Plato, and consequently the oneness of its action. Some might argue that if the soul were a complete unit, and one, and immortal, in the rational aspect only, then how could the soul operate on the lower powers after death? But this most decidedly is not Plato's intention.

Now, it was all very well saying as he did, that the soul was immortal. But the stage was bound to be reached when proof for this statement was required.

Plato held that an opposite produced naturally its contrary effect. For example, one goes from weakness to strength, waking to sleeping, light to dark, etc. In like manner, of these opposites, death produces life.

But this idea leads to obvious drawbacks. For one thing, creation *must* take the pattern of a cycle. Is the soul in a state to receive a happy eternal life when it leaves the body or not? No suggestion is offered on this point. Neither would this concept prevent a person being born over and over again into this life.

It is possible to attain absolute standards in life; this is clear from the manner in which it is possible for me to compare their standards or values. But again, they cannot be applied to sense. Plato assumes that man knew of these perfect standards in another life. Conversely, sense knowledge does not provide us with universal concepts. However, by a method of questioning which can be a form of teaching, it is possible to arrive at the particular. This method was adopted widely by Socrates. In the Meno, it is sought to demonstrate that particular truths of mathematics can be arrived at in this way. An argument is proved in the Phaedo where the soul is shown to be superior to material things by its contact with the Forms; it would appear from this indisputably that the soul was meant to rule the body.

In another discussion in the same work, a question is put by Cebes. Is it not possible, he says, for the soul to deteriorate with its variety of physical existences? Socrates replies that the presence of one Form would naturally preclude the presence of any contrary Form. One such Form could not thus be cold and hot at the same time. To continue this idea, the soul, because it shares in the life of the Form, will not admit of death. When, however, death does occur, it seems that two alternatives are open to it. One is for it to die, the other to go back to another state. It is taught throughout that the soul does not die, therefore, this is taken for granted; the conclusion of the whole argument being the incorruptible nature of the spirit.

Plato is certain that a soul cannot be destroyed except by something bad within it. Lack of righteousness, ignorance, cowardice, etc., are some of these. Yet it is obvious the bad quite often outlives the good. From here, he argues that it is unreasonable to suppose that if it could not be destroyed internally, there is little likelihood of it being so externally. This argument is laid out in the Republic.

Next, Plato considers motion. If a thing is not always moved by another, it may cease to live, because of the lack of movement. But we know the soul can move itself, and this is a principle of motion in itself. So it can become the beginning of motion. This leads him to suppose that the soul is uncreated because of its aspect of principle in motion. But if this is asserted, then we must say that it has always existed, but not much progress would be made in this way to prove that it is immortal. It illustrates, if anything, that the individual soul returns to the World Soul after the physical death. The Phaedo, Georgias, and the Republic all reveal that

Plato was quite genuine in this belief in immortality. What of the myths in this respect? They are pictures that Plato wishes to give of the after life, but how far positive certitude can go with them is not certain.

From what has been shown, it seems that Plato introduced no system into his study of the mind, but nevertheless he produces some profound observations, which can be found at various places throughout his work. Examples are of the operations of the memory in forgetting and remembering and memory and recollection, the former in the Theaetetus and the latter in the Philebus.

CHAPTER 21

PLATO AND MORALS

When the end to which Plato directed his teaching on ethics is considered, it is found to be the happiness of man. The attainment of this would appear to be a balanced development of the whole personality, rational and mortal, inducing a general well ordered behavior. But it is necessary for man's soul to be in a good condition in order for him to be happy. An idea of what is exactly meant by this statement is found in the Philebus. We have Protarchus on the one hand maintaining that pleasure is the end of the good, whilst Socrates believes the good is to be attained by wisdom. Socrates illustrates that if one were to take pleasure in its commonest sense, i.e., physical pleasure, this would entail an operation in which neither mind nor memory could share. Protarchus surely does not advocate an existence on such restricted lines.

But man is not a pure intellect. Consequently it is not fitting to consider him in this capacity only. The true human good therefore, consists in part intellect and in part sense pleasure. Plato thus makes clear that he teaches the mind is paramount, but satisfaction of human desire is not wrong, provided a middle course is followed, not veering to excess or defect. An example is given of the mixing of honey and water for a tasty drink, in like manner, pleasant sensation and intellect should be mixed.

For a realisation of the good, true knowledge and what is important, application of this knowledge, is absolutely necessary. Otherwise, it is doubtful if an action could attain its proper end. This application involves the employment of less true knowledge or knowledge of a subordinate type in the material world. It is important that a man always realises these subordinate truths for what they are, and realizes they truly *are* subordinate to a higher and true good. The material world then, cannot be ignored; but it must be considered rightly as an inferior to the true type of knowledge.

A problem is evident here. How much sense pleasure to allow? What actually does constitute a middle course? The amount must be submitted to knowledge for direction. It will admit of that sense pleasure to make for a sober mind and natural health.

From this, it would seem that measurement and the proportion which follows are the absolute basis of a good life; when these are not observed, there is consequent disorder. The beautiful element in the good is thus clarified by measure and proportion.

And, or course, if man is to lead a happy life, he must have knowledge of God. God's work can be seen everywhere in the world, and true happiness would include a recognition of this. Thus God forms the pattern, and man follows it to the best of his ability.

What path does a man follow in order to become as like to God as possible? He must travel the path of virtue. In a statement in the Laws, Plato insists that God is the measure of all things, and is higher than any man. Temperance in a man makes him like God. It is a fine thing to offer sacrifice to the gods, and he goes as far as to say the sacrifices of the wicked are displeasing. So we find two more parts to happiness. They are worship and virtue, though actually virtue is intermingled with happiness. The good considered in itself is a state of the soul, but one has to be virtuous in order to achieve this happiness.

In the light of what has been said, it would seem that to Plato the double ideas of knowledge and virtue complement each other. That is to say, one cannot be virtuous without knowledge, and to have knowledge is a sure way to virtue. In the Protagoras, Socrates is depicted as speaking against the Sophists to this effect. Further, lack of temperance causes a man to choose what is really harmful to him, whilst the temperate man strives to preserve those things that will prove of benefit to him. Now, it is clear that to choose what is harmful is foolish, and what is of benefit is a wise course. Next, example of valour and courage is taken. Valour is standing one's ground when the dangers involved are realized. So courage and wisdom are related, just as are wisdom and temperance. Certainly, there are individual virtues, made known by their objects, and the soul upon which they operate. All this is but a manifestation of good or evil as much as the ratio of knowledge is to these properties in the individual. The role of prudence is to unify the individual virtues in the light of knowledge as to what is really good, or wherein his end truly lies. The Meno says that providing knowledge or prudence is virtue, and it can be taught. This idea is expanded somewhat in the Republic when Plato says only a philosopher can expound virtue. The sense in which the word philosopher is used here is of one who possesses accurate information on some science. This is contrary to ideas and beliefs which are generally current amongst the less learned. All virtues relate to goodness which is not to be thought of as changeable; it is completely without change.

The view that virtue and knowledge are a complement to each other, and convertible, remained with Plato always. In the same manner, did his view on good and evil remain. No man would choose evil because it was evil; he chose it because of some aspect of good which he thought he perceived in it. In addition to this, Plato made allowance for the strivings of human appetite which strains to carry all before it, no matter what the cost. Going back to the example of the man in the chariot, if he lets the bad horse get the better of him, it is because of the lack of knowledge or onrush of passion. A man may seek to do another harm; but the idea is that in doing harm, the attacker would see a good. It seems the aspects of good and right are not very well clarified with the Greeks.

Plato teaches four main virtues which he outlines in the Republic. They are wisdom, courage, temperance and justice. Wisdom is the rational part of the soul, courage is the spiritual part, whilst temperance is the result of a unity of the appetite and reason. Justice is a general virtue, the object of which is to see that the soul operates in a balanced manner.

According to Plato, good and evil are not the same as pleasure and pain. It is also wrong to teach a morality which is beyond the power of man to attain, as indeed had been taught by Callicles. Socrates had shown that to be tyrannical was a worse fault than injustice because to do wrong, and get away without punishment is worse for it has the tendency to fix the soul in its wrong doing. Callicles remarks that Socrates is only appealing to ordinary convention. A mass of people or majority will agree that a certain action is morally wrong, but this is simply saying what everyone else is saying. The majority hold together to maintain as right certain actions of others, and maintain as wrong actions which could prove harmful.

Socrates is grateful for these remarks. He points out however, that if the majority *do* hold together over the "strong minority", then indeed they themselves must be tyrannical, in the speaker's own words. Further, if a single person is going to maintain moral behavior against a majority, it is necessary to show why the individual is to be preferred to that majority. Callicles defends his position by maintaining the wisdom of the individual, and because of his wisdom, should rule over others. In this case, says Socrates, the doctor should have more to eat and drink, and the shoemaker the largest shoes. Callicles says what he really means is that those who are wise should rule the State. But, asks Socrates, should the strong man bring himself under subjection? Callicles says his passions should have full rein. Socrates replies that in that case Callicles' man is like a leaky barrel. He is always filling himself but is never full. This leads to Callicles admitting of a quality in pleasure, which is subordinate to good. Pleasure then is good in so far as it brings happiness. But pleasure for pleasure's sake interferes with the good order of the body. There is always a question of judgement after death.

It is wrong to do good to friends and evil to one's enemies. Polemachus had said this in Book One. For evil cannot be good. Socrates considered evil as actual harm, as different from a punishment. This would result in making a just man unjust, and the bad man worse. It is impossible for this to be consistent with good.

CHAPTER 22

STATE AND STATESMANSHIP

The State has a great influence on ethics. Plato considered them almost as integral parts of one another, so greatly did one affect the other. Ethics naturally concerns the individual, consequently it seems that the individual had a part to play in the State's progress. Without the State, it is difficult to visualize man as happy; he is meant for society. It involves a natural existence for him, and we find this idea in both Plato and Aristotle. It thus becomes necessary to lay down what is required for a well run State in order to procure man's happiness. The State may be corrupt; in which case individuals will find conditions difficult. On the other hand, if the individuals were corrupt, the notion of an upright State could not be achieved.

The idea of separate laws for State and individuals are not practical; there must be one uniform law for both. There must be a single law applicable to both, and it is impossible for the State to develop properly without paying attention to some moral law. This in turn will justify the actions of the State, whether it be favourable or unfavourable. In the first book of the Republic, Socrates says he is uncertain as to what justice is. Consequently, in the second book, the suggestion is put forward that the notion of justice be examined. Socrates also suggests this be done in a specific way, that is starting with the State's justice, and proceeding to that of the individual. This constitutes a movement of the imperfect to the more perfect. But it also illustrates that one Law is valid for both. This is because if a person lives in a State, then if there is an ideal Law for that State, both must of necessity fall under it.

But perfect justice is hard to find. Consequently, Plato was more concerned in showing the perfect State, and this is one of the objects of the Republic. He was compelled in the Laws, however, to make various changes of an elastic nature, which would permit of a certain degree of give and take.

Should Statesmanship be scientific? Plato replies yes. A statesman must have intimate knowledge of the State and the proper life; if this is not the case, the statesman can bring the state to ruin. Plato had had some bitter political experiences; yet he always sought to sow the seeds of right thinking in those that studied under him.

Naturally, the State will act for an end. This end is to serve the individual person. As individuals are not independent, they need the help of their fellows. For this reason, they form communities, and so give rise to the formation of cities. The city exists primarily for economic ends, which is given variety by the various callings different persons follow. One task alone is sufficient for one person, and if he maintains this work, the quantity and quality will be high. A laborer will not make the tools he works with. They are made by someone else. Thus in a city, there is a conglomeration of trades and callings, each of which is really dependent upon the other. As the city advances, there must not only be labourers and traders, but teachers, poets, musicians and thc like. Gradually, as the city expands in population, more territory is needed, and this leads to wars with the cities' neighbors. Plato comes to the conclusion that the root fault of war is economy. But these observations are not to be taken as referring to aggression.

The rise of war will mean that there will be those who will direct operations of war. These people must be gifted with philosophy, being able to distinguish the true situation. But all this requires knowledge, and knowledge must be taught, thus they must be educated. This education must be well chosen, for the ancient poets were fond of depicting the gods conducting themselves with flagrant immorality. Little respect is shown for simple promises in these writings, which would thus set bad examples. The representation of God must be shown as the Author of all good.

In each case in the Republic, Socrates tips off the discussion by finding that the State supplies some human want. Economy is mentioned, and then education. But the State's aim is not one of economy. It primarily exists to make man happy, provided that he lives according to the annals of justice. Education is necessary to achieve this aim. This education must be aimed at the good in all things, and the true in all things. There are those who organise the education of the State, i.e. what each shall do and so forth, and this position belongs to those who really know the true and good, that is to say, philosophers. It is for this reason that Plato decided to exclude poets and artists from the Perfect State. Not that he did not appreciate Homer or Hesiod; but it seems to him that the emotion roused by the very limpidity of their respective arts would prevent people as a mass from seeing the truth. Certain lyric poetry will be allowed under the supervision of the State. But in general, Plato was disinclined to permit artists in his concept of the Perfect State for the reasons given above. Again, according to him, they often held immorality in a favourable light. We may think today that Plato over-emphasized this point, but he was always so utterly sincere in his search for the truth.

Those who take care of the State or guard it must take care of themselves physically. But their exercises must be carried out in moderation. Plato was quite aware however, that a system set up for the benefit of the State was open to abuse.

There are two classes in the State, i.e. workers, and those who guard the State itself. But who is to rule the State? Plato replies that they will come from the class of guardians. They will have reached an age of sense, and not be young men. They must have a love of the State, and must put it first in their considerations, even when they are liable to suffer by doing so. This type of person is considered by Plato to make an adequate ruler; so the consequence now is that there are three classes of State, guardians and rulers, and artisans. This does not include slaves.

With respect to the Middle class, life must be communal, and they must possess no property. Plato thinks that if they acquire property, it will result in making them bullies to those beneath them.

Plato had found that to define justice was hard. Here, however, it was at least possible to fix the foundation of it in the State. It was the duty of the rulers to administer it. The conclusion is arrived at that as the person is rightly ordered when all the faculties of the soul work together, with the lower in obedience to the higher; so in the State, it must function properly, when all the parts act in their right place in order.

Plato next deals with an aspect which is repugnant to the Christian mind. It is the idea that woman are capable to be trained for war equally as men. In Book Five of the Republic, the care of children is illustrated as being not the only task for women. After all, Plato asserts that the only real difference in the sexes is their different roles carried out in having children. Gifts of nature are found in both sexes, and there is no reason why they should not both share in the progress of a perfect State. Marriage among the middle classes should be controlled by the upper, and by this control thus imposed, Plato does intend any idea of free love or loose morality to be understood. The lower class or workers maintain their belongings, which in thes case of the two upper classes have to be surrendered for the State's welfare. The marriage control suggested is a very strict one. Wives will be chosen for the person concerned, and the couple will have sexual relations at given times, and thus have children, and relations are forbidden at all other times. If the husband should form associations with other women, and children are born as the result of the union, Plato suggests that these children should be disposed of. Further, children who are born into the upper classes, but do not find their particular niche, will, from then on, be included as members of the working class.

What can be said of this teaching? Certainly, the philosopher's intentions were far from barbaric, but he totally ignored the dignity of the person. Also man is superior to an animal, and it does not necessarily follow that measures carried out with respect to the latter will be successful with the former.

It is pointed out that it would be impossible for a state to reach the condition of perfection by means of these proposals. The reply is that one does not expect perfection in anything with every attention to detail. A suggestion is put forward that the solution would be a ruler who also would be a philosopher. Plato did not appreciate government by the people. A king must rule with knowledge and that knowledge must be true. As a general principle, Plato seems to consider that if a ruler is wise, he will be able to guide others, and infuse them with his wisdom and thus guide the State. If, however, he is not wise he cannot diffuse wisdom among others, and so will be ill fitted to guide the State.

In the first place, it is necessary to educate such a person to a high degree; his instruction must include everything from physical culture to astronomy. The overall purpose of such an education would be mainly the appreciation of intelligible things. Plato speaks of such candidates being drawn from truth and being of a true concept of philosophy. In like manner, a man passes on to the absolute by means of his intellect and not his senses. If this operation is achieved, his intellect will be fully developed, far beyond those examples such as the people in the cave which Plato had given previously. Thirty years of age seems to be a convenient age at which to start to study dialectic, which study must be continued for five years. After this study, they would be required to hold some governmental post in order to ascertain if their will was strong enough to withstand worldly temptations. This posting should continue for fifteen years at the end of which time it should be possible for them to work towards the absolute with intellect alone. Thus their main pursuit at this stage, would be philosophy, and they should labour for the public benefit. It seems that Plato considers such an existence to be very well worth rewarding in the after life. He goes on as far as to say they are worthy of honour being shown them by those left behind on earth.

The remainder of the Republic is devoted to a summary in metaphysical form. The ideal State is one ruled by Aristocrats. When there is a combination of the other two classes, a State known as timocracy develops. This shows the force which is uppermost. The outcome of this is an oligarchy and a poverty class. But there will always be a reaction, and gradually a favourite among the people appears. By degrees such a person shows his true disposition and becomes a dictator. So it seems then that the happiest State is one ruled by the aristocratic idea for through them reason can be exercised, as through the philosopher, it is also manifest thus allowing him to become a happy man.

Plato, in the Statesman, is very decided on the point that ruling a state is a task superior to other callings. Further, no community can govern adequately; balanced government is found in a few or in one person. Laws are general and should be adapted to various cases. It would be equally foolish, Plato says, for a doctor to maintain certain treatment for a patient, when the condition of the sick person no longer required such treatment. Taking human nature as it is, it is necessary to imply means which are operative, yet still provide room for improvement. Such is the concept of Law, under which all must become subject in order to live happily.

There can be various forms of rule; by one, by a group, or a community. Plato certainly considered the first as the best type; he also thought the rule of the community was the least desirable. At the same time, it is obvious that the worst type of government can also be that by one person — when that person is a dictator. When Plato considers democracy, he thinks best of the governments outside the law, and worst of those within it. His reason is that actual offices in the ruling of the State are shared among many people, instead of being in the hands of a single person. If he saw the dictators of modern times, Plato undoubtedly would say that they considered themselves as gods and actually were shallow personalities.

In the Laws, it is suggested that the best formula for the formation of the perfect State would be co-operation between a wise statesman and a learned king. Plato's personal experiences at Syracuse undoubtedly led him to taking this view. It is true, too, to say that Plato took the history of a city or State into account when making this suggestion. The history of Athens, for example, was a great influence upon him in this respect.

It is not a good thing, Plato says, to have a State ruled by classes of people. If such a state would so seek to govern itself, then it would become a political party, and could not be therefore truly called a State any longer. People thus called upon to govern do not realise their true responsibilities. All rulers must themselves be subject to a law, and this is difficult for some persons. Thus the law must be superior to the ruler, and the ruler must be below the law. In this setting, all will go well.

From these remarks, it seems that the state exists for the common good. Plato here alludes to the convenient size of a state. He says it should consist of 5,040 persons. It is interesting that he also refers to the same number of houses, the inference being that it was 5,040 *families* as an ideal state. The philosopher also safeguards the finance of the state, not allowing it to accumulate too much wealth. His plan is for a currency which is only valid inside the state itself.

The legal faculty of this perfect State must work smoothly. Plato is very involved upon this. There shall be thirty-seven magistrates who, when they take office, shall be less than fifty, and they shall hold their posts till the age of seventy.

They should head a Council of 360 who will be elected from those who are property owners. This Council will provide for several Ministers, the most important of which will be the Minister of Education. This post will be responsible for all boys and girls, and the person holding the position must also be the father of children himself. The education of children is one of the most important factors in the State's development.

Married couples will be supervised for a period of ten years after their marriage. This supervision will be carried out by a female committee. The marriageable age for men is thirty to

107

thirty-five, and for girls between the ages of sixteen and twenty. Offences against marriage are to be punished.

The ages between twenty and sixty are considered the best years for military service; but neither are the women exempt from this task, the only exception being childbirth. Thirty is the youngest age a man can hold an office of any kind, whilst the same would not apply to a woman until she is forty. The best that can be said for Plato's views on marriage in general, is that its first fruit would be healthy children.

According to Plato, the emotions are soothed in a child by being rocked to and fro. Up to the age of six, the sexes will play together. After that they must be separated. However, Plato holds fast to the idea that the education for both boys and girls should remain the same. The former will need extra supervision, and they will be instructed in athletics and music. Schools will be built, the teachers in them will come from other States; children must attend daily at school, and mathematics, astronomy, etc. will form part of the syllabus.

One day must be set aside for worship. One of the ruling class should offer up sacrifice to the gods for the rest of the citizens. Plato goes as far as laws for farming and prison law. Roughly he divides law in this manner into what we should know today as a civil or a criminal action.

Next, the philosopher deals with the problem of nonbelievers, and false belief. Some had said the earth was the product of physical elements, but this is wrong. In fact, it is atheism. Plato on the contrary, teaches there must be a source of primary motion and so on to a First Principle. This First Principle which he also refers to as Soul or Mind must therefore be the cause of the universe. Since it is obvious there is discord in the world, it is feasible to posit a second Principle to account for this. In Greek religion, heresy involved the idea that the gods did not care for man. Against this, Plato makes three points. Firstly, the gods if they attend to big things cannot ignore the smaller things. Secondly, surely God will attend to minute things, when a human workman will do so. Thirdly, there is no interference by God in men's lives. God's justice will be fulfilled in the next life.

A second Greek religious heresy involved the idea that the gods could be bribed, and consequently, bring about a miscarriage of justice. Plato replies by saying it is wrong to consider the Gods merely as pilots of a ship, men that could be bribed purely on a human level. Such belief is punishable as a crime. This punishment will consist of imprisonment for five years during which time efforts must be made to induce the offender to mend his ways. If a person offends again, the punishment is death. It is possible to lead others astray if heresy is peddled for gain, or for the purpose of immorality. In such cases, the person responsible will be imprisoned in a wild countryside and will not even be buried at death.

To prevent such occurrences, no superstitious rules must be allowed. It is necessary to decide if an offence is intentional or is a childish prank.

In Books Eleven and Twelve, Plato deals with law in general.

An example of this is:

1. There is a law against persons becoming beggars; if this person is a beggar, then he will be banished.
2. Lawsuit for gain is wrong; if a person commits this offense, he will die.
3. Embezzlement is wrong; certain classes of persons commit this offence, consequently, they will be imprisoned.
4. Accounting to the State is necessary; the ruling class will thus account; an ordered financial society will result.
5. It is necessary for the main Council to meet daily; they have a knowledge of God; thus there will be an ordered society.
6. To travel abroad is a good thing; men of middle age can do this without permission, then they can bring home new ideas.

Plato fully condoned slavery. The slave belonged to his owner, and moreover, seemed to be capable of alienation. Anyone who married a slave in Athens, that marriage was free; Plato says any children from such a marriage will be the property of the slaves' owner. Democracy, never a strong point with Plato, showed to his way of thinking, the laxity with which they were treated. On the other hand, he did not advocate a barbaric treatment of such people. They should be punished as punishment is deserved and no more. To ill-treat a slave is wrong; through the love of justice and hate of injustice, should they be afforded treatment equal to our immediate circle of acquaintances. Plato seemed to strive to follow a middle path towards slavery; between the Athenian softness on the one hand, and that of the brute, common in Sparta.

According to Cleinias, all the regulations in the City of Crete were for the purpose of war. This is found in the first book of the Laws. In the process of this conversation, others are found to concur. However, a stranger points out several aspects. Firstly, a good lawmaker will make laws that do not make for strife, and secondly, the aim of the lawmaker is to find the best laws. The State's welfare will rest upon this. It would be foolish to permit war for the sake of peace, conversely it would be equally wise to sanction war for the sake of peace. Plato also takes pains to point out that in war, the victorious are often in a poor state, even suicidal, but education can never be suicidal.

Social relations are bound up with happiness. It is obvious that man is born into a society, the purpose of which is to lead him to an altogether fuller existence. Thus he is by no means a solitary being, and if he remains in his loneliness, he can never completely fulfill himself. What happens if a man must consider himself as part of an authoritative power? He has to serve this power either in paying taxes or serving in the forces. But under these conditions, he can hardly be expected to take an active interest in political life. A politically minded person on the other hand will work *for* the state, whilst the unpolitically minded in all probability will feel antagonistic towards the same state.

Attention has been drawn before to the importance of politics in Greek life; to the Greek mind, a good life and a political life went together. Consequently then, Plato speaking in philosophical terms, should naturally look for a good life, and in looking for one, he will equally naturally seek one in which politics are included.

The teachings of both Aristotle and Plato will furnish the material for future speculation on the State. We must not think their ideas were perfect, for they were not; but with their mighty intellectual scope, they showed the way others should take. Indeed, when St. Thomas came to write upon this subject, the Greek view became his view. Both the Greeks and St. Thomas in this way showed that the state is for the benefit of man and not the other way about. This is in sharp contrast to the French and German philosophers of the latter half of the nineteenth century who upheld this latter view. The notions of Aristotle and Plato are resplendent with nobility when dealing with the State, whilst those of the latter philosophers, though forming a part of the natural development of an original idea, nevertheless, seem harsh and dictatorial, under which man could never teach the "good life" as the Greek philosophers termed it. The Christian thinkers took the Greek idea then, and showed that the Ideal Community was for the benefit of the individual, and in this condition, there must be perfect poise between the Church and the State itself, to guarantee this fullness of earthly life.

CHAPTER 23

PHYSICS

There is one book which deals with Plato's teaching of physics. It is the Timaeus, and belongs to the philosopher's old age, and was to be the first of three books dealing with physics. The other two books were to be the Critias and the Hermocrates. Of these, one was partly finished, whilst the third one was never started, possibly due to Plato's advancing years. The Timaeus, however, starts with an account of creation including that of man. Athens is described as represented in the myths defending herself against mythical cities; phenomena of nature are dealt with to show the development of an overall Supreme plan.

But why did Plato wait till his old age to write something about physics? The answer is that he did not. It had been a life long interest, though it is possible that scientific enquiries at the Academy influenced him in no small measure. Plato's main concern was centered upon morals and metaphysics, but an exploration of the material world gradually became necessary to give these arguments added weight. Due to the changing and becoming of bodies, physics can never be an absolute science. The Pythagoreans had said everything is number; Plato now says everything shares in number.

There is another reason for Plato writing the Timaeus. An ordered world will show an ordered Supreme Intelligence and, of course, the converse is true. By illustrating this order in the world, credence could be given to a Supreme Intelligence. Also there is the question of why man shares in things he knows and in things he senses. But in the idea of the supremacy of the Mind is contained the notion of the divine origin of the human soul.

Various writers have, at particular times, doubted whether the material contained in the Timaeus, is either mythical or factual. There seems little room for doubt, however, that the views expressed are the facts as Plato believed them to be. Proof of this lies in the fact that discerning people like Aristotle and Theophrastus at no time give any indication that the writings of Plato were false. A point like that would scarcely have gone unheeded. Further, it has already been pointed out that Plato did not consider the theory of physics as absolute; therefore he would allow for a certain latitude in definition and so forth.

The world according to Plato was generated. All the while the material world is becoming, and that which becomes does so by some cause. This is the line of argument. This cause then is the Demiurge, whose task was to introduce order out of chaos.

But why did the Demiurge act in this way? Because he wished good for everyone and wished others to approach his in likeness. A limit was imposed by the material that was fashionable, nevertheless, he wished as high a grade of good as possible to be sustained.

But how is it possible to relate the Demiurge to God the Creator? Broadly speaking, the former corresponds to reason, and this is clear from what Plato says himself in the Timaeus, to the effect that generation was the result of the combined forces of necessity and reason.

Now in taking into account the concept of necessity, Plato did not think of something *necessarily* fixed, as a fixed law or such like. He adopted the atomist view to this, seeing it as a state without purpose. Now, if it were without purpose, it must be contrary to intelligence since intelligence acts for a purpose. Also, the atomists did not discount chance; so the two, necessity and chance, are easily related. Today, it is true these two ideas are of an opposite nature, but in Plato's mind, it was possible to unite them, on the grounds that they both were conditions which were deprived of intelligence.

This is the reason Plato speaks in the Laws of the world existing not by mind, or the action of a God, or art, but purely from necessity and chance. Neither does this view end here, for we find Aristotle in the Physics saying that the world was generated from Spontaneity. His view is that since all movers are subject to a first mover, the notion of necessity is very prominent in creation. Thus spontaneity, chance and necessity have obvious relation, despite their individual or concerted ends, they do not in any way reach to the concept of purpose. So it is convenient here to introduce the element of reason which can serve purpose, and thus is explainable Plato's action in introducing the Demiurge.

It was accepted at the Academy that chaos had never existed. There may have been one or two minds who disagreed, but in the main, this was the view accepted by Aristotle who was quite content with the idea of creation in time. The pupils of the Academy gave this theory as an explanation to facilitate understanding, but according to Aristotle, it is doubtful if they were sincere in this belief. Proclus and Simplicius also did not have conviction in this explanation. What can be made of Aristotle's interpretation of the Demiurge? Simply that he has become less actual and more symbolic. Again, in the Timaeus, Plato says that it is difficult to find a Father of all, and if He is found, He cannot be spoken of to everyone. So there is room for symbolism.

The Demiurge is referred to as taking over various aspects, presumably he took over the task of fashioning all becoming though this is not at all clear. Space plays the part of a Receptacle wherein becoming can be fashioned. But things are not made from Space, but are formed in it.

Earth, fire, water and air which had hitherto been considered as elements were discarded by Plato for the reason that they are subject to becoming as are all other material things. But how are they to be described? Quality would appear to Plato the best description. The Demiurge then took over Space or the Receptacle into which were placed these qualities; thus proceeded to fashion things in accordance to the ideal of Forms.

The same power is responsible for the distribution of shapes. The elements combine and recombine and Plato adopts as his lowest denominator in shapes the notion of triangles. The answer to the reason for this choice is found in the Laws, when he says that not until a thing has reached its third dimension, does it become susceptible to our senses.

It is possible for the elements of fire, air and water to be reformed into other things. Fire, it would seem, is particularly active in breaking down the element into triangles. The exception however is earth. The explanation provided is that its particles are particular to it alone, consequently can never mix with others. Aristotle condemns this idea on the ground of insufficient proof.

Apparently, the Demiurge is responsible for what Plato calls the world-soul though if taken literally this phase is liable to sound nonsensical. It is a kind of intermediate existence between the Forms themselves, and the Becoming in sensible matter. Since the Demiurge has created the immortal souls in the same fashion as the World-Soul and both worlds, i.e. mortal and immortal. The celestial bodies are also considered in this way as possessing souls. The actual beginning of the human Soul is left unanswered in both the Phaedrus and the Laws.

Plato does not consider it possible for the human reason to trace the genealogies of Greek deities. This task is too large. It is best to follow custom in this respect. But, in this way, he does not reject them completely, and encourages the visual workshop of the gods. Plato put little credence, however, upon the stories in which the gods were supposed to have been created.

When the Demiurge created, he sought to make his creations as much like himself as was practicable. Since this was not possible in a complete sense, each created thing bore the character of eternity upon it. Now, eternity is a unity, and if a likeness will last always and will move according to number, we have Plato's idea of Time, i.e. likeness of movement of a world, the sun providing the unit of Time. The cause of night and day is the light given out by the sun which acts in co-operation with other heavenly bodies.

Plato does not enter into a discussion on the formation of the human body. He does, however, point out that the gods thought the front a better place to lead man to than the back, and for this reason, movement was introduced to lead creation in this direction. This naive observation is found in the Timaeus: as the world was completed by the galaxy of creation as a whole, it bore the reflection of the eternal God who thus acted in such beneficence.

CHAPTER 24

PLATO AND ARTISTRY

If we consider the attitude Plato adopted to art what can be said? Certainly, the evidence is scanty, and is confined to two works, the Phaedrus and the Laws. On many occasions, Plato had expressed disapproval of various dramatists and poets, but this is no criterion to say that he did not appreciate art. It is a certain fact that he did, and in support of this statement, we only have to examine extracts from the Symposium and the Phaedo to show the complete artist at work. It is not work that falls in line with a conventional mode; it is the utterance of an artist making his point.

It would be wrong to think that Plato did not consider beauty as something objective. If there is Supreme Beauty, then it must exist in external objective things. This is shown in the Hippias Maior where relations are discussed.

Beauty is by participation in greater or lesser degree, further it is subsistent in itself. From this observation, we may assume that pure Beauty according to Plato is not participated. But this fact necessarily puts artistic work on a very low level of actual beauty and this is for two reasons. First, an artistic work of art must be a thing. From this, it follows it must also be material. All this being granted, pure or absolute Beauty is then immaterial, and is not a thing, on account of its lack of participation. Now this is a lofty concept, so lofty indeed that it is hard for a material being conditioned to sensible matter, to hold a completely perfect notion of beauty solely on an immaterial plane.

It is true that the point is made that what we can use is also beautiful. Very well. Let us accept that statement. If, however, beauty is efficiency, then the immaterial Absolute Beauty of which Plato spoke must be capable of being used by creatures. As it stands, it is absurd. However, Socrates considered it a beautiful thing which could be used for a good or bad purpose. But if beauty

116

will produce something, as according to Socrates it will do, then we can no longer consider beauty and efficiency the same. According to these ancients, beauty is that which appeals to the sight or hearing; let us accept that statement. But music could never be beautiful on this basis; for it is not seen and therefore cannot be completely appreciated sensibly. Conversely a fine painting is not beautiful; for it will only be seen and not heard. This position will arise because there is nothing that is shared between sight and hearing. There is nothing common between them.

How does all this harmonize with the rest of Plato's views on Metaphysics? The answer is that it is incompatible with it. Confining ourselves to purely an historical standpoint, we may say that Plato does not define completely natural or supernatural beauty. Certainly, he makes references to them, as in the Philebus, when he speaks of lines and curves giving pleasure. He goes on to note the difference between the pleasure arising from the beautiful thing, and the thing itself. He also says that symmetry of line goes into beauty, but this is the furthest his definition goes. From his remarks, however, it is certain that Plato believed in a supernatural and natural beauty.

There is an instinct for expression common to man. Plato takes this as a beginning of artistic effort. He continues that all art is but a copy of the Supreme Art, i.e., the original man. Pure Truth is found in the Pure Form, and so the artist will start with a disadvantage, his primary materials being removed from the Form. As a result of this teaching, Plato is bound to hold art in not too high esteem, and indeed this is the case. The ruling force in Plato's life was the search for truth, and obviously he was not going to bother himself overmuch with what he considered a discipline removed from the truth. This form of drift is found in the Republic and the ultimate conclusion is that anybody who prefers shadows for the real, has made, to say the best of it, a gross mistake in values.

Music is good when it is an imitation of the good; it is not to be gauged by the amount of sense pleasure that is gained. Always do we find Plato returning to this theme of the true when he says that songs and the like must have a semblance of the true. This is found in the Laws.

In both of these works, i.e. Republic and Laws, Plato is quite certain that music is an art of imitation. Nevertheless, he lays down certain principles whereby a good critic may judge. They are (i) whether the imitation is accurate, (ii) its degree of truth and (iii) if appropriate rhythms and words have been properly applied.

It would seem that Plato first considered what he called an ideal order. Natural objects came next in importance and finally works of the imagination. Now, art belongs primarily to the sphere of imagination, its term being the individual emotions. If this art form is considered as is a photograph, for example, we will see that the exactness of copy attributable to a photograph was not an absolute factor in Plato's artistic estimation. Certainly there was the eternal quest for the true, but possibly it would be truer to say that the art form "stood for" its prototype. In other words, it was a symbol. Thus the imagination gives rise to a specific symbolism, which has its terminus in human emotions.

Plato goes on once again to specify that some emotions produce good results and others produce bad results. Consequently, it is the role of reason to decide what is good and separate it from the bad. A point should be given emphasis here that throughout his consideration, Plato is concerned with moral effects of art, far more than he is with the notion of beauty appealing to the soul. No doubt his intentions were of the best, but he seems to outweigh the purely beautiful in favour of morality. A more balanced conclusion would be arrived at by considering both these factors equally.

Music is to give pleasure; Plato realises this view, but apparently he thought it a mistaken one; since he shows disagreement with it. When music as a thing can have no use, no utility and no truth, it cannot be good. It must possess these elements, particularly truth. Now, truth cannot be perceived by sense, thus to Plato it is unpracticable to consider it as a sense pleasure. This rule applies to other art forms. At the same time, it would be a mistaken notion to think of Plato decrying all pleasure in art or music. He merely requires a qualification, that is, that music for example, shall procure some profit. Undoubtedly, as some writers have said, it was the educational view that prompted the philosopher in this regard. But music can and should be used, by men and women alike, as a welcome diversion.

In the Laws, the scope of art is given a wider sweep, wider than is found in the Republic. But the basis of Plato's thinking has not altered, that is to say, the moral aspect is still uppermost with concern shown for censorship in that it is of the right kind.

The conclusion is that although art does not occupy a very high place in man's activities, it nevertheless is an integral part. It helps man to express himself and provides food for the imagination. It would be wrong to conclude that Plato ignored art although it would have to be admitted that his ideas are left in a comparatively undeveloped manner.

At the beginning of this portion of narrative devoted to Plato, attention was drawn to the contribution he would make to the development of philosophy. An attempt has now been made in a most imperfect way to present that contribution to the general reader and we can look forward at some of the influences Plato will have in the years that follow. We will have occasion to recall this influence when we deal with Christian philosophy. The human mind with its marvellous capacity for judgment will now see the degree of development philosophy has undergone at the hands of Plato. To do this, it will have to generalize, compare, adjust, classify and so on. The view of philosophy now adopted will have to be in accord with these adjustments brought about by Plato.

Now an idea which stands for some notion or objects represents the total sum of its possible aspects. These aspects will vary according to different persons, and thus it will be that the same notion will appear with greater depth and strength to some than to others. But this depth and strength is of great value, for under its guise the *variety* of a certain science can become very evident. Just as with some physical object which will not become clear until viewed from every material angle. These remarks are not meant as a useless digression; on the contrary, they are included to show the basis of the extraordinary influence Plato was to have during the next thousand years. He devoted his life to the search for Truth. He was speculative in a brilliant fashion, but he could be practical also, as is shown by his ideas on morality. In short, a person should live and act his life in accord with reason. He showed that man could become a small ordered world within himself provided there was submission to the all important reason.

Aristotle in a touching fragment said of Plato that he was unique, and the wicked should not speak his name, for theirs is not the right to praise him who showed that a virtuous man is he who is truly happy. None of us can equal him.

During the thousand years of Plato's influence that followed, St. Augustine was undoubtedly the greatest adherent, receiving the doctrine as he did from the Neo-Platonists. Many discussions St.

119

Thomas Aquinas conducted were on topics originally proposed by Plato. In later years, a Platonic Academy was formed at Florence. St. Thomas More showed Platonic influence in his Utopia.

In our own times, all spiritualistic philosophy finds its root in Plato. His influence can be seen in all branches of philosophy, metaphysics, ethics, idealism and epistemology alike.

However, he left no complete system. We mentioned earlier that his lectures are not available; probably in these lie the solution to many unsolved difficulties. But what is left shows a life dedicated to the sincere search for what is truth and goodness. Not all men even start on such a hazardous journey, and fewer still succeed half so well as did Plato.

CHAPTER 25

THE ACADEMY AFTER PLATO

What happened in the course of time to Plato's school is now our main concern. Its corpus of teaching modified over the years, but in the main, it was the Pythagorean content that seems to have been maintained. After this, there appears to be a period of choice or eclecticism when various trends are developed at the expense of others. The men who led the school along this path were such as Speusippus, (348/7-339/8), Xenocrates (339/8-315/4), Polemon (315/4-270/69) and Crates (270/69-265/4).

Speusippus who was a nephew of Plato modified the doctrine of ideas and accepted number as the norm of reality. Some have considered that Speusippus changed the concept of knowledge and perception, but Plato had himself taken steps for these same modifications.

The actual drift of teaching of other members of Plato's school is not clear. We have Aristotle's observations and other ancient literary work for information. According to these, Speusippus held that One was responsible for substances and the many also acted as a substantial principle. The One is also responsible for reason where are found the first glimmerings of Neo-Platonism in this doctrine. Human souls are immortal. The creation of the world, according to Speusippus, is merely an account in the Timaeus and nothing more. Time does not enter the picture of creation at all. The traditional duties were material, and so Speusippus laid himself open to charges of impiety.

Xenocrates of Chalcedon was the next head of the Old Academy. To him, ideas and numbers were one, and came from the One, and an Indeterminate principle. The former was a masculine element, the latter a feminine element.

In a somewhat confused teaching, Xenocrates said that the Demiurge was produced by the addition of Self and the One who are added to number and are self moving as number. There are three Worlds, he said, viz. The sub-human, the heavenly, and the super-celestial. These worlds were peopled with demons of good and bad character. In this manner by attributing immorality to the demons and not to the gods, Xenocrates explained immorality. He also agreed with Speusippus that the soul was immortal even to its irrational parts. It is interesting to note he deplored the eating of fleshmeat on the grounds that irrationality may triumph over the rational. Polemon who followed him also held this view.

Next, we have an adoption of Pythagorean philosophy by Heraclides Ponticus. He maintained that the world was made of particles, which he probably took to be separated by space. These material operations occur through the action of God. Consequently, the soul is a body. He maintained that Mercury and Venus revolve around the sun and suggested that this was also probably true of the earth's action.

Eudoxus (497-355 B.C.) was one of the greatest mathematicians among the ancients. Two of his views are worth mentioning. They are (1) that Ideas and things intermixed, and (2) pleasure is the supreme good.

Commentaries were written on Plato's works from the earliest times. The first was by Crantor (330-270) where the concept of creation was again treated with complete absence of time, that is as a timeless process. In this, Crantor, Speusippus and Xenocrates are of one accord, the former mentioning that the passions must be modified which was the contrary opinion of that held by the Stoics who said the ideal was an apathetic one.

CHAPTER 26

LIFE AND WORKS OF ARISTOTLE

We come now to Plato's partner in philosophical fame, Aristotle, who represents the summit of speculative thought of ancient Greece. He was born at Stagira in Thrace in 384/3 B.C. His father was Nicomachus, a doctor at the Macedonian king's court. The name of this king was Amyntas II. At the age of 17, Aristotle went to Athens to further his studies and entered Plato's Academy in 368/7 B.C. Aristotle remained at the Academy for twenty years, and thus was able to observe closely the manner in which Plato sought to solve his philosophical problems. About this particular time, two forces were actively at work in Plato's mind. They were dialectic, and the spirit of religion. Aristotle studied the natural sciences; gradually branching out on lines of his own, and away from the original Platonic ideas. Some have held that there was violent disagreement between these two, certainly two of the greatest minds the world has ever seen. But to hold that there was contention between them is wrong. Plato was always willing to guide and advise Aristotle if he so required, and Aristotle looked upon Plato as more than a friend. The change in direction of thought was not achieved at once by Aristotle. It took time, and he, like any student, would appreciate the guidance of a master.

When Plato died, Aristotle decided to leave Athens. This was because Aristotle did not agree with some of Speusippus' views. Also he may not have wished to stay in an inferior position. Consequently, he went to Assos in the Troad and founded a branch of the Academy there. He was greatly respected by Hermias, the ruler of Aterneus, whose adopted daughter and niece Pythias, Aristotle married. During his stay at Assos, it is possible that Aristotle began to work out his own ideas. After three years, he went to Lesbos where he met Theophrastus of Ephesus who later became one of Aristotle's most prominent followers. Hermias was even-

123

tually kidnapped by the Persians and tortured to death. This was probably the reason Aristotle wrote a poem about him.

Philip of Macedon, in 343/2 B. C., invited Aristotle to Pella to instruct the young Alexander then thirteen years of age. Great opportunities were open to Aristotle to widen his perspective, but little seems to have been accomplished in this direction. Aristotle always remained faithful to the idea of the small Greek City-State as the ideal one. Be that as it may, when Alexander became king, and Aristotle probably returned to Stagira, the former rebuilt the philosopher's native town, in gratitude for the wisdom he had received at the hands of Aristotle. Various incidents after this, tended to separate the ways of Alexander and Aristotle. For example, in 327, Callisthenes, Aristotle's nephew, was executed by Alexander, who had accepted the man in his service in the first instance on Aristotle's advice. The execution was for alleged conspiracy. In addition to this, Alexander's compromising attitude to the Greeks in general did not please Aristotle.

Consequently, in 335/4, Aristotle returned to Athens and started his own School. It was situated in the north east of the city in a gymnasium consecrated to Apollo Lycaeus. It was called the Lyceum. Aristotle walked to and fro with his students whilst lecturing, and thus they became known as the peripatetics or walkers.

This school would seem to have a greater spirit of dedication than did Plato's Academy; in short, it was a complete university, complete with library and efficient teachers where lectures could be given.

Alexander the Great died in 323 B.C., and Aristotle was compelled to leave Athens on account of his close associations with the dead ruler. In his own words, he left because he did not wish the Athenians to sin a second time against philosophy. He went to Chalcis in Euboea, where he lived on the land belonging to his deceased mother. In 322/1, he died of a stomach complaint.

In considering Aristotle's works, three main divisions can be seen. Firstly, when he was with Plato; secondly, during the time at Assos and Mitylene; and thirdly, the time he spent as head of the Lyceum. Again two main divisions may be observed, that is, those works that were for general consumption, and those which provided material for lectures. The former are very rare, and it is the lectures which have provided us with the bulk of Aristotle's ideas. They are remarkable for their austere setting which may be explained by the fact of the attitude of their author. He was interested in philosophy, but not in a flowing style. In the first group of works, it would be reasonable to say that Aristotle stayed close to the style to Plato; where there are dialogues it appears as if Aristotle himself is in a prominent position. It is true that Aristotle has been credited at this period with Plato's Ideas. This was attributed to him by Cephisodorus, a pupil of Isocrates.

Undoubtedly, at this stage, Aristotle followed Plato in his belief in the pre-existence of Ideas. The Eudemus is ample proof of this. Also, Aristotle takes the Phaedo as a model when he proves that the soul is immortal. He says the soul is not a harmony of the body; further harmony has an opposite known as disharmony. But it is not possible to find the opposite of a soul. The conclusion obviously is that the soul cannot be called a harmony. Aristotle goes on to explain that as people fall sick and lose their memories, in like manner, the soul after death, remembers the body. Actually, life apart from the body is the natural habitat for the soul; its union with the body can be likened to a grave illness. Now these views show how much at this stage, Aristotle depended upon Plato, and he is hardly recognizable as the same Aristotle as when he matured.

Another work of this period, the "Protrepticus" also shows the influence of Plato's forms. It is actually a letter to Themison of Cyprus. The work is interesting for phronesis retains the Platonic idea as contrary to the practical one Aristotle will display in the Nicomachean Ethics. Also Aristotle shows that worldly goods are limited in their value. True happiness is depicted as beyond death. We must conclude, however, even for those who follow philosophy, that material goods have their place.

The first parts of the Physics and also those of the "De Anima" date from this period. Originally, the Physics were two monographs, and we can ascribe the first two books of this work and also Book Seven to this early period.

However, Aristotle gradually became aware that the teaching of the Academy was at variance with his own. A representative work at this time is "On Philosophy"; which is notable, for in this work we find the first recorded criticism of Platonic methods.

Despite the fact that Aristotle always considered Plato as the main teacher of early Greek philosophy, he attacks the doctrine of Forms with great fervour. He argues that if the Forms had any extreme other than a mathematical one, we could not understand

125

it. Also, the famous doctrine of the Unmoved Mover makes its first appearance, though not with the precision of the later metaphysics. It is mentioned in relation to the Heavens.

Another doctrine that will become more familiar later on is the concept that "generally if a number of things are better, among them will be a best. Now among things that are one, a best thing is found, and this would be divine."

Firstly, it seems that Aristotle derived his concept of the existence of God from ordinary phenomena such as sleep, and walking, the stars, etc. However, this is not in accord with Aristotle's later teaching, and still shows Platonic influences. In the Timaeus, there is the argument for the eternity of the world. This, along with other distinctly Platonic teachings, Aristotle proceeds to criticise more and more fully as his own ideas advance.

The first books of the Metaphysics would seem to date from about this time. This would be Book A, Book B, Book K1-8, Book A (except c-8), Book M (9-10), and Book N. The pronoun "we" is constantly in use in these books, suggesting that technically at least, Aristotle still regarded himself as a Platonist. Some eminent writers have considered that these first works of the Metaphysics were directed against Speusippus, with whom Aristotle had disagreed earlier.

Aristotle's stay at Assos probably was the setting for the Eudemian Ethics. But differences from Plato are to be noticed here. For example, whilst he still holds to the idea of Phronesis, we find God as the transcending Power set down in the Metaphysics. In addition to the Ethics, it is likely that Aristotle also wrote an outline of the Politics, where he again disagrees with Plato's idea of the perfect State. "De Caelo" and "De Generatione et Corruptione" also date from this time.

The years 335-322 represent Aristotle's third period of development. In it, the progress made and sustained is astounding, to say the least.

By this time, Aristotle had started his own School, and the thoroughness of investigation in this establishment reached a rare level. Certainly, there had been organized research at Plato's Academy; the reason for this being to build up a logical corpus of thought. But although Aristotle may have copied this idea, he far exceeded it. The fact too, that this effort was a sustained one into the realm of history and nature puts the Middle Ages and our own civilisation greatly in Aristotle's debt. The great danger here

126

is to consider Aristotle purely as an observer of history and natural philosophy. But he was more than this, for he never lost his absorbing interest in Metaphysics.

Aristotle formed a system of teaching at the Lyceum whereby his lectures were distributed to students. Andronius of Rhodes was the intermediary from whom the general public received these works. These particular works are extremely difficult to edit in modern form, owing to unexpected breaks in the texts. The reason for this is that originally they were lectures, and probably not meant for general consumption. However, progress can be somewhat labouriously made in presenting Aristotle in modern dress, by grouping various lectures under one common heading. Aristotle himself never completed the grouping of his works; but it was done by Andronicus of Rhodes and others.

Works of this last period are as follows:

1. *Logic.*
   The Categories (wholly Aristotle), De Interpretatione or on Proposition and Judgement. The Prior Analytics (2 books on proof, knowledge and principles). The Topics, (8 books on dialectic and probably proof.) The Sophistical Fallacies.

2. *Metaphysics.*
   A collection of lectures of various dates. It acquires its name from before the time of Andronicus.

3. *Natural Philosophy.*
   Natural science. The Physics. Eight books, the first two of which reflect Aristotle's dependence upon Plato in earlier times. Metaphysics A983 a.23-3 refers to the Physics in the theory of causes in Physics 2, Book 7, also to an earlier period, whilst Book i is really not included in the Physics at all. This is inferred when Aristotle refers to explaining a point in the Physics. Thus the work is a series of monographs, in addition to which the Metaphysics mentions two other works as Physics. These are "De Caelo" and "De Generatione et Corruptione".
   The meteorology in four books.
   The History of animals in ten books consisting of anatomy and physiology.
   The last books were possibly completed after Aristotle's death.

A lost work in seven books.

"De Incessa Animalium" in one book and the "De Moto" to Animalium also in one book.

"De Generatione Animalium" in five books.

"De Anima." The psychology of Aristotle in three books.

"Parva Naturalia", a work containing discussions upon perception, memory, sleep and waking, dreams, life long and short, life and death, breathing, divination in sleep, etc.

"Problemata", collection of problems collected by Aristotle himself.

4. *Ethics and Politics.*

"Magna Moralia" in two books.

"The Nicomachean Ethics" in ten books. Edited by Nicomachus, Aristotle's son, after the death of the philosopher.

"The Politics", books, 2, 3, 7 and 8 refer to Aristotle's second period of development.

"The Constitution of 158 Greek States." The one referring to Athens was discovered on papyrus in 1891.

5. *Works on History and Literature.*

"The Rhetoric" in three books.

"The Poetics," part of which is lost, thus the work is incomplete.

Also works concerning plays at Athens, and the territorial rights of the State.

It would not be correct to assume that all these works were written by Aristotle himself. Some were writtem by various people, Theophrastus for example, who produced a work on natural history, under Aristotle's direction. Another example is a treatise on mathematics and astronomy carried out by Eudemus of Rhodes. By glancing at the list above, we can see that the scope of Aristotle's interests was enormous. A point of difference may be seen in comparing the works of Plato and Aristotle. The former treated the world to a very great extent as an illusion and adopted a deprecatory attitude towards it. The latter on the other hand tended towards science and empiricism. This difference would appear to be the basis of contrast between two of the greatest minds of the pagan world, and furthermore, the gap has widened with the years. Now that there is truth in this view is undoubtedly so, but it must not be forgotten that Aristotle was developing the views held by

128

Plato. The fundamental idea of philosophy did not change, for we have the preservation of idea and philosophical type. We have had occasion to point out the stages of development before in this work. They apply to Aristotle just as much as they did to Plato; the logical sequence continues, just as does the chronic vigour of the discipline itself.

This process of development is not considered by some writers who consequently tend to treat these two philosophers as opposed. But they are not; one merely completes or corrects the prior content of thought. Further, weight is given to this view by the fact that a unification was attempted in Neo-Platonism, and the great thinkers of the Middle Ages, such as St. Thomas, whilst giving pride of place to Aristotle, would always consider a Platonic idea if it helped to solve the problem at hand. Both St. Bonaventure and Duns Scotus also worked with both doctrines.

One common factor to both Platonism and Aristotelianism is that they both terminate in Metaphysics. For this reason, Goethe could compare Aristotle's thought with a pyramid, broad at the base and rising to a pinnacle, and Plato's with an obelisk, leaping up as a tongue of flame.

CHAPTER 27

LOGIC

In writing his works, Aristotle appears to have followed a definite plan. Firstly, Theoretical Philosophy in which knowledge itself is the end. This includes subdivisions thus:

1. Physics or natural philosophy concerned with material things which include motion;
2. Mathematics concerning things not moved and not apart from matter;
3. Metaphysics concerning natural theology.

Secondly, practical philosophy which concerns Politics and has as its subdivisions Strategy, Economics and Rhetoric, since it appears that these subdivisions have their end in Political Science. Included in this survey also is Political Philosophy which concerns production as opposed to action as would be the case with practical philosophy.

The prefix "formal" is often used to designate Aristotle's logic. This is because he undertakes an analysis of thought in its various forms, from which idea is derived the word "analytic." But Aristotle's work is entirely objective; it does not rest in the realm of the subjective only. His aim is scientific proof with relation to the real. The syllogism — all men are mortal; John is a man; therefore he is mortal — would have for Aristotle a basis in pure reality. Not only does this example obey formal laws of thought, but the real must be present. We feel we cannot stress this too weightily, on account of present day trends of subjectivity in philosophy. Aristotle accepts reality, and his subsequent thinking will contain the idea of reality within it.

A further step would be to say that the philosopher accepts too, the doctrine of universals. Things exist outside the mind in a non-universal state. In other words, they exist in a particular state with their attendant accidents. The categories show this point well. They illustrate the normal procedure of thought, they also show how things actually exist. The categories are therefore a metaphysical study.

In brief, Aristotle does not tend to isolate the idea purely in the mind as Kant does. He will go to reality, to that which exists, for his information. This will rule out all critical ideas on thought with Aristotle; his epistemology is real.

In two works, the Categories are numbered differently. For example, in the Topics and Categories themselves, there is man or horse; three yards long, white, double, in the market place, last year, lies or sits, with shoes, cuts, is cut or burnt. In the Posterior Analytics, they appear as eight, sittings and habit being included under other headings. The conclusion is that Aristotle did not lay down a hard and fast rule as to the number of Categories. But there is a definite order in this list. They are a collection of concepts governing the acquisition of knowledge. They always predicate something in the manner in which we think of a thing as existing. For anything we think of must fall under substance. Aristotle thought of the Categories as indicating genera, species and individuals from the universal to the particular, and that is just the way the human mind works. First, it considers a genus, then a particular species, then an individual in that species, and finally the subsequent accidents of the thing.

Aristotle foresaw that the Categories could bridge the gap between Logic and Metaphysics for on the one hand, they represented external reality, on the other substance, which is the object of Metaphysics. Thus both have their roots in being as well as Logic. We have said to exist something must be a substance. Singulars exist materially, and for something to do this, it must be a substance. But there is also the addition of accidental forms such as colour, extension and so forth. Consequently, it is possible to consider the first three categories which are substance, quantity and quality. Now these are interior possessions of the object. The dog has the same substance as other dogs, and will not equal them in quality and in quantity. Now if we consider, we note that the dog must be in a certain place at a specific time or period, and must stand or sit in a certain way, that is to say, its posture will be specific. Since substances belong to the natural world as parts to a whole, it is clear that they themselves act and are acted upon. This will make it possible for two divisions in the Categories, firstly interior determinations and secondly exterior determinations. This is because of the relationship of one object to many and vice versa. But at no time is order lacking in this arrangement since, as we have pointed out, it is the method adopted by the human mind in discerning various objects.

There are two works "The Posterior Analytics" and "The Topics" where Aristotle discusses how a universal group is related to a particular object. The largest group is known as a genus, the next largest a species, and then there follow difference, property and accident. In the latter book, "The Topics", Aristotle shows that it is possible to divide predicables according to the relation they have with the subject. In this way, if the predicable is substantially the same as the subject, then the essence of the latter can be obtained from this same predicable. On the other hand, if it is not substantially the same, then the accidents or attributes may be derived only from this source. Following this through, he further says that then these attributes are part of the definition as genus or difference, or otherwise as an accident only.

Definitions are arrived at by the genus and difference, involving a secondary species mentioned by Plato. Aristotle always allows for these secondary definitions even though the results obtained from them are somewhat inconclusive. In physics and natural science, they are widely used, but do not act as completely as a descriptive definition favoured by the philosopher.

It is true language has played a distinctive role in philosophy; when I talk of whiteness, I naturally think of whiteness inhering in some subject, that is to say, in its substance. So it is with the Categories; substance and accident as expressed in language are expressed in this way because of these limitations. But language follows thoughts which in turn follow things. Thus language is not a prior consideration.

Aristotle concluded that scientific knowledge meant deducing things from their causes; it was then obvious that a link must be formed between the two. Scientific knowledge is possessed by the knowledge of causes, upon which are based dependent facts.

It is always true that this relationship of cause and effect is valid; nevertheless, it is possible to know a thing slightly, and on the other hand to possess a deeper knowledge of it. Aristotle was quite decided in this difference. Another way of expressing this truth is to say that knowledge by sense is first, and afterwards, according to the capacity of the person intellectually, the same thing is known by the intellect in a greater degree of perfection. Induction is necessary for this operation, even at sense level. This leads to sense perception and memory. But the sense does not make a mistake; error in individuals rests in the judgement. If a heavenly body appears smaller than it actually is, the senses are reporting correctly. But error will occur as the result of lack of knowledge about the heavens, and this example illustrates the relationship always occurring between sense and judgement. Consequently, Aristotle treats of both forms, i.e. induction and deduction.

Now, if induction is scientific, it is complete. Oratory makes use of incomplete induction. In the case of deduction, Aristotle instituted the syllogism. This he developed very much, but he did not carry induction to the same level. He described the syllogism as "discourse in which certain things being stated something other than what is stated follows of necessity from their being so." The syllogism is demonstrated in three stages, viz.

1. The Middle Term is subject in one premise and Predicate in another. Thus: every man is mortal; Peter is a man, therefore he is mortal.
2. The Middle Term is Predicate in both premises. Thus: every man can laugh; but no dog can laugh; therefore, no dog is a man.
3. The Middle Term is subject in both premises. Thus: every man can laugh, but every man is an animal. Therefore, some animals can laugh.

The difference between demonstrative reasoning and dialectical reasoning is that in the case of the former, the propositions involved are more basic whereas in the latter, knowledge is more indirect generally by way of opinion. These views are set forth in the Topics.

There is yet another form of reasoning, and this is termed contentious, the explanation of which is where a number of opinions are held which appear to be valid, but in actual fact are not. This view is discussed in a different work, the "De Sophisticus Elenchis", the main point of which is to bring various forms of fallacious reasoning to light.

Now, in the process of deduction, it is necessary to obtain proof. Nevertheless, it is not reasonable to expect every principle to be proved, otherwise this will be an unending process, which in turn will mean nothing is proved. Aristotle, because of this fact, claimed that there were various principles which we can term self-evident. The best example of this is the principle of contradiction. If I assert that a circle exists and is round, then it is impossible to assert that the circle exists in any other form except in its existence and in its roundness. That circle then must exist and no one could deny this existence. I cannot say a circle exists, and it does not exist. It either exists with the properties mentioned above, or it does not exist at all. The same principle applies to all manner of being. The attribute of roundness cannot be possessed by the circle and not possessed by it. Such a principle is the basis of thought, and is taken for granted.

In effect then, there are self evident principles; then there are other principles which are derived contingently. But, if a syllogism is taken into consideration, the first premise is required to be proved. It depends for this proof upon first principles and induction. How is this done? By a reflection of the universal, which, Aristotle says, is shown clearly in the particular.

Without doubt, Aristotle made a tremendous contribution to human thought in general by his observations upon logic. It is not a complete survey, yet no one before had attempted such a comprehensive treatment of this subject as the Organon provides. Aristotle omitted apparently to consider the position that the mind also reaches conclusions from various concrete facts. It may well be that he took this for granted; in any event, later on, in Christian times, St. Thomas Aquinas was aware of this point. But to all great achievements, there must be a beginning, and it was to Aristotle that we owe this fundamental work in the study of the human mind and thought. The philosopher himself says at the end of the "De Sophisticus Elenchis" that, while much has been said before him on the subject of logic, he is treading new ground in his observations.

How does modern logic compare with its Aristotelian counterpart? There have been writers who would relegate the latter to a thing of the past, and there have also been authors attacking the modern logical concepts. Firstly, the logic of Aristotle is incomplete, yet there are many outside the realm of scholastic philosophy who gain inspiration from it. Secondly, modern logic may be able to add to Aristotle's original, but it is not an opposite.

The name given to the complete body of Aristotle's logical writings is the Organon. But it would seem that many things are discussed under this title. In the Categories, there is a wide discussion on Subject and Predicate, in "De Interpretatione" there is another, showing how propositions can be opposed. Also through this discussion of model and assertoric forms, comes the reference to the excluded middle. In the "Prior Analytics", pure propositions are dealt with, also those of necessary and contingent character. The syllogism is also shown in three ways — truth and falsity in these matters as found in the conclusion. These analytics also include a discussion upon the enthymeme.

In the "Posterior Analytics", science is shown to be able to be discovered by deduction. Then there is unity, diversity, distinction, ranking of various sciences, ignorance, error and invalidity. In Book 2, there are definitions, demonstrations, the fact that an essential nature cannot be demonstrated, how truths are known and so on. "The Topics" describes predicables, definition, and the art of dialectic. The last, "De Sophisticus Elenchis," as already mentioned, concerns fallacy.

CHAPTER 28

ARISTOTLE AND METAPHYSICS

In the last section we said that logic and metaphysics were related through the Categories. Because of this relationship, it seems at this stage, fitting enough to give consideration to a most famous work of Aristotle, "The Metaphysics." This work is extremely difficult to study on account of Aristotle's particular style, and in translated versions, undoubtedly the transition of language adds to the already great difficulties; nevertheless, possibly no work has influenced Western thought as much as the "Metaphysics" has done.

After observing that all men desire to know, Aristotle goes on to demonstrate that there are two ways of knowing. The first by experience which really means to have knowledge without knowing *why* a certain thing is so. The second way is knowledge by act which means to have knowledge of something, and also to know *why* such a thing is as it is. In other words, experience is knowledge without reason, and art is knowledge with reason. The end of art is an effect of some sort, but Aristotle says that Wisdom at its highest level does not aim at producing anything. It cannot be used, and for this reason modern writers, following Aristotle, have spoken of the "uselessness" of Metaphysics. This is what they mean; the great point is that it cannot be used, and is an end in itself. Anyone who studies the highest type of wisdom is superior — at least in the mode of study — to anyone who studies a particular science for a particular end. This is because Metaphysics can be desired for itself. The other sciences cannot.

It is simply a science of first principles, prompted by man's desire to know. Man wished for an explanation of sensible things, and thus philosophy came to be out of a desire to understand. Whatever *use* could be made of knowledge, this was essentially secondary. Consequently, because it was sought for itself, philosophy was essentially free, and in this science the highest part is

Metaphysics. Since this is so, Aristotle concluded that Metaphysics marked the summit of man's ability to perfect himself. Such a person could be a lover of wisdom desiring to know the ultimate in all reality. Further, Aristotle maintained that such knowledge is attainable, though he did not propound ideas without proof.

We gain information in this life by means of the senses which concern particulars. But Metaphysics concerns universals, which will mean that it is furthest from sense, and consequently the most abstract. It is in this that lies the difficulty to be overcome when it is studied. According to Aristotle, there is no wisdom in sense perception, since it is common to everyone. Also Metaphysics is an accurate science. This is because when fewer principles are involved, greater accuracy results, since there is a narrower margin for error. In addition, Metaphysics is the most knowable of all sciences, since it deals with first principles.

Now these principles are reality in the manner of their application since the latter are absolutely dependent upon the former. As we work from sense, we are not always conscious of this fact of knowledge of first principles, as our appreciation of them will depend upon the power of abstraction.

There are four causes with which wisdom is concerned, and these we find in the Physics thus:

1. the substance or essence of things;
2. the matter or subject;
3. the beginning of motion or efficient cause; and
4. the final cause.

The first book of the Metaphysics starts with a form of historical survey. The point of which is to discover if any other cause existed besides those already mentioned. The conclusion of this historical opening is to find that no one has previously clearly set out the causes as mentioned. Aristotle regarded his own philosophy as a development of what had gone before, though in a somewhat advanced form. Other philosophers have taken this view of their predecessors, notably Hegel. However, Aristotle does not render to those former thinkers what is rightly their due, and this fact should be noted in regarding his conclusions about them.

The object of these first philosophers had been to find an absolute base as it were, or substratum which stands by itself, and is open to neither generation nor corruption. In order to achieve this, they had employed material means, and it was in this way that Thales, Anaximenes and Heraclitus proposed some particular material element. Empedocles listed four elements. But material things could not possibly provide the answer for which they were looking. It still remained what is it that is an ultimate mover, and what is the cause of becoming? Empedocles and Anaxagoras had answered this question in their way. In Aristotle's opinion, this last philosopher, whilst he did maintain Mind as a mover, when he was confronted with a difficulty he could not solve, posited mind as the solution. But Aristotle appears to think that in many cases, it was only when a suitable explanation was not forthcoming did Anaxagoras fall back upon the concept of Mind. In this way was mind pressed into service to hide the fact of ignorance. Empedocles had used two principles, Friendship and Strife, but he was not logical in his use of either.

We find moreover, that the conclusion is that two of Aristotle's four causes have been identified, i.e., material cause and source of movement. But these early philosophers had not developed these ideas.

It would seem that Aristotle did not hold Pythagorean philosophy in very high regard, for he passes over it in a somewhat cursory fashion, and comes to the philosophy of Plato. Now in this philosophy, we find the Form outside the essence of the thing itself, so according to Aristotle, Plato used but two causes. They are that of essence, and the material cause. Treatment of the final cause is very incomplete, though Aristotle overlooks the fact that in the Timaeus, Plato had mentioned the Demiurge as having an influence upon finality. On the other hand, Plato, it is true, could not because of this teaching, arrive at the idea of an immanent essence as the final cause of substance.

In Book 3, there are some main problems of philosophy, and in Book 4, Aristotle says that the main object of Metaphysics is to study being qua being. The particular sciences take only isolated attributes and work upon them, but Metaphysics does not consider this or that particular attribute or thing; it takes being as a whole. This is also simply to consider being as one, so we find unity as essential to being. The Categories all contain being, in like manner so unity is contained in them. Goodness also is applied to being and thus to all the Categories. Unity and goodness will be called by the Scholastics "transcendent," for the reason they are not confined in any way to any one category. Thus, if man is defined as a rational animal, being will be predicated of both "rational" and "animal." From this, it is obvious that being is not contained in a group or genus, and consequently the same will apply to unity and goodness.

Aristotle next considers that it is not possible for everything to possess being in exactly the same way. This brings in the notion of quality, and so a substance possesses being in accordance to a certain quality. What categories then apply to being? The answer is that of substance, since this is primary to all the others. Again we may add at this point, there are many different kinds of substance. If this is correct, with what kind does Metaphysics deal? Aristotle replies that it will be a substance not open to change, for since Metaphysics studies being qua being, one can only really arrive at an accurate idea of being within a substance which does not change. Undoubtedly, such a being is in existence, which causes other things to move; this will be a divine being, the study of which is called theology. This idea will be used by St. Thomas Aquinas fifteen hundred years later, to prove the existence of God. The science of mathematics, in spite of the fact that it is possible to consider it separately, has its roots in matter. So it cannot exist apart from matter. Physics is the science which deals with bodies and with movement. Metaphysics considers substances completely apart from matter and without motion in themselves.

There is a division made by Aristotle into changeable and unchangeable substances. This is in Book E, but in Book D, he shows three kinds of substances, thus:

1. sensible and corruptible;
2. sensible and eternal (the heavens etc.)
3. without sense and eternal.

The conclusion is that Metaphysics studies being in itself and not by way of attributes. It does not study being as truth. Why? Because truth and falsity are in the mind and not in things. It is possible for it to lay down various truths, which it does do unerringly — such as the principle of contradiction for instance — which it would appear forms the basis of all knowledge.

Now if it is said that Metaphysics studies substance, that is non-sensible substances, we can discover what non-sensible substances exist. Are they mathematical, universal or ideas of being and unity? Aristotle is quite decided that they are none of these, and this leads to his attacks upon the Platonic theories.

Firstly, Plato's arguments merely show that the universal is real and nothing more. Logically, it includes negation and relation, which are not dealt with. For if one Form is applicable to many things, it necessarily will be related to those things, and a system of negation will have to be considered if all things are not the same, which in fact is the case. Secondly, the doctrine of Forms is of no value.

This conclusion is reached because the notion of Forms involves a necessary doubling of things that are seen. It seems that Plato, since he cannot solve the problem in smaller members, turns equally fruitlessly, to larger ones.

Again, the Ideas cannot produce knowledge, and do not have substance. If they had, they would be present in various things. As it is, they are not. Aristotle seems here to take an interest in what is around him; Plato regarded the sensible world purely as a stage whereby one reached the Forms. There are, however, various types of things; from these, we can gain some idea of the fullness or completeness to be obtained. This view Plato regarded as most necessary. For instance, the realisation of a lily could lead to a Perfect Idea of a lily. The lily would have imperfections, it is true, but from it we can gain an idea of how perfect it could be.

Can the Forms explain motion? No, replies Aristotle. The reason for this, according to him, is that the Forms provide no principle for coming to be, or passing away. The Forms are depicted as without motion. In that case, the things of this world should be without motion too. But this is absurd, since it is evident that they do move. Therefore, in the Forms, there is no explanation of motion.

This criticism, subtle as it is, needs further examination. Plato realised the Forms were without motion, and it was for this reason he resorted to the Demiurge. So it would actually appear that Plato attempted to account for motion, realising that he had depicted the Forms as being motionless. It is not clear how the Forms explain sensible things. For example, the Perfect Man would have to be sensible in order to explain man existing in matter.

There would seem to be a great divergence of meaning here. For while Aristotle kept his reasoning strictly within the realms of sensible matter, apparently he did not consider Plato's meaning a truly spiritual entity. The Forms are described as subsistent concepts, and concept *as such* is not corporeal. Further, it is shown that the Ideal Man is but an idea, and neither is an idea *as such* corporeal. Could God have in His Mind a purely corporeal Ideal Man? It is certain that later writers following Plato would not think so.

Aristotle says that the theory of Forms is impossible. This is so because the substance of a thing is both the thing and its substance. They do not exist separately. It is not shown how the Forms as substance exist, and also the subject as substance exists. How can the latter obtain any essence in order to exist? Plato replies that the subject has essence in imitation or participation. But this explanation will not do; Aristotle says it is empty and metaphorical.

This criticism is a deeper one than the previous objection; nevertheless, what sort of separation is meant? Is it merely local, or a complete independence? To Aristotle, participation would have little meaning except if it meant an immanent essence of some sort. This would mean that the essence of the object would exist in matter — a point to which Plato did not agree. Actually here, Aristotle argues against both Plato and himself. Against Plato for not admitting the co-existence of object and matter, and against himself for not providing any higher principle to stabilise the essences of which he was speaking.

If all the senses in which the word "form" is used, are taken into consideration, it is not possible for all things to come from the Forms in all of these ways. This brings into play the relationship of the object to that which provides the Form, and Plato uses metaphors to cover up this weakness. Undoubtedly, it is a weakness in Platonic teaching, and Plato himself seems often to be at a loss to explain it. We have to note, however, that when Aristotle speaks of Plato in the Metaphysics, he does not speak of the Demiurge at all. Various reasons can be given for this however. Aristotle would consider a prime mover as a final cause, and the notion of an intermediary in the nature of an efficient cause would not be adequate.

The nature of the Forms should be universal; but this is not the case. They are eminently particular in character. If the Ideal Man is like Socrates well and good, but the problem does not end there. We will have to bring in a third man who bears resemblance to Socrates, and also to the Ideal Man. This process can go on indefinitely which is absurd.

What can be said of this criticism of the Forms? First, we have to be certain that Plato meant the forms to refer to things. But we are not at all sure this was what he did mean. Of course, if they (the Forms) are universal and subsistent, then they cannot be particular. On the other hand, there is the mighty intellectual effort on the part of Plato in trying to bring an overall system into material creation. A system that would be overall and complete, and would conform to reason; this was Plato's aim, though no claim is made here that he ever achieved this. With such concepts in mind, it is hard to see how he could avoid speaking metaphorically. However, later philosophers have followed Plato in seeking such an overall explanation of the universe.

The idea that the Forms are numbers is wrong. Aristotle's objections to the "number theory" are well known, particularly when he says that "mathematics have come to be the whole of philosophy for modern thinkers, though they say it should be studied for other things." Most of the objections can be found in the Metaphysics A991, b9 to 993a, 10 M & N.

It is not clear, if Forms are numbers, how they can be a cause. If one number is a man, the second is John and the third Peter, how does the first number become the cause of the other two? Apparently, Peter is the sum of all these elements, in which case, neither will be in the true sense, a number. This is because Plato considered the Forms as exemplars and not efficient causes as Aristotle would do.

Neither is it clear why there should be two kinds of numbers; that is, numbers applicable for Forms, and numbers that apply to objects. Aristotle held there was only one class of numbers. Plato would say there are two, and Speusippus would follow him and say there were mathematical numbers and numbers pertaining to an object. Aristotle attacks these theories by saying if Forms are numbers, it is impossible for them to be singular, as the elements composing them are alike. Secondly, the object of mathematics does not exist separately. The reason for this objection is that it will involve a regress into infinity if the existence of mathematics must be constantly separated from its matter. There cannot be an end to such a process.

If we grant that substance is mathematical, how then do we explain motion? If things are to be moved, the Forms must move. But they are said to be motionless. Therefore, from what source is motion derived? We have spoken of the Demiurge of Plato which was his endeavour to explain movement.

Broadly speaking, what Aristotle says of Plato's mathematical observations, resolves itself into the fact that apparently Aristotle thought that his predecessor considered that the Forms and things were one and the same.

In addition, Aristotle had to meet the selfsame difficulties. For example, it is impossible to arrive at the idea of a perfect triangle. This is because the perfect triangle does not exist. How then are we to arrive at a basis of perfection in drawing our triangle?

Aristotle would possibly answer that the most perfect triangle that can be drawn looks perfect to the eye. This would be adequate to produce what naturally could be called a perfect triangle. You cannot abstract a perfect figure, when that figure as regards its dimensions does not exist. Neither can we say that the world as we know it is but a copy of a more perfect universe.

This really shows that Plato and Aristotle are indispensable to philosophy. What they taught must not be split up, but treated as a continuous whole. This will be the Neo-Platonic approach to philosophy. Plato said the Forms were exemplary Causes; these later thinkers described God as possessing all exemplary causes. No doubt this is correct, for the Divine Essence contains other exemplars as St. Thomas points out. He also explains that these ideas do not exist outside the Divine mind as Plato had thought.

This can be illustrated as follows: Plato was quite certain that it was possible to have direct knowledge of the ideas; yet it is impossible to have *direct* access to the Divine Mind here on earth. Certainly in this life, we can have knowledge of universals, but again these universals are known through various particulars. The perfection of the thing remains in God, whilst we possess the abstract universal quality. On these grounds, Aristotle could be justified in his attacks, since the *direct* knowledge we have is nothing other than the nature of some particular thing. It is necessary to absorb Plato's Demiurge with the Forms of Aristotle which must find their reference in God; this, together with the theory of abstraction, must all be included in order to get a complete historical and philosophical picture. Grave injustices have been done to both Plato and Aristotle, and also to philosophy by past writers extolling one thinker at the expense of the other. Credit must go to Aristotle for his criticisms; but what he criticised — the Forms for instance — were not a meaningless jumble of ideas. This great mistake, that is, accepting one philosopher's ideas against another, we find demonstrated in Augustinian thought, where the original weighed heavily in the favour of Plato, despite its later Neo-Platonism.

Now, with respect to Aristotle's criticisms of the Forms. Did he fully understand what Plato meant, or did he misrepresent this particular theory?

Probably, an answer to this question would come from reading Aristotle's Metaphysics. Here he would appear to attack Plato himself, as distinct from the Platonists. Again, while attacking the general teaching on the Forms at the Academy, Aristotle knew that a number of his objections had come up in the Parmenides. Despite these attacks of Aristotle, Plato did not withdraw what he had originally taught. Neither had Plato ignored the mathematical aspect of this problem. So Aristotle included the mathematical view within the scope of his attacks, in other words, as doctrine he ascribed to Plato. The Metaphysics is not a continuous work; this much must be realized. It is also doubtful if various sayings of Aristotle are all of equal gravity, bearing in mind the nature of this particular work.

Now, what is the position? Either Plato maintained his stand on the Forms despite the objections voiced in the Parmenides, or on the other hand, Aristotle did not understand Plato's intention after twenty years. It would be a most uncharitable gesture to consider either Plato or Aristotle as imbeciles, not knowing what they were about. In addition, it would be absolutely at variance with actual fact. Probably, the most we can say is that Plato never solved the problem of a first mover properly, whilst Aristotle could not take mathematics as one of his truest weapons. Aristotle could see that the doctrine of Plato involved difficulties with regard to the Forms; consequently he (Aristotle) was not going to assess it from *that position*. As a result, he developed a position of his own, which manifests itself in criticism. This had to be; for since he could not accept Plato's position as his own, Aristotle had to change to a position that was particular to him. It will not be the only time that the weakness in a doctrine will be exaggerated for polemical ends. Actually, hardly anything is easier than this procedure. It may be a fact that due to this exaggeration, Aristotle became the heavy critic, but that is all. If the concept of mind always remained vague, how could he accept the Demiurge as the perfect answer? On the other hand, he was mistaken in ignoring it altogether, and it is not suggested that the solution offered above will meet all requirements, but as the consequence of it, we no longer may look upon Plato and Aristotle as two men not responsible for their actions. Aristotle says there is "imitation" and "participation" in things, and in this he is right. Plato could not prove a theory of substantial form. Aristotle pointed out that the Forms were inadequate to supply this, because they were separate. But this led to Aristotle's ignoring any exemplars in Plato's teaching completely. This was taking criticism too far, but looked at from Aristotle's *own position,* the position can be understood.

The seven stages of development as outlined previously, are to be seen again here; but a distinction must be made to avoid possible confusion. Hegel had spoken of a *final* philosophy as "the result of development and truth in its highest Form." Now no claim for a final philosophy is made here, merely the action of seven individual notes or stages working simultaneously on a developing organism, a structure of philosophy that is still in the process of vitality and growth. With philosophy, thus developing at the hands of Plato and Aristotle "The Preservation of Type" is seen, as is the continuity of principle. Thirdly, there is the power of assimilation of one to the other, these facts following in logical sequence. There is anticipation of the future, and a conservative action upon the past thinkers, finally there emerges the chronic vigour of philosophy.

Judgements are always passed by the mind on the things that pass before it. Some fact is noted and at once judgement is passed. This is done in Aristotle's case, as it would be in the most ordinary occasion of judgement by a process of contrast, abstractions, generlisations, connecting, adjusting and classifying.

Nevertheless, there was agreement between Plato and Aristotle as to the nature of the universal. It was not a subjective equality. The essence was separated by the action of the mind. It does not exist in objective reality, but in the mind and also in things. Things of the same class are substances indeed; but they do not share in an objective universal. This is because the essence is different in each member of a specific class. But again, the individual essences will agree in so far as the individuals agree in a species. This latter observation has its foundation in the universal, which is the same in the mind and agrees with the individual essences of a particular group. From this emerges the definition of a science, that is, research directed to the universal element in things. If a scientist discovers uranium, the philosopher will not be concerned with individual pieces of uranium. He will be concerned with all uranium everywhere, wherever it may be found. In other words, he will be concerned with uranium as a universal. Socrates gave the lead in this form of thinking, but did not carry it through to universals. It is essential moreover, to possess the universal, otherwise if it is not possessed, there is no knowledge to be had. In a *precise form,* the universal does not exist objectively with Aristotle. What it does do is provide a basis for the concepts of things held by the mind. If I think of "cat" for example, there must be objective evidence of a cat to agree with the mental concept I have formed of the "cat", otherwise, I have no means of knowing if any thoughts be true or false. Further, if my concept of cat in the universal is found to be true, I can apply it to other objects within the same genus. If it is a false concept of "cat" that I hold, then obviously in the service of truth, I do not apply it.

But it is certain that individuals are substances. But what of the overall or universal element. Are we to call this a substance also? According to Aristotle, it would be wrong to do so, except as a secondary measure, and derived from something else. The individual thing alone is the subject of predication. By itself, it is not predicated from other things. It is permissible to call the species a substance, and it is rightly so called since the essential element is of higher quality than that in the individual, since it pervades an entire species. Observe that the philosopher has been misunderstood in his teachings on this point. If, says the statement, Aristotle teaches the individual is substance, and science is concerned with substance, then the individual must be the concern of science. But say the detractors, Aristotle in fact says that science is not concerned with the individual, but only the universal.

The reply to this contradiction, as read by some, will depend upon what was Aristotle's real meaning. He will no doubt talk of the individual as substance, but when he does so, he is refuting Plato's teaching that the universal element is by itself and separate. He does not mean that the specific nature of things is not real. If the individual is substantial, this quality will mean it can become this or that. Absolutely retained then, is the overall element or form of the thing, which is the object of science. This the mind will abstract, and consequently form its ideas of the universal. In point of fact, Aristotle has only pointed out that the substance exists separately. In the individual, it becomes a real thing, but in the case of objective reality, it is not transcendent, but merely immanent and concrete in the universal sense. The individual alone then has substance, the sensibles are compounded, but despite this, the intellect goes straight to the dynamic element existing concretely as an element of the individual. Notice too, the philosopher gives weight to the fact that whilst individuals die, the species continues. Individual cats may perish, but the species of cat will endure, because this endurance is carried by individual cats throughout the whole of this particular species. It is certain that neither does Aristotle contradict himself in the terms he uses. In a primary sense, substance is that of matter and form; secondarily, it means something specific corresponding to a universal. The specific substance will combine with various accidents. Moreover, when Aristotle speaks of primary and secondary, he means as far as we are concerned not in nature and not in dignity or time, but in universal concepts.

A compound is formed from the substance and essence. When this substance becomes individual, it corresponds to the nine other categories as laid out by Aristotle. But we still have the universal as the object of science, whilst at the same time existing in the particular. But no way is open for the mind to grasp the universal, save by this particular existence.

What of the question as to whether the universal is the object of science as suggested by Aristotle? We may reply in the affirmative here, and we may go as far as to include Wisdom in our perspective. When a philosopher considers anything in a specific manner, he does not just consider this or that. He considers the whole genus or species in its universal aspect. To illustrate: a philosopher regards contingency. In doing so, he will include every contingent being, contingency being in this case an essential or universal. A particular investigation could only lead to particular conclusions, and this does not suffice for philosophy, for in this science, a universal conclusion is always sought.

How does this fit in with the modern outlook on science? True, it is an advanced knowledge to know the universals of particular sciences, but most particular sciences today, are content to define within their own sphere leaving the ideal of completeness for the philosopher. Again, there are two kinds of essence. One is nominal, and the other real. The first kind contains some characteristics engendered by a part definition, the other is a full definition resulting in all the relevant characteristics as far as they are known.

So it is quite clear that some knowledge is necessary, otherwise no definition will be possible. There is always the suggestion of the universal, even in a nominal definition. It must in fairness be said that modern science can do without universal definitions. But when Aristotle talks, it is of these universal types that he speaks. In this respect, Aristotle and John Stuart Mill are poles apart, the latter admitting of nominal definitions and views.

As a result of this position of Aristotle, to him the objects of mathematics or of universals are not substance. This is the position in the metaphysics where he refutes Plato, yet it is possible for him to refer to them as secondary substances when discussing them in the Categories. The main point that emerges from these apparently confusing views is that Aristotle considered the individual as substance, and other considerations as secondary. But the philosopher makes another observation. He says that matter makes it impossible to define an individual thing, on account of the fact that matter perishes, and makes things opaque to knowledge. It is the substance wherein we can discover definitions, since it acts as the principle which makes an individual thing what it is. However, God and Intellect are beings found to be independent of matter. Man's active intellect can also be included in this group and so it is here that we truly find substance. This will lead us to note that metaphysics studies substance, and in doing this, it is at one with theology. If Aristotle did not accept the Platonic Ideas, he maintained part of Platonic doctrine. The philosopher considers that matter stands in the way of knowledge, only the form being capable of intelligibility. From all points, this would appear to be a development of Platonic thought. By referring to the seven notes of development, this can be clearly seen.

There are four principles thus: matter, form (which moves), the efficient cause and the final cause. Naturally for these to integrate involves change, as from a change from this to a change to that. Such phenomena are facts despite the remarks and teachings of some of Aristotle's predecessors.

To see this idea of change fully, several factors must be considered. First there must be an underlying basis for change, generally referred to as the substratum. Then there is always the thing that changes. To do this, it must be in *potentiality* to its new form. It must be moved by some cause, thus we have the efficient cause, which, as said before, acts as a mover. The well known instance of the marble being acted upon by the sculptor who produces a statue out of it, is the best example. It also shows potentiality as a capacity for something. But granting the marble has changed, it has acquired only the form of a statue. The substance still remains marble. Consequently, the change brought about must be accidental. But this is not always so. To illustrate: a cat drinks milk. The digestive juices of the cat act on the milk and change its substantial form. Thus in this case, there is a new substantial form. If we take this reasoning a step further, it is possible to see that anything is capable to change into anything else in an absolute sense. There must be some fundamental substratum which is in potentiality to everything. To explain this, Aristotle gives the explanation of prime matter, which was so widely used by the Scholastics. This then was the basis of change, but no efficient cause has direct action upon prime matter. There is always a definite thing, some particular substratum. The carpenter works upon wood, that is his particular matter, and the cat will drink milk which will become cat, but in neither case is it prime matter that is being acted upon. Therefore, prime matter never exists by itself, but only joined to some form, which gives it its definition and character. As prime matter cannot exist by itself apart from form, it is only distinguishable from it in a logical sense. Nevertheless, it must be considered as an essential element of matter, and the absolute basis for change in material objects. Mistakes could occur in thinking of it as a body, but it is not. Aristotle mentions that air, earth, fire and water are changeable elements, and these were regarded as the simplest bodies. Now, for example, air could be, by change, fire. But now, it possesses the actual form of air. But again, it is possible for it to change into many other definite things, therefore at the outset we must perceive of a naked potentiality of all things.

A thing which exists is only capable of development through change, not definitely, but in a manner that tends to something else, though as yet it is not that other thing. The potency must become actual, but this form of potentiality involves something else existing which lacks some quality, or in other words, is deprived of some form. Steam must have a principle which is water. But water as it stands, cannot produce steam. Steam comes from a condition of water which when acted upon by heat, inclines towards steam, since as yet it is deprived of the form of steam.

It does this not only because it is deprived of the form of steam, but also because it is natural for it to have that particular form. Thus there are three elements in change, viz. matter, form and privation. This latter is not positive, but is essential to the nature of change.

Individuality comprises matter and form. But the formal element, which makes a thing definite, is the same throughout a particular species. But this formal element cannot supply the principle of individuation as well. There must be another principle involved, and according to Aristotle, it is matter. We can say that Peter and Richard are the same in form, that is to say, in nature — but differ from each other in that separate matter is involved in each. Of course, it follows that the matter referred to, in each and every case, is unified and made active by the form. St. Thomas Aquinas will accept this idea with several improvements. St. Thomas saw it was treading on difficult ground to say that prime matter itself became a principle of individuation. Therefore, he will say that matter is quantified, and consequently, will be individual on account of this quantity. Subsequently, in union with the form, an individual entity is set up known as the person or material thing.

Interesting conclusions will follow from this. St. Thomas will teach that provided the form remains pure, only one form will make up a species. He goes on to say that this is the principle of angelic existence, each existing as one particular species. In consequence, there are not two angels belonging to the same species. Not all the Scholastics were in accord with this theory — notably St. Bonaventure. But referring to Aristotle as the source of these ideas, we find him saying that as many things depend upon matter, a first mover will have no matter, and will be one. This is a most penetrating observation on the part of Aristotle.

Taking these conclusions a stage further, the philosopher will say that it is true that matter individualises, but at the same time, it does not know itself. So we are faced with the problem that an individual thing is unknowable. Also, the individual thing has no definition. But definition is one of the objects of science. It follows that the concrete thing is not an object of science. But if, says Aristotle, an individual cannot be defined, it can be known by intuition. He keeps this as a bare suggestion, with no elaboration whatsoever. It seems that we have arrived at an impossible situation, but such a view as Aristotle holds is quite fitting. Why? Well, I may know Peter's character, but all the knowledge I have of it, I will not obtain through scientific reasoning. Aristotle's love of science and of definition is possibly a shred of his learning he acquired during his years with Plato.

Aristotle contributed to the development of philosophy most considerably. One of the places this can be seen at its best is in the ninth book of Metaphysics, where he discusses potency and act. There were some schools who denied potency, but it is foolish to say that if I am not digging in my garden now, I cannot dig at all. Obviously I will not dig when I am not actually doing so; if this were possible then it would be a contradiction. The point is I have a capacity for digging, and ability to employ that power when I wish to do so. Nor is potency the negation of actuality. If a man is asleep, he is not thinking. He awakens and he begins to employ the power of thought. The table upon which I am writing is not actually thinking; further it has no capacity for thinking whatsoever, and subsequently no potency for thought. A natural object will be in potency to its form or a full realisation of itself. Potency is a power to influence another or oneself, and so to move further from non-being and closer to actuality. Thus potency is half way between non-being and actuality.

We find that actuality precedes potency. Why is this? Because the potential thing is always reduced to act by the actual, or that which is already acting. So in a temporal sense, actuality comes before potency and in a logical view, the same view holds, for the end for which the potency exists is the actuality. In a worldly sense, the boy precedes the man; but in a logical or final sense, the man is prior, since it is for the sake of manhood, that the boy exists.

Further, that which is final is more substantial than that which changes, and for this reason is to a higher degree actual. God as a final end must be a complete Act, as the eternal unmoved mover reducing potentiality to act. Eternal things are good; in them there is no privation of any sort. There does not exist a separate principle of corruption, since that which is not in matter is pure form. To Aristotle, God was something of the same character as Plato had conceived of the Ideal Good. If this Unmoved Mover is the source of all movement, then this is the reason potentiality is made actual, and why goodness is endowed with that peculiar quality of spreading itself over the things it contacts.

In this doctrine of act and potency lies the answer to Parmenides' assertions many years before. Parmenides would not admit change; thus he would says that air produces air, it can never produce fire, because it is not fire. But with Aristotle. we have

151

the notion of the capacity of the air to become fire. It has been truly said that a thing becomes to be out of its privation.

Now, it is necessary to note that a thing does not come into being merely out of non being or privation as it is called. It simply does so in a subject. It could be objected that this implies a being coming from being. In reply, we say that it is being certainly, but it is non-being also, that is to say, it is not yet what it *could* be.

In this manner, matter, form and privation are made distinct, but these differences are generally referred to as act, potency and privation. From this separation, we arrive at the idea of ascendancy in the scale of existence, which evolves from the fact that if a subject has a terminus *from* something, then it will be in potency as regards a terminus to something. For example, a table is in act if compared with a table as yet to be made. The same holds for the soul in its sensitivity acting on the body, but it is still in potency as regards the mind. In a summing up, we find prime matter which cannot be known, never existing without form. It unites with opposites, and thus there is earth, air, water and fire. These relatively simple bodies combine to form minerals, and the tissues of simple living bodies. Thus the rungs of the ladder of living things are gradually ascended until we arrive at the human intellect. Above this, there is only God. All this does not concern evolution, as pure form does not come from matter. Further, Aristotle held all species to be eternal.

Aristotle has next to explain how change begins. It is clear that some agent outside the table brought the table to act by change. Thus, although we possess a formal as well as material cause, we must also acquire an efficient cause. But this agent need not be exterior as can be seen from the action of the four elements in the world. Any element will move with natural motion unless it is prevented. The form of the element will incline it to what is natural. So the formal and efficient causes meet. But they are not always the same. Certainly, they act as one in the case of the soul when there is movement. When a man builds they are not the same. Neither are they in the case of generation, where the efficient cause, the father, is only specifically and not numerically, the same as the formal cause of the offspring.

As Aristotle saw the position, he was the first to speak of a final cause. Now, despite the fact that greater emphasis is laid upon it by him, he does not intend an eternal formality only. The notion of interior finality, or immanence as it is called, occupies him as well. An individual object will strive after the most perfect form which is natural, and will often entail the unification of the final, formal cause and efficient causes. Thus in living substances, the Soul is the formal cause, or that which determines. The acorn all the while is inclining towards a fully grown oak. This will be its final cause. Apparently, it is the final cause which moves by attraction. In the example of the tree just cited, the final and formal causes are the same, the former drawing up the acorn to full development.

We may say that the final cause, as yet, does not exist and so it is not possible for it to act upon the acorn. Aristotle's reply is that the acorn is the oak in germ, and it has an immanent tendency to its own perfection.

It is true that there is a tendency in Aristotle to run the four causes together. Generally, he reduces them to two, i.e. formal and material. Nowadays, we consider the efficient cause and final cause only, in everyday use.

If we consider a final cause, is there any reason to conclude that mechanical causes exist? Aristotle will reply that there is, and will go on to assert that sometimes mechanics and a final cause act as one. The example is given of light passing through the glass of a lantern, which prevents the holder from falling. But, in other cases, mechanical causes seem but accidental. Nevertheless, it is vital to look for a final cause, since many things are explainable by material or efficient causes.

If a thing passes from potentiality to act, it must have some exterior principle to act upon it. Now, if every created thing is in the process of movement, and thus changing from something, it is clear that the world as a whole will require a First Mover.

When he spoke in this way, Aristotle thought of a mover in a worldly sense, since motion is to him eternal. If movement were to disappear, that would in itself be the result of movement. But the sense meant here is completely primary to everything else — even to eternal motion. Again, to Aristotle, the world had existed from all eternity; therefore, it is not possible to think of a First Mover as a *Creator*. But it is correct to say that God *forms* the world. How is this done? By acting as a final end attracting all movement through His role as final cause. Following Aristotle's line of thinking, he could say if God were the efficient cause of the world — pushing the universe — He must of necessity change

Himself. But this is impossible, since the lesser thing would react upon the greater as effect to cause. God then is to be desired by others as a Final Cause.

If this Mover is a complete mover then it must be pure act. Potentiality does not exist in it. If we conclude the world always existed, then time always existed. Otherwise, if the world commenced to exist, then time must have commenced to exist also, in which case it is possible for the notion of time existing before itself to be held. Such a view is absurd. Now, change and time are related; if time is eternal, so is change. Thus there must be a First Mover causing change, without itself being changed. If this Mover were changeable in itself, then it could cease to cause motion which would also affect change. But these are eternal. Consequently, this First Mover must be Pure Act, since to be pure act involves no matter whatsoever. Now where there is materiality, there is change. So it is clear that the First Mover is Pure Act, and because of this is changeless. Aristotle also considers that the irregular movement of the heavens is proof of motion without cessation.

Aristotle has already said that God is desired by all outside Him. How is this done? By moving the first heaven, and inspiring love and desire. What is desired and what is known are identical in the world of the spirit. This leads to the notion of an Intelligence in the first and other spheres. There are spiritual entities and the sphere, through desire, wishes to emulate the Intelligence. Thus it cannot be complete, and is forced to perform rotating actions.

As to the number of unmoved movers, Aristotle does not seem to be very concise. Both in the Physics and in the Metaphysics, different numbers of movers are given. In chapter seven and nine of the latter work, Aristotle speaks of One unmoved mover. In chapter eight, he speaks of fifty-five subordinate movers. Later on, Plotinus will say that the relationship of the One to the fifty-five is not at all specific. Another objection held by the same philosopher will be that it is not clear how they are individual, since Aristotle himself had said that matter is the principle of individuation. In chapter eight, he mentions this very objection, but unfortunately does not offer any answer. The general drift among Aristotle's followers was to cleave to the idea of an unmoved mover.

In the Middle Ages, the philosophers will find in Aristotle, material for the proof of God and the angels in what he had said of the Intelligence and the spheres. They were made to be subordinate to God as First Mover and relation exists between Him and them by intelligence and desire on the part of the spheres. It was a Neo-Platonist move to establish an ascending scale as it were, culminating with God. But God is spiritual, and He is also intellectual, so what will be the object of His knowledge? This object will not imply sensitivity or anything of this sort, but will be none other than God himself. In short, only God is fit for the contemplation of God. Thus we have Aristotle calling God, Thought of Thought. God then, only thinks of Himself. St. Thomas Aquinas interpreting this, said that knowledge of God did not necessarily exclude knowledge of this world since God is everywhere. In this, he was right, and others have followed him. This idea includes the notion of Divine Providence.

As the result of Christian teaching, we look upon God as personal, but the Greek mind was not particularly worried about the particular number of Gods. Consequently, would Aristotle think of God as personal? He had the idea of God as Thought, and most people's thought is personal. Whilst it possibly would not be accurate to visualise Aristotle's thinking of God as personal in a *theological* sense, he probably did so in a philosophical way. Worship was not however a part of Aristotle's thought for a First Mover. Neither did he conceive of God as a Person to pray to. As a result, it seems that the philosopher thought of God as self contained entirely, and if this were so, it would be difficult for men to be related to Him. In a work called "Magna Moralia" Aristotle is quite decided that contact with God is impossible, and this for two reasons. First, God would not return love, and secondly, in no sense could man be said to love God.

God can also be proved by the natural phenomena around us, particularly the heavens.

In this same work, there is the germ of what St. Thomas would later utilise as his fourth way of proving God's existence. The notion is that where something is better, a best must exist. Always there is something better, until one arrives at a best which is supreme. But this idea demonstrates the Perfect Good only by relation. A cause must be introduced in order to conceive of things sharing inexistence. Then it is quite possible to consider a fullness of all Perfection contained in one thing. Without causality, this notion is lost, as is the idea of participation. St. Thomas realized this, and consequently when speaking of a passage from the Metaphysics uses Aristotle's own illustration of fire being the hottest thing; other things will be hot, but only by sharing the heat from the fire.

By the time Aristotle wrote the Metaphysics various changes in his style can be seen. The religious drift is not nearly so pronounced, and he tends more to everyday speech. Not only this, but he never put his ideas of God into a system.

However, Aristotle advanced on Plato with his ideas upon God. Plato would not ignore divinity in the world which is necessary to theology based on reason. Aristotle conceived God as totally apart from the world, and as its sole cause. There are no Divine operations in the world, but in this, Aristotle shows up in an inferior way to Plato. But if this were so, Aristotle demonstrated the complete movements of all things towards a fullness of being, reality became clearer, and a purpose was given for change. Overall, the idea of philosophy was kept intact as always, it absorbed, it grew in strength, and all this in a logical sequence. It was more vigorous than before, on account of new ideas, and the assimilation of older ones; in short, it was healthy development.

CHAPTER 29

ARISTOTLE AND PSYCHOLOGY

At the beginning of his treatises upon material things, Aristotle in the Physics, looks upon Nature as the complete sum of objects. This has to suffice for a definition in this case, for he provided no other. But what does Aristotle really mean by this statement? Presumably, he is referring to those objects capable of change and attaining their natural end through this process. Objects which are not simple cannot move themselves. The table at which I am writing is an example of this. In the form of a table being compounded of parts, it cannot of itself move. However, the simple objects of which it is constructed can move. To illustrate: The table is made of wooden parts and as a table it cannot move itself. But wood as a simple object can move for a tree grows. A distinction is thus drawn between simple and artificial objects, the former also being considered as "natural". It is necessary also to mention that bodies without life are necessarily moved by a force outside themselves. But an apparent contradiction to this can be shown. If I carry a bucket full of water, and the bucket suddenly develops a leak, then the water will begin to move out of the bucket in a downward motion to the ground. On the face of it, the water moves of itself. Actually however, the movement is caused by the agent that produced the hole in the container which would remove impediments to the natural action of the water. Also hot or cold conditions would be responsible for the density of the water.

Two forms of movement may be recognized. That which adds to a thing's perfection, and that which takes away from perfection, i.e., decay. In an action involving decay, three subsequent kinds of movement must be considered. They are: qualitative movement, quantitative movement, and lastly local movement.

The question of movement naturally leads to a discussion on Place and Time. In respect of place, Aristotle says that air has a definite "place". This place can be taken over by another of the four elements. Also, the four elements of themselves, will have their proper places. For example, fire always goes up, whilst earth will fall down. This brings us to the definition of place which is described by Aristotle as a limit in which the body is, this limit being thought of as without motion. This definition excludes all idea of an empty place, since place is the inside limit of a container. There is a difference between a thing contained and the container. Aristotle illustrates this by the example of a boat on a river. The river moves and is really the container, more so than the place of the boat. From this, place is an unmoved limit, if we reckon outwards. According to Aristotle, the river is by far the most appropriate place, since the river is immobile. All objects thus occupy a place whilst the world does not. If a body changes place, it does so by motion, and so there is change. Aristotle concluded from this it was only possible for the world to rotate; it was not possible for it to change place.

A body is only moved by contact with another body. The first mover passes its impetus to secondary movers, e.g., air or water, and thus to the thing moved. There is a proportion existing between the force used and the distance; when the force used is an *exact* ratio to the distance the body will come to rest. We can gather from this that Aristotle did not believe in the principle of inertia, and in this connexion, he concluded that force tended to slow down, whilst a natural action tended to acceleration. St. Thomas Aquinas will follow him very faithfully in all this.

We must realize that whilst there are many movements, Time is one. Nevertheless, there is a definite link between them. Sometimes, changes go by unnoticed, if that is the case, the time will also be unnoticed. Aristotle defines time as "the number of motion according to before and after." The great point not to be missed in this definition is that Aristotle conceives time as continuous as movement is continuous. There are no isolated points in either movement or time. If a thing is at rest, then it is capable of being moved. This will mean its movement will take place in time, from which follows the eternal concept of time.

Local motion is not the only motion involved in change; the change of a person's state of mind can influence a lapse of time. Again, when the philosopher talks of time being as it were numbered, he does not mean this in a literal sense. What he means is that we recognize many phases at once, following one another.

158

Without time, it would not be possible to be aware of these particular phases.

A straight line is not enough, according to Aristotle, in order to measure time. The reason given is that it is not always the same. A forced movement will be slow, a natural one will be fast. We must then look for some movement that is natural and the same. Aristotle's answer to this is to mention the circle as a figure that is uniform and is certainly natural as is shown by the movement of the heavens. Thus, if a man tells the time by the sun, he will follow a proper course.

An interesting point is raised here. If the human mind did not exist, would time still exist? Aristotle does not develop this idea in any way, but he provides an answer. He says in a proper sense, time would not exist, but there would remain the substance of time. What is meant here is that in a continuum, there are only potential parts. Now, if there were no mind, it could not distinguish one phase of time after another. But, of course, the substance of time would endure. All parts attributed to a continuum are only potential. The human mind will actualize them. This action of the mind breaks the flow of time and duration. Aristotle always thought of human beings as existing. Therefore, it did not occur to him to think of a time when there was actually no human mind. But the parts already numbered constitute parts already in existence. Change in any case, is inconceivable without time.

Aristotle had said that time really cannot be separated from the first and last in motion. Consequently, it is possible for time to exist outside the mind since motion does this. The latter is assisted by the mind's action. The notion of time is only potential in this, that it cannot be conceived as actual without the assistance of the mind. Aristotle and Kant are not related in their views on this; the Greek philosopher at all times being objective.

The next question is, what is the infinite? Aristotle's first observation upon this is to state that since a body is bounded by a surface, it is impossible for a body to be so bounded by surfaces of an infinite character. Therefore, it is impossible for a body to be infinite. Neither could a body actually existing be infinite. This is because it is not possible for it to be simple or composite. The reason for this is slightly more involved. If I have an infinite substance, and a finite substance as well, the infinite must of necessity possess the finite, in somewhat of the same manner as a lesser body is contained in a greater.

Nevertheless, it is possible for the infinite to exist in potentiality. No material extension is infinite, but it can be potentially infinite since it is capable of division to infinity. A line is but a continuum, and is not a number of points only. This will be Aristotle's answer to Zeno's objections raised earlier. But a line, though it be divisible to infinity, will never be completely actualized in this manner. We can describe time as infinite as it admits of infinite extension. But it never *actually* exists in this way for it is successive. It never has all its parts together at the one time. But time also is capable of potential addition which fact separates it from extension which cannot be thought of infinitely. Extension has a maximum but not a minimum. Number is to be considered in potentiality, since it can always be added to, as it is impossible to think of a number beyond which it is impossible to count. But number is not capable of infinite division like time or extension for it possesses a minimum in the concept of unit.

Now, nothing acts except for an end; it is evident there must be some single and specific end in all nature. It is the development of a thing from potentiality to actuality in as complete a form as possible.

Both Plato and Aristotle associated Nature with various ends, but in different ways. Plato had spoken of the Demiurge who thus brought various acts to conclusions, whilst Aristotle often spoke of nature as a unifying principle. This in itself does not seem sufficient, for it does not explain the relationship between God and nature. In Aristotle's view, God and nature are a long way apart, and the gap does not seem to be bridged satisfactorily by him, throughout his observations.

When one considers the cosmos or universe, we see that it is divided into two parts, the first consisting of the stars which do not change except for local motion. They have a circular movement and arm made of either which can be taken as a fifth element. This element is superior to the other four, on account of its resistance to change.

Now if the earth is a sphere, it is at rest at its center, whilst around it are various layers of water, air and fire. Outside of these are found the heavens, the extremes of which owe their movement to the First Mover. Aristotle also took from Calippus, the idea of thirty-three as the number of spheres. He added: the number of twenty-two count for the spheres progressing backwards. This provided a stabilising principle for the plane. The total thus made was fifty-five which is the number given in the metaphysics for the spheres.

Individual things come to be and then pass away, but the species and genera are eternal. This doctrine excludes at once the notion of evolution in Aristotle's thought. If modern thinkers would attribute any evolution whatsoever, to Aristotle, we find an ascending scale of perfection ranging from organic matter to God. This ascendancy is caused by the gradual perfection of the form. Even plants have souls, however, and because this is a common factor, all being is thus interlinked. The soul, Aristotle described, as "the first entelechy of a natural organic body".

As it is the act of the body, the soul is identical with form. As form, it is a principle and an end. The body exists for the soul, every organ having its own specific end or purpose.

In view of this, it is necessary to examine the soul as Aristotle states in "De Anima." But the position of this examination is not easy; the reason for this being that a wrong method could be used. In this discovery, the philosopher and the natural thinker occupy different positions. Consequently their conclusions will be different. This explains why even today, different sciences will take different viewpoints on a subject, find their results do not agree. It is impossible to see an object from the same angle from different positions. Yet, that is what in many cases the particular sciences seek to do. Nevertheless, it is not true to imagine that their individual findings will go for nothing, for each will contain a part of the truth not possessed by the other.

If a substance is composite, then its principle of life is called the soul. We do not say a body is life. Why? Because the body *receives* and therefore *has* life. A long discussion is possible on the ancients between those who believe the body to be life, and those who did not. Aristotle thinks of himself as a Platonist in this matter, and so ranges himself against the Atomists. Following upon what Aristotle has already said on this subject, it seems that the body is matter, whilst the soul is the act of the body. So Aristotle will call the soul the act of a body which possesses life in potency. Thus the soul is the principle which the body seeks in fullness of its being. In this manner, one cannot think of the body separately without the soul, or the soul without the body for they make one unity. The soul then is the source of life to the body, and this in three ways, viz., as movement, final cause, and as substance of living things.

161

In all types of the soul, the higher includes the lower, but this does not apply in an inverse way. A distinctive mark of the soul is its ability to acquire nutriment, and to generate itself. The existence of a thing is dependent upon these properties. Plants do not seek nourishment, but draw it from the ground in an automatic fashion. But animals, once given the power to move, must experience sensation in order to seek after food.

Thus the animal soul can nourish itself, generate itself, and in addition possesses desire and movement. From this develops imagination and also memory. Now, if the animal is looking for food, some power must be possessed by it to distinguish this food. So there is touch, to achieve this. The animal must decide if the food is good or otherwise. For this purpose, taste is introduced.

The human soul is at the highest peak among animal life. Once again, all the lower faculties are included in it with additions not found in the inferior species. The human soul possesses an intellect which it can apply in two ways. By thinking decisively and willing. Thought has truth as its object, whilst things are willed for practical purposes. The intellect alone is incorruptible, all other powers perishing with the body. But as well as the active intellect, there also must be a passive principle, a tablet so to speak, upon which things can be recorded. This is the role of the passive intellect.

Aristotle is quite clear however, that the soul and body are one; the Platonists did not follow this line of thought; they considered the intellect as the true man and the body as a form of prison. But this was not Aristotle's view, and fifteen hundred years later, St. Thomas Aquinas will follow him and say the soul and body are one. However, many teachers and writers will demonstrate that the Platonic tradition will die hard. St. Augustine is perhaps the most famous example of this. But in Aristotle's view, Plato and his followers did not sufficiently explain the union of soul and body. Apparently, they thought that a soul would fit inside any body. But Aristotle says this is absurd because each soul has a definite character peculiar to it and to it alone. Neither would we say that Aristotle would agree with Descartes who thought of the soul as a certainty which achieved existence later. "The *whole* man, soul and body alike, is something given and not questioned."

It remains to enquire what Aristotle really meant in his

162

doctrine of the Active Intellect. Unfortunately, his actual meaning is very difficult to arrive at. For this reason, we will tread warily and present below what Aristotle says on the subject of the "De Anima". "This Nous is separable, and impassible, and unmixed, being essentially an actuality. For the active is always of higher value than the passive, and the originative is identical with its object; potential knowledge is prior in time to the individual, but in general, it is not temporally prior; but Nous does function at one time, and other time not. When it has been separated, it is only that which it is in essence, and this alone is immortal and eternal. We do not remember, however, because active reason is impassible, but the passive reason is perishable, and without the active reason, nothing thinks."

We will attempt to cut a swathe through the mass of views resulting from the above. We will appeal to St. Thomas Aquinas in his commentary on the "De Anima" where he says that it is wrong to interpret Aristotle as Averroës would do. The active intellect is an active principle. It is not affected by passion or emotion, and does not remember species. It is not possible therefore, for the separated human reason to function in the same way as it does when united to a body, and in any case, Aristotle does not treat of this state. But this does not mean Aristotle denied immortality, or said that the separated intellect spends its time in enforced idleness or inactivity.

CHAPTER 30

ETHICS

We move on now to consider Aristotle's Ethics. Action is its keynote, and it seems that this action is bound up with man's ultimate good. For example, a good action will lead a person towards good. Conversely, a bad action will lead towards a lessening of the good influence. But it is not sufficient to take good merely as good. It is necessary to point out that there are different kinds of goods, each applicable to different actions.

These kinds of goods are further split up into subordinate goods, which naturally serve those others ordered to more final ends. Thus, medicine may induce sleep, which is subordinate to the final end of which is health. The lesser ends serve those other ends which have a wider scope. The question will arise if there is any good that is needed for its own sake. If such a good exists, it will be the ultimate in all goods. Aristotle wonders if there is such a good, and if so, what is the science in which it is found.

He answers the latter part of the question at once. It is the science of political or social life which is concerned with man's good. There is good in the individual certainly, but that found in the State is superior. This may be interpreted as a development from Plato's Republic where the State and justice are hand in hand. To Aristotle's mind, it was first necessary to treat of the individual, then advance to the State.

We can say a man is good; but the question is how to assess this goodness. It is impossible to treat it as one would say, for example, a mathematical problem. It lacks the preciseness for this form of treatment. Further, the gulf separating mathematics and ethics is one of the principles and conclusions. As the former starts with principles, so does the latter start with conclusions. In ethics, it is what a person has actually thought and judged to be correct. From this, it can be assumed that human nature has certain fixed tendencies, but once this is recognized for Aristotle, it becomes more and more difficult to reconcile human action with the laws laid down by God. From an historical standpoint, it is interesting that the great thirteenth century thinkers actually tried to bridge this gap. If, however, we consider Aristotle's Ethics, as they stand, we see that it is essentially rational, the conclusions dealt with being based on ordinary judgements of which any normal person is capable. If there are found any contemporary Greek ideas in morality for instance, the overall plan was to see human nature as it actually is. Undoubtedly, Aristotle would always affirm to the particular tendencies of human beings, in the face of what has been taught by later philosophers.

It is certain man's end is to be happy. However, this statement as it stands is vague and undefined, particularly since different people have different ideas on happiness. One man will equate wealth with happiness, another honour and yet a third with carnal pleasures and so on. Moreover, these different people may not agree as to what makes for happiness at all times. Sickness can make a person believe that health is happiness, and consequently he longs for it. A poor person will think that to possess riches is happiness. In regard to honour, this is dependent upon the one who gives and thus we do not really possess it.

Is it possible that honour safeguards virtue? Aristotle says no for in this case in an absolute sense, all that is needed is inactivity. With inactivity, there is unhappiness. Accordingly, the true end of life consists in activity and happiness.

Having thus established that activity enters into the happiness of man, we must find out what action is peculiar to man. If we think of reproduction, growth, or sensation, we will be wrong. Why? because these are shared by animals below man. Thus this activity must be one that is particular to man alone. It also must be reasonable. But surely this describes a virtuous action. This Aristotle would not deny, but there are intellectual virtues as well as moral virtues. Furthermore, when most people think of happiness, they think of justice and things akin to it. What is aimed at here is not so much an ethical end as a virtue as such; but an action performed in a virtuous way. This leads to an understanding of the moral and intellectual virtues. Moreover, if it is to be true happiness, it must be spread over a lifetime and not be an experience we have from time to time.

But are we just to consider happiness merely as an activity performed in a virtuous way, without so called "popular" ideas of happiness? Aristotle would say no. Why? Because any action performed in the way described must bring pleasure with it. Pleasure accompanies a natural and free action. But if a person is to perform this activity of which Aristotle has spoken, material goods are necessary in order to carry out this operation. The cynics did not agree with him in this. But by the employment of externals, this activity is kept in a certain manner. Also, it is not necessary in this case to exclude outer manner. Also, it is not necessary in this case to exclude outer prosperity. Great credit is due to Aristotle for this matter of first teachings; quite different from the vast imaginative flights of fancy of some of his predecessors.

It is necessary to determine the nature of a good character, and also of a good action. Also we must know what is a moral virtue, and also of those virtues which are in accord with reason. Finally, there is a consideration of the intellectual virtues, and what makes for an ideal life.

To commence with, goodness of character; Aristotle says there is a capacity for it, but it must be worked at if a person wishes to obtain it. What form is this work to take? By performing actions which of themselves are virtuous. But a difficulty seems to arise. If a person is to act virtuously to attain virtue, how can he start a virtuous action, without already possessing virtue? The answer lies in an objective viewpoint. If our actions are directed to things outside ourselves at first, latterly this produces an interior habit of virtue.

To illustrate: a child is told that he or she must not tell lies. The child will obey without realizing the tremendous moral imposition of this direction. Gradually, it will form a habit of truth telling which of course, is virtuous. The true answer to this objection then, is that there are two kinds of acts. The first creates a good disposition, and the second flows from it. It is possible to arrive now at a definition of virtue. It is a disposition arising out of a capacity, by reason of the proper development of that capacity.

The opposite of virtue is vice. While virtuous acts are orderly, we can say that one can err by excess and one can err by defect, but the ideal or mean is the most desirable. This is how Aristotle defines virtue. But if we speak of excess or defect, what material will make up this excess or defect? The answer is according to the way a person feels or acts. Once again to illustrate: if a person feels too confident, this excess will be rashness. On the other hand, no confidence leads to cowardice by defect.

It is clear that in the exercise of virtue choice plays a great part. A person then, can choose between excess and defect, and the resulting action will be one of virtue. Aristotle lays emphasis upon practical judgements made by a rational person, much more than he does on academic calculations. We must note here that in his definition of virtue Aristotle uses the expression "relating to us". He does this to show that we cannot think of a golden mean by reason of mathematics. So many things depend upon a person's character, mental make up, and what he believes, and so on. All these have bearing upon human action. Sometimes excess could be employed with advantage and sometimes defect. Moreover, it is possible for Aristotle's idea of the mean to be taken for the purely ordinary. Far from it, for in the order of excellence, virtue is the highest point. Why then is it called a mean? Because it has an essence and a definition. A definition, we find, is a formula having parts; each of the parts must correspond to the essence of the thing. Thus the definition of virtue may be considered in either a vertical or horizontal way.

What is meant by this? Firstly, virtue can be looked at in two ways. From the point of view of ontology it possesses a mean, in a vertical sense, it can be considered as an extreme. Neither is virtue made up of contrary views; since it unites good points which, if unchecked, would run to excess. To illustrate: If a man has courage, this is a combination of (a) boldness and (b) forethought. It can be clearly observed that the virtue of courage prevents in the first case boldness becoming rashness, and in the second the prudence or fear.

Aristotle felt that no single virtue could stand on its own; if it did so, it would degenerate into excess or defect. The ideal was a synthesis which would ensure stability.

The attitude to virtues adopted by Aristotle is one peculiar to the pagan Greek mind in that the expansion of soul of man is greatly elaborated. The greatness of Christ crucified would mean little to him; it is quite possible he would think of it as not in accord with human reason. This need not surprise us, since Christ crucified was essentially an act above reason.

Fundamentally, the first requirement for a human act is freedom since it is from this that a person derives some degree of responsibility. Thus if a person were to act under coercion or force, the responsibility would be lessened in proportion to the force applied. Such a force is fear; since it prompts a person to act in a way he would not do if full freedom were open to him.

Ignorance can be looked at in two ways. Firstly, a person acts from ignorance, and secondly a man can act in ignorance. The difference is that if a person loses his temper, he is in the grip of ignorance which will affect his actions. Secondly, the ignorance is incurred from the loss of temper. But it does not necessarily follow that a person on seeing the error of his ways will show his true nature. By this latter statement, Aristotle means whether a person is wholly good or bad, according to his human nature.

Aristotle realized that life was a moral fight in resisting temptations. He says however, that when a person actually is performing a bad act, at the actual time of doing it, he does not realize it to be bad. In a strict sense, this is but a half truth, since a man can act from passion in the way Aristotle described, yet on the other hand a person may will bad acts deliberately. Owing to this deliberation, one would be quite conscious of the moral value of what was being done. It would be wrong to overlook the purely human element in Aristotle's ethical outlook where right and good are as one. Under these circumstances, fornication or adultery appear as a good to a particular person. Nevertheless, that person may quite well know of the rightness or wrongness of the act he or she is performing. In short, Aristotle in these sections set out to refute Socrates' moral theories. But by doing this, he came under their spell. The concept of duty or obligation was not well formed in the Greek mind. Reservations can be made with Plato in certain customs, but in the main, the idea is not a vigorous one. Aristotle was by no means an exception. The Stoics will provide for this deficiency.

From this, it is clear that the idea of will in Aristotle will be but imperfectly formed, since he expresses it simply as reasonable desire and in a number of other forms. Thus he inclines to choice, but he does not set choice in the lap of either desire alone or reason alone.

An act progresses in the manner suggested thus: first, the agent wishes an end, and secondly, the agent weighs for and against, seeing one will produce the other as B will produce A as means; thirdly, it is seen that some action is possible here and now which affect the ultimate end, and fourthly, the agent chooses this means which appears at the time practical. A simple explanation used by many writers (Aristotle among them), is the question of health. A person desires health. It can be obtained by exercise. A walk will induce health through exercise. It can be taken here and now, therefore a person chooses to go walking for health's sake.

Our actions then are clearly ordered, and the above is a fine logical sequence. But it provides no sense of obligation or duty to which we have already referred. It will need later writers to add their contributions to it in the way of real moral necessity.

The action of voluntariness lies within us, and we can choose the paths of virtue or vice. This proves Socrates was wrong. It is quite true to say that a person may be in the grip of a sinful habit and unable to stem the acts which flow from it. However, that same person need not have acquired such a habit in the beginning. Further, a person's conscience may be so numbed by sin that he cannot know what is right, but the ultimate responsibility lies with that person for the ensuing ignorance.

The general drift of Aristotle with respect to morality is as the above; but again, he fails to show clearly that there is a cleavage between moral weakness and malicious wickedness.

Generally however, when treating of the virtues, Aristotle is characterized by admirable poise and moderation. The phrase "relatively to us" shows perfect balance in demonstrating what is applicable to one is not to another, neither can it be defined in any way mathematically. In another way however, it is difficult to reconcile Christian thinking with the concept of one ashamed to receive gifts; in addition, giving greater and larger return gifts in order not to appear inferior.

Justice is dealt with in the fifth book. By justice, Aristotle means various things. First, what is lawful and secondly what is fair and equal. The concept of a universal justice comes about through Aristotle's understanding of the supremacy of the state in matters of law. This view he shared with Plato. As a lawgiver, the state is also an educator. Now these views will differ sharply from those held by various thinkers and writers in England and Germany, where the personal view towards both law and education will be thought of as an ideal.

Justice can be divided in two main parts. These are Distributive Justice and Remedial Justice. The first was applicable to the way the state apportioned out its goods to the citizens and the second was further divided into civil Law and Criminal Law which explain themselves.

These forms of justice work in a proportion to the manner in which they are required. Finally, there is a commutative Justice. This form regulates the "give and take" between members of the community.

Aristotle refers to justice as a mean between acting unjustly and unjust treatment. The reason he speaks in this way is to make the definition uniform with the other virtues. But as it stands, it can be misunderstood. For example, if I sell two books for the price of one and am content with the deal, I am hardly acting unjustly. The position is clarified somewhat when the philosopher mentioned that justice is not a mean as are other virtues, but really an arrangement of things halfway between when A has too much and B has too much.

It seems that there are two kinds of action which are not just. First, there is the action which harms someone else, despite the fact that the harm was not intended. Secondly, there is the action which does harm to someone, that particular harm being intentional. The consequence of this distinction is to show that equity is superior to legal justice, as the latter cannot supply the complete need in all particular cases, but only generally.

The powers of the intellect are divided according to the faculty of reason. Thus the intellect considers the necessary, that is, those things that are independent, and those that are dependent and of which opinion may be held. How are intellectual virtues and science related? The answer is that an intellectual virtue is "the disposition by virtue of which we demonstrate."

Proof and intuition do not count as negative forces here. This is because it is possible to grasp something in its wholeness — though confusedly and by reason of previous experiences, to judge it. At this stage, any proof would be self evident.

The intellect is directed to the highest objects including as they do mathematics and natural science. These contribute to the happiness of man and philosophy or wisdom may be defined as the combination of intuition and reason. Objects give dignity to that which is known about them. Aristotle is quite decided that political science is not the highest science. It would be so only on one condition. This is that those participating in it were above others — indeed the highest of all. Aristotle does not believe this to be possible.

Intellect and wit are related — the latter being a disposition to make things by a true rule — in that the intellect will direct the art. Practical wisdom is concerned with things as they are good or bad for individuals. This practical wisdom is further subdivided according to the objects concerned. Firstly, there is the individual's good, secondly concerned with household goods and management, and thirdly as regards the State. This last can be divided thus: with respect to Politics as a purely legislative body, or administration to the people. Administration is divided into two groups, deliberation and judicial. It should not be missed that throughout these divisions, practical wisdom is the same for the individual and the state. In connection with the State, it is called Politics.

A is the end of something. B is the means to achieve it. Therefore B should be done. This represents the cardinal syllogism upon which practical wisdom hangs. This in no way impedes the general inclination to good which pervades mankind, and it does not ignore the fact that many people know the right course of action but do not know the principles from whence comes that particular action. Thus Aristotle remarks it is better to know the conclusion without the major premise, than the major premise without the conclusion.

Socrates had said that virtue was a form of prudence. Aristotle partly agreed, and partly disagreed with this view. All virtue is a form of prudence, but it is not correct to say that virtue exists without prudence. While Socrates maintained that virtue was a form of reason, Aristotle says that virtue is reasonable. The difference here can be clearly seen. Virtue is a right, and as such, it is reasonable. It encourages an attitude to right which must be commended. Leading to a right, and a reasonable choice is what is meant by prudence. From this, it is obvious that if a person wishes for virtue, he must employ prudence as a means. Further, no proper choice can be made without the co-operation of both prudence and virtue.

Does all this include cleverness? The answer given is no, because cleverness consists in choosing any right means to a specific end. A dishonest person or a criminal of any sort can be clever in choosing the means to gain the end for which he is striving. So cleverness is a difference from prudence which stands for virtue, and which can be compared to insight existing in the moral order. In order to be prudent, one must be clever; but it is impossible to reduce it to cleverness for it stands in the

171

moral order. Looked at in another light, prudence is cleverness when the acts implied lead to the end of man; but an act of cleverness does not *necessarily* presuppose that the act is for man's betterment. Under these conditions, it is possible to follow a certain line of action without being morally good. However, when the question of moral choice arises, the action becomes a good one, if preceded by a good moral choice and not a bad one. If it is a bad moral choice, then again the act is a bad one. The change from a good to a bad act is effected by a loss of prudence.

Aristotle says if a person is to be reasonable he must have prudence. He goes further than this. He says given prudence, all other virtues will follow. Socrates had thought that virtue was consistent with knowledge which would mean if I learn a language for example after class, I am more virtuous than before having acquired more knowledge. This is obviously incorrect, since many have knowledge and are not virtuous.

Distinctions must be made between that which is a theory and that which is a product. We are told if a person understands justice, this does not necessarily make him just. Aristotle further illustrates as follows: A person who thinks he becomes good on theoretical knowledge alone, is like those who listen to a doctor's orders, but do not obey them.

Pleasures in themselves are not wrong. But we must not think of it as a perfect good as Eudoxus thought. This is because pleasure accompanies a free action, but it is the action which is to be aimed at, and not the accompanying pleasure. Shame is attached to some pleasures and this will affect their attainment. But it is quite easy to say if some pleasures are shameful, then all pleasure is wrong. This view is foolish. Aristotle makes various observations on pleasure which are mentioned above, and pleasures differ by the objects they are derived from.

Some have maintained that pleasure was a "filling up" as it were to the natural state, but Aristotle does not agree to this. Certainly where there is this "filling up" there is pleasure as also the result of exhaustion is pain. But this principle cannot be held universally as regards pleasure, as coming after pain.

Pleasure can be obtained even from mathematics or sense, or smell, but there is nothing here to indicate the presence of pain. We must conclude therefore, that pleasure is positive in the sense that it perfects an action. A good man will indulge in good pleasures and not bad, and so some notion can be obtained of the pleasant and the unpleasant. Again, pleasure and pain can be used as a sure guide against injury on the one hand and safety on the other, somewhat in the form of a rudder.

Throughout his teaching on pleasure, Aristotle has at all times kept to the centre of the road as it were. He neither inclines too much to excess or to defect, whereas teachers like Eudoxus had taught that pleasure was a complete good, whilst Speusippus had said that pleasure was wrong.

Friendships are valuable to everyone, and Aristotle discusses this topic in the eighth and ninth books. Firstly, it is a virtue and is absolutely necessary for life. Unfortunately, it seems that friendship is portrayed mainly for selfish ends. This would appear so as Aristotle says that when a person has a friend, he is really loving himself. Later on however, Aristotle somewhat tones this idea down by saying some look for the good of wealth, or the pleasures of the body, and we think little of them. On the other hand, people may give away sums of money, but in spite of the fact that they are undoubtedly self loving, no one belittles them. In this latter case, the gift goes to the friend, but the act to the giver; thus he obtains a greater good. Aristotle is showing here that self-love can be of two types, i.e., good and bad. Considering the fact that Aristotle was a pagan, it is startling to find him making the remark that a man's relations to his friend are the same as his relations with himself, as the friend is the other self. A result of this statement would seem to be that the being of each person — the friend and the befriended — is very considerably enriched. This and other remarks of the philosopher would reveal that in the last analysis his concept of friendship was not a matter absolutely for the ego.

There are three types of friendship — firstly in the lowest class is the friendship of utility, where a friend is not loved for himself, but for some gain the other will obtain. Secondly, friendship of pleasure, characterized by feeling and common to young people. Lastly, there is friendship for the good. The first two do not hold their attraction, but the last is enduring.

Friendship if it is true is an act of mind, whilst affection is concerned with feeling. It is almost impossible here not to adopt this last idea to the friendship of Our Lord for everyone. Also, there is a desire for increase of friendship.

Happiness and virtue together bring out that which is best in a person. Aristotle agrees with Plato that the ideal is the contemplative faculty. Without a sound morality, it is impossible to exercise this highest function.

There are quite a number of points to show how happiness is connected with reason. Firstly, because it is the highest part of man; secondly because this activity can be maintained long after bodily activity tires; thirdly because pleasure without doubt is an element of happiness; fourthly, a philosopher is sufficient for himself, despite the fact that he cannot do without necessary material things, but he is able to pursue his studies by himself, and the deeper his studies go, the more capable is he of being able to do this. Others may co-operate in his thought, but if this is lacking, he can do without it; fifthly, philosophy can be loved for itself alone, and not for properties that seem to flow from it; sixthly, leisure would appear to accompany happiness.

The faculty of reason would seem in the face of this, to be the principal source of happiness. Accordingly, it would also show the divine element in man. Moreover, we must not listen to those who exhort us to listen and cling to that which is purely human and mortal. If we can concentrate upon that which is highest in us although it be so very small it surprises all others in excellence. Furthermore, it would seem to be more truly fully a man's self as it is superior to all other faculties. It would be odd if a man chose something else, other than his true self for his life.

There are various other disciplines which assist contemplation. Among these are metaphysics, and also mathematics. God is the end of metaphysics but Aristotle does not include this in his ideal life, as laid out in the Eudemian Ethics. In the Nicomachean Ethics, he certainly does not say so. Despite this, what he did record was to show that intellectualism was sufficient to fire great Christian thinkers notably, of course, St. Thomas Aquinas to conclude that the Vision of God lay in the intellect and not the will as by the will we obtain, but by the intellect we rest in what is obtained.

CHAPTER 31

ARISTOTLE AND POLITICS

We do not possess all the works that were once extant relating to Politics in Aristotle's time. If we did, it would be an easy matter to show Aristotle's progress from his youth to old age. For example, a lost work entitled "Alexander" or "On Colonization" would show the concern with which Plato was watching the younger Aristotle's activities in a royal court in Asia. Again, how far did these great changes affect Aristotle's political outlook? We cannot tell; but as the subject stands, our main interest is where he would show signs of differing from Plato. To decide this problem, we have eight books of Politics to rely upon, but a detailed study could not be complete unless as is the case with the Metaphysics and Ethics earlier works were noted, in order to show his complete progress in relief.

Unfortunately, such historical research as this requires cannot be undertaken in an overall survey of this kind, but for the advanced student, it is a very fruitful path.

We may begin then by considering Plato's aim in Politics. His idea was to combine politics with virtue, bringing about a complete Good. The Republic which is an enquiry on justice became the model for Aristotle to follow when he wrote his books on Justice. Later these were to be utilized by Cicero. In Aristotle's Ethics, the Good was no longer integral with ethics, or political science, yet in his earliest works, it was his central theme, just as it was in Plato's Republic. This is clear from a fragment from the Statesman where the Good is described as the most perfect of all forms. Plato's concept of ideas is consistent with this, and it is emphasized in the Protrepticus where politics and theory are thought of as theoretical knowledge to be used by the Statesman. We can also discover that particular state is not to be treated by all kinds of experience. This idea is wrong, as Aristotle states in the fifth book of the Politics. One cannot become a good lawgiver by merely copying Spartans or Cretans for a copy of a thing is not its ideal. Someone who looks to the Laws of nature can provide a stable form of lawgiving. By "law of nature" is meant "what is" and what "ought to be", as Plato laid down in his Metaphysics, what is the relationship between theoretical and practical knowledge as applicable to the Statesman? To illustrate: the eye does nothing, it produces nothing, except to distinguish external objects without which we could not move. In brief, this was the political thought handed down by Plato and accepted by Aristotle. The former had tried to find an ideal which is not found on the level of experience.

The second step will be to consider what Aristotle himself says of the Politics, in the eight books. Firstly, it exists for a purpose. This purpose is the good of man, a good which includes his moral and intellectual life. The family is the smallest unit that exists to produce life, and to supply needs, and when several families band together, there is a primitive community or village. Furthermore, when several villages combine to form a large community, there is the State.

The State differs from the family or village in three ways; firstly, quantitatively, secondly qualitatively, and thirdly specifically. Only in the State can man find his natural good, and for this reason the State may be called "A Natural Society." The fact that man has speech has fitted him for social intercourse, and in Aristotle's view, the perfect form of this in the State is before the individual or the family in the sense that the latter two are not self supporting, while the former can be. One who tries to be self sufficient according to Aristotle is "either a beast or a god."

The teaching of both Plato and Aristotle on the State as leading man to a good life, and also being naturally prior to the individual and the family has had far reaching repercussions. It led the thinkers of the Middle Ages to the idea of a perfect Society within the Church, whose end was higher than that upheld by the State. One can but conclude that the Greek idea of the State did not perish with Greek freedom. Moreover, its logic was far sounder than that of many concepts propounded in all seriousness in recent times.

The Politics as we know them are incomplete, and Aristotle discusses the family on a master-slave basis, and also speaks of ways of acquiring wealth. In his view, some people are marked out to rule, and others must be slaves. It is right that some are free and some are not. This appears a barbaric view to say the least, but we must not forget that Aristotle was a pagan, and in fact what he aims at is to demonstrate that people differ by their natures and capacity. Some are alike and some quite unlike. Because of these vast differences society is widened, and a complexity of human persons is thus formed, which is so interesting.

Aristotle, like any human person, was a product of his times, and slavery was an accepted thing in those times. A master must not abuse his authority by ill-treating a slave. Moreover, all slaves must hope for freedom. If a slave has a child, then that child is not naturally a slave. In Aristotle's view, slavery by conquest is wrong because superior power and superior excellence are not the same, and war itself may not be just. On the other hand, Aristotle does not accept slavery from an historical standpoint, and on the other, he will attempt to justify it. Here is a unique case of possibly one of the greatest minds that has ever lived, falling into a simple contradiction.

Aristotle shows that there are three ways of obtaining riches. One is natural, by which is meant collecting things that are needed for life such as farming, hunting and so on. Then there is the way of exchange, where a thing is employed apart from its natural use. But as much as it is employed to support life, it may be referred to as natural. Finally there is the way which Aristotle called unnatural by which he means where money is used for the exchange of goods. It is undoubtedly true that Aristotle took this view of commerce which would look extremely odd in the world of today, because of the Greek attitude to trading which they did not consider fit for a free man. Aristotle hits hard at usury. He maintains that money is for exchange, but not for the purpose of making more money, or interest as we should know it. By this, the philosopher means that preying upon the ignorant and foolish by various means which make them the victims of the unscrupulous. St. Thomas Aquinas will follow Aristotle very closely in this, but in short, both thinkers are against the idea of the unnecessary being made to appear necessary by resorting to cunning and other ways of persuasion. This usage of money is maintained to be unnatural.

Plato had envisaged an Ideal State. But Aristotle was critical of this idea, for he felt that what Plato proposed such as crèches for the wealthy was not needed. Any form of communal idea, a pooling of individual resources to make a monster State. What we today would know as communism can find no hold in Aristotle's mind. He says an organization like this would be fought with inner disputes and discord, and lack of efficiency. To possess property brings a man pleasure, and it is foolish to assert that the State would be happier if all property were owned by it, as this sort of ownership belongs to individuals and it is this that helps them to be happy. Otherwise, they are not able to enjoy life to the full. Unity had been Plato's aim. Aristotle found no use for the accumulation of riches.

When Aristotle comes to speak of democracy he takes the qualifications from the Athenian democracy, which is not the same as in a modern democracy with its various representatives. Aristotle considers that all should take a turn in ruling and be ruled by others in turn. This is the very least one should expect as the right of a citizen. But the idea of ruling in the assembly led the philosopher not to consider tradesman and labourers as citizens, because of their lack of leisure time. In addition to this, manual toil fetters the mind, making it unsuitable for perfect virtue.

A Government may have as its end that which serves a common interest, or that which serves its own interest. These are further capable of sub-division. As opposite to Kingship there is Tyranny, Aristocratic Oligarchy, and Democracy. The way Aristotle treats these three, is indicative of the political ideas. The ideal would be that one man, highly disposed, should impose rule on all the others, maintaining throughout a perfect ideal of virtue. But Aristotle is alive to the fact that human nature in a single person cannot maintain such loftiness and because of this he advocates a democracy as the best fitted for the purpose of ruling. He does this because he thinks that rule by an aristocracy would ask too much of a community. He suggests what really amounts to middle class rule, operating as it does by a majority. If one serves the State as a hoplite or warrior, certain means are necessary and in this conclusion Aristotle was probably influenced by the Constitution of Athens in 411 B.C. At this time, the Five Thousand had a political grasp, but all the Five Thousand possessed heavy armour, which was dispensed with under the Constitution of Theramenes.

Government of this kind attracted Aristotle; nevertheless he realized that middle and rich classes mixing together were far more liable to produce a stable community.

Aristotle was a student of history. By its means, he could show where various Constitutions had come to grief, and the necessary future measures against a recurrence. It is possible, for example, for oligarchies or democracy to push their authority too far. The result is political discontent leading perhaps to graver issues.

The question would naturally arise; what should the ideal State be? The answer is found in the seventh and eighth books. The community must be neither too large nor too small (actually this observation does not bear reference to our modern times, with the accent upon large cities). It must be able to achieve its own end however, and not too large to be hampered in this. The number of persons to achieve this cannot be fixed with mathematical accuracy.

The same principals apply to the territory covered by the State. It must be big enough to encourage leisure but not large enough to encourage laziness. Money should not be an only end, but also importing and exporting should bring their due rewards.

Next as to the people themselves. Thadesman and labourers are essential, but they do not possess citizenship. The soldiering class are truly citizens. Fighting men in their youth, they will be public figures in middle life, and priests in advanced age. Each citizen would own two plots of land; one in the city itself, and one outside it which would be worked by requisite labourers. The idea of two plots is that ownership will inspire people to defend the city, particularly if they own land outside the city.

Both Plato and Aristotle agreed that education should play a big part in the life of the average citizen. It is to begin with physical training, because the appetites develop earlier than the intellectual faculties. All physical training is to be subordinate to the soul and the appetites must be controlled by reason. Thus there is a strong moral tone to Aristotle's ideas on education.

As stated at the beginning of this chapter, all the works on Politics in Aristotle's time are not extant. But we can form a fairly accurate idea of the loftiness displayed by both Plato and Aristotle with respect to the State. The State is good if the citizens are good; that is, if they act in accord with reason. This gives rise to moral goodness, and consequent soundness of character in the State itself. Conversely, if the State is immoral, it does not give the individual a chance to become good. An individual achieves perfection through the State, whilst the State attains perfection through individuals. The State is not a great monster upon which good and bad can have no effect. Neither is war and conquest the end of the State. It exists for the good of everyone, and this is borne out by both reason and history. A military state is well fitted for war, but not for peace, and war is not the end of man. Military forces may acquire empires, but they do not keep them, for a process of disintegration sets in and nothing is left. It is a question to wonder if Aristotle was influenced by the crumbling empires around him. Again, the point is left open to wide speculation.

CHAPTER 32

AESTHETICS

In three books, i.e., the Problemata, Metaphysics, Rhetoric, and again in the Metaphysics, Aristotle describes beauty, and the pleasant in various ways. In the first case, beauty is shown as the outcome of desire. In the Metaphysics, he says that there is a relationship between mathematics and beauty. If the beautiful is related to mathematics, then it cannot remain in the domain of purely sensible pleasure. In the Rhetoric, Aristotle says that the beautiful is pleasant because it is good. Under these conditions, there is little to distinguish between beauty and morality. Referring once again to the Metaphysics, we learn that something can be beautiful without desire. This would seem to imply a condition of pure thought. The most stable definition is given in the Metaphysics where Aristotle concludes that the forms of beauty are order, symmetry and definiteness. These qualities give mathematics their relationship to beauty, though one can only conceive this in a geometrical sense. Aristotle promises a fuller explanation of this subject. If one were ever given, it has not come down to us.

There is a reference in the Poetics to beauty containing size and order. Something living must have a symmetry of its parts which must not be too large or too small. Thus some argument is arrived at between the Metaphysics and the Poetics on the subject of beauty. Desire on these grounds would not hold claim to inspiring Aesthetics.

Comedy, according to Aristotle, is the ridiculous. This is a species of the ugly, he says. What is its definition? We are told that it is a mistake or deformity which does not harm or hurt others. This art form could then be used as a means to produce a desired effect. But we are not told of the relationship, if any, of the beautiful to the ugly.

The end of morality is some particular act; whilst art produces something. Further this can be considered in two ways. First, the art that assists or perfects nature, such as implement making, as nature only provided man with his hands in this respect. Secondly, art that copies nature. This is an imitation of the real. Both Plato and Aristotle were in agreement on this latter idea, although whilst Plato would persist in the Ideal being over and above the thing itself "out there" as we have remarked before, Aristotle adopted a more realistic approach. To him, it almost seems the ideal is the thing itself, translated by artists into various media. Moreover, Aristotle asserts that to imitate is natural to man, and to delight in its results. Psychologically we can take pleasure in what in actual life is painful. Recognition is a source of pleasure in this way. But these remarks though true, do not assist in forming ideas upon art.

In the Poetics, poetry is considered superior to history. The reason given by Aristotle is that the former deals in universals, whilst the latter contents itself with particular observations. A particular thing or act is a singular thing; whereas a universal act is that which introduces the notion of possibility or the necessary. This principally is Aristotle's demonstration of factors which cause the poet and historian to differ.

A type is close to the universal. These ideas can be associated well. An historic figure can be described by his particular acts. The artist would display the same person in a broad sweep of language as a type. Actually history can assist poetry, but little, although subjects may be taken from history by the poet, and used to advantage.

The statement that "poetry has rather the nature of universals" is interesting. It indicates poetry tends towards universals, without necessarily becoming a universal concept or idea. In this way strictly speaking, poetry is not philosophy, for in addition, it lacks the characteristic abstract approach of philosophy.

In this work (the Poetics) Aristotle describes only three things, e.g. Epic, Comedy and Tragedy with the accent on the latter. His remarks on other arts are useful to give an insight into Aristotle's ideas upon imitation.

In his view, the most imitative art of all is Music. Drawing is imitative also, but only as far as gesture will allow. In this way, it is imitative of prevailing morality. In the case of music however, the moral tone is contained in the music itself. He inquires "why should what is heard alone of the objects of sense contain emotional import?" The answer would seem to be that the stimulation of music is more direct and can go as far as to include symbolism as to what is really felt. Again, a dancer is assisted more by rhythm than by harmony. By the former, he may imitate the various emotions which the human soul undergoes.

Drawing and music are desirable requirements for the young in their education. Probably, it is true to assume that Aristotle was interested in art from the point of view of its contribution to education and morality. This does not mean, however, that he ignored the fact that music can be used for recreation. But including this purely sense pleasure aspect, it was also necessary to draw attention to its higher possibilities.

In the Poetics, there is according to Aristotle, the definition of tragedy. Firstly, it is an imitation of a serious act. It has size being in complete form, in language which will provide pleasure; additions are brought in to form the complete work; the work is dramatic, and is not a narrative, finally, the scenes must arouse fear or pity to provide a climax to the emotions.

The above definition contains so much, it will be of great advantage to look at it in greater detail.

The general tone of the tragedy can be serious, noble or good. This it has in common with Epic Poetry, and thus both are separated from Comedy and Satire, which have the foolish or ridiculous or ugly as their ends.

A play of this type is in complete form when it can be described as a whole consequent upon the unity of plot. Mistakes have been made in the past when writers claim that Aristotle demanded three unities in drama. He did not. He simply spoke of tragedy, unlike poetry, "endeavours to keep within a single circuit of the sum or something like that". "When language will provide pleasure" this is taken to mean that there will be rhythm and songs if necessary.

Additions are brought in to form a complete work. Aristotle is referring to Greek tragedy where song and speech alternate. If a work is in dramatic and not narrative form, then this separates it from epic poetry. It is reasonable that the play will have a climax to give satisfaction to the emotions.

Further, there are six notes which go to make up a tragedy. They are plot, characters, diction, thought, spectacle and melody. The philosopher concludes that the whole action revolves around the plot; therefore this is of paramount importance. All the actions are subordinate to the plot. Aristotle is quite decided that a tragedy is an imitation, not of people, but of life itself, of enjoyment or misery. All human happiness or misery takes place in an action; it is certain that our end is some form of action, not a quality. The latter is provided by characters, but it is in action that we are either happy or miserable. Consequently, action is prior at all times.

Nevertheless, the action must be clothed by appropriate characters, and this, he states, is of utmost importance.

The intensity of thought is brought out by showing it is speech proving or disproving something. It is not speech that reveals a character. Euripides used it in this way, but a danger would seem to be the sacrifice of plot for long discussions.

It is possible, says Aristotle, to use fine diction to illustrate fine thought, but unless it is directed towards a dramatic end, the end is to a great extent lost.

Possibly melody is the most pleasant of all additions to tragedy. Aristotle maintained that the Spectacle was alluring; nevertheless, the part played in tragedy was entirely secondary to that of the plot.

In respect of the plot itself, it must be a unity. Also it must be large enough to take in all the characters easily, and yet not be cumbersome. On the other hand, it must not be cramped, for this would impede the characters' actions, and consequently, the drama. It is wise not to have one character around which the whole plot revolves, but several incidents strung together. The probable happenings of such incidents adds to their interest. So does necessity. Why is this? Because of the contrast between what will happen and what has happened.

It seems that tragedy contains an element of Discovery. This is illustrated when the secret of Oedipus' birth is made known, and he discovers that he has committed incest. This change from ignorance to knowledge greatly heightens fear and pity.

Now, if tragedy imitates, and it arouses fear and pity, the plot must not take one or more of three forms. Firstly, an honourable man must not be depicted as passing from happiness to misery. Aristotle says this idea is revolting to the human mind. Secondly, a bad man must not be depicted as passing from misery to happiness and for the same reason as given above. Thirdly, a man who leads a very bad life must not be depicted as moving from happiness to misery. Although human feelings are aroused, these do not include fear or pity, since pity is aroused by something not deserved, and fear for someone like ourselves.

What then is left to portray? Just an ordinary person who passes through various trials brought about by bad judgement, but it would seem that vice or depravity must not be portrayed.

The emotions of pity and fear are to be aroused by some brutality. This leads to what has been described by writers as catharsis. Its effect is psychological, but what Aristotle meant by it is a favourite topic among authorities. The actual meaning is certainly a difficult one to discover, for the second book of Poetics — where Aristotle may have given an explanation — is not extant. It seems that in the main, the points of view are two. Firstly that of a purifying action on the emotions, and secondly, the idea that pity and fear be obliterated. Of these two, the latter is the most generally accepted today. How is fear and pity then obliterated? These emotions are excited in the audience by the plight of the hero and the dangers, etc. that befall him. Everyone or nearly every normal person, experiences fear and pity sometimes in excess of what is good for him. Thus tragedy gives an outlet — a very necessary relief for some people — which is at the same time pleasurable. As a result, the excess of fear and pity disappears, and this would be Aristotle's version of tragedy. Plato also had described tragedy in the Republic. It is not possible to consider Aristotle's ideas on the intellect with relation to this, as in all probability his views were included in that part of the Poetics which is lost to us.

It seems clear however, that the effect would be purgative and not moral. For example, the flute is exciting, and because of this, should be played by those who are capable, and at times when a "catharsis" of the emotions is fitting.

Harmony is useful for again it calms what would be excess emotion. There are three reasons for education of music. Firstly, for instruction, secondly to purify, and thirdly, for enjoyment of the mind. Also, it is useful for recreation after heavy labour. The distinctly ethical and purgative elements are further distinguished. Fear, pity or enthusiasm are very strong in some people, others in a greater or lesser degree. The former upon hearing music will have like experiences, whilst the latter with not such strong feeling, will nevertheless find pleasure also. We may assume that this catharsis of which Aristotle speaks is not ethical. Following this, it would seem that the ideas of purification of ethics are nothing but a metaphor drawn from medicine.

At this point, it is only fitting to mention that Aristotle's ideas on tragedy are not universally accepted. Some thinkers maintain that the soul is purified not *through* but *of* pity and fear. It would appear, they say, in much the same light as when the human body purges itself of unwanted matter. What is the value of such a position? It is not a question if Aristotle's view was right or wrong. It is simply Aristotle's view. That is the limit to which an historian can go.

Aristotle traces out the history of both tragedy and comedy. The former began with an impromptu part for the leader of the Dithyramb, followed by the chorus dividing into two groups. Its object was to worship Dionysius in much the same manner as the renaissance of drama in Europe was connected with mystery plays of the Middle Ages.

The beginnings of comedy were identical. The material used was generally of an erotic nature in song form.

Drama developed by developing the role of the principal actor. The actors were increased to two by Aeschylus and later Sophocles increased them yet again to three with the addition of scenery and parts for the chorus were limited from thereon. Spoken dialogue was iambic, this being the most suitable for speech.

The above is but a brief summary of Aristotle's views on drama. His whole viewpoint would seem to rest on the discussion of interpretation and correctness of a particular art form. Aristotle was followed as head of the Lyceum by Theophrastus in 322/1 B. C. Whilst the old Academy of Plato staunchly retained its mathematical emphasis, Aristotle's followers will agree with him broadly speaking in Metaphysics and Ethics.

Theophrastus came from Lesbos and he continued in his position until he died in 288/7. His work is marked by his following of Aristotle's experience in the beginning of philosophic study. Right up to the Middle Ages, he was considered an authority on botany, and noticed that some animals change color according to their surroundings. He wrote probably one of the first Histories of Philosophy to become widely known; unfortunately it is now only partly in existence, other parts being lost. He must have been a student of human nature, for he left an interesting work in which he discusses no less than thirty types of character. The work is called the Characters.

A native of Tarentum, Aristoxenus believed that the soul was a harmony of the body. This doctrine he realized from the Pythagoreans. Ultimately it led him to deny the immortality of the soul, but he followed Aristotle in his empirical outlook on nature, and also on music.

Others came in Aristoxenus' footsteps. One was Dicaearchus of Messene who wrote a work on Greece from the earliest times. He believed contrary to Aristotle that the practical life was superior to the theoretical. He laid down that the best form of government was one based on monarchy, aristocracy and democracy. Sparta, he taught, was an illustration of such government.

Theophrastus had a pupil named Demetrius of Phaleron, who left many writings and was noted for his political activity. He actually was head of the Government of Athens from 317 to 307. He encouraged a library and a great school at Alexandria to be built where he himself went in 297. As result of this project, Demetrius founded a link between Athens and the Greek community in Alexandria, and undoubtedly helped that city to become a haven for the scholar, and those wishing to acquire knowledge.

CHAPTER 33

A COMPARISON

An idea whether it be material or immaterial actually represents the sum total of its possible aspects, however much they may separate and divide under the influence of various minds. Now, such is the working of the human mind that except for this variety, the idea in question would lose force; that is to say, it will not be thrown sufficiently into relief, as for example, black is by the presence of white. Thus an idea, philosophic or otherwise, is given power to possess a mind, and when it does this, it can be truly said to live. At first, a time of confusion ensues, due to the multiple agitation of thought among many people. This happened in the case of philosophy, until a firm concrete structure was founded by Socrates and later on by Plato. Into this environment came young Aristotle at the age of seventeen and stayed for twenty years. It is mostly noticeable that any idea of Aristotle's development is often ignored. Why is this? Because his philosophy appears as set conceptions, and yet it must have developed. His austere style is possibly the only and main link which have sewn his demonstrations together so to speak. Again this is because of the separation of his logic and his Metaphysics, an event that did not occur with Plato. Indeed Plato is regarded as considering logic and ontology as one entity. Aristotle's letters and dialogues which would give an insight into his development are now lost. Tradition then did the rest. It became a question of a set formula, a set style, a particular demonstration. No one has ever revived Aristotle partly because his personality was lost with his dialogues and letters. Further possibly throughout the whole course of history, no genius has remained for so long under the influence of his master as did Aristotle with Plato. There is no safer guide to the creative power of a pupil than the length of time he remains with his teacher. Now, Aristotle was a man nearing forty when he left Plato. This influence upon his development was great. It was thus

188

a united effort of mind that gave Aristotle his gifts in their full maturity. This maturity is bound up with development. The variety of thought which we have had occasion to mention is collected, sifted, rejected and gradually separated from it in the minds of individuals and of the community. This process, whether it be long or short, is development, and is just as applicable in the field of philosophy as anywhere else. It cannot progress without cutting across and so destroying existing trains of thought, but with itself, it also unites other ways of thinking and operating.

These remarks are very appropriate when we consider these two great philosophers. But in what way did Aristotle's thought "cut across" that of Plato?, and, in what way did he assimilate from the latter those notions of philosophy later to become identified with him?

Plato took from Socrates the fact that an idea must be based upon ethics. From this standpoint, he developed his doctrine of ideas. But this did not come at once, for Plato realised that if one took an ethic, that ethic must have foundation in something. The "something" in this case proved to be objective reality. Why did he come to this conclusion? Because ethics are realisable only in reality. They must apply to the real. Moreover, Plato concluded that if this were the case, then moral values were not changeable, indeed they were in the nature of an ideal. These ideas or ideals all share in common goodness which is derived from an absolute goodness. This goodness is God.

Plato thus utilised some of the teachings of Socrates. It is understandable that for this reason his doctrine was put in the mouth of Socrates in the dialogues. But in his pursuit of the ideal, Plato did not stop here. He applied his dialetic to concepts of all sorts. His reason was as all good things share in common goodness, so do individual good things. What was the result of this view? Primarily, it was not a break in doctrine, but fundamentally, it forced Plato to associate the Idea and the thing more closely. He consequently developed a scale of goodness from the Ideas to the least of things. These things all shared to a greater or lesser degree the goodness contained in a perfect way in the Ideas. In short, one was Being in the complete sense, whilst other things are Becoming, the mere fact of which made the latter imperfect.

Some have said that the hierarchy of values in Being could but show a relationship between Being and Becoming. Probably, this is accurate, but the emphasis Plato laid on Being at the expense

189

of Becoming cannot pass unnoticed. Lack of reason and Becoming were associated in Plato's mind; such was to be expected in a man who thought of logic and ontology as one. Thought concerns the universal, the universal concerns being; thought therefore concerns Being, and if this is so then the particular cannot represent Being. Being does not change, which cannot be said of a particular. It changes and dies, and therefore is not Being.

From this, the conclusion is that philosophy concerns Being and is interested only in Becoming insofar as the latter imitates the former.

It is undoubtedly true that Aristotle attached great importance to Metaphysics. The statement, for example, of the presence of an unmoved mover, and the observation that man's highest function was contemplation of unchanging things, could well be interpreted in this way. At the same time, Aristotle pointed out the immateriality of form, and so it was that natural theology made great strides.

In the main, Aristotle taught that the gap between the "Idea" of Plato and the sensible object was too wide. Plato did not admit of any interior principle which would draw the Idea and the thing closer together. But by not doing this, he allowed Being and Becoming to fall into two great classes which it seemed could never approach each other. On the other hand, Aristotle identified the particular thing with a particular immanent form, which in the case of man was rational, and this form, together with its matter, made up the object. It is by this form that the object is understood at all; also the activity of the thing is realised from this form. It shapes the end desired at the same time maintaining a unifying effect upon the whole organism. Thus is all nature seen as an ascending scale of being culminating in a supreme unmoved mover, who is completely actual pure Being or Thought, self subsistent, and contained in itself. Nature is therefore a process of perfection and development of the individual thing.

Aristotle does not occupy a similar position to Plato. His views on Becoming are different, for he will say that everything *is* insofar as it is actual and this actuality involves Being. There is actuality unmixed with potency; but there is also in the world actuality always being realised in matter directed by an Unmoved mover. Consequently, the answer to Becoming is to be found in Being, particularly as the former is for the sake of the latter. Through this doctrine of forms, Aristotle was able to give a meaning to the everyday world, which we do not find in Plato. Moreover, he was insistent that the end of man is an activity and not a quality.

Aristotle had perfected Plato's teaching of transcendental essence, and secondly, his teaching on finality helped to a great step forward. At the same time, in this perfection or correction of Plato, Aristotle omitted much valuable material, e.g. Plato's conception of Divine Reason.

Also Plato's teaching on exemplary causality went by the board. It may be that Plato's handling of these questions was not as thorough as Aristotle would have wished. Nevertheless, it is a truth that when Aristotle passed over Plato's treatment of this world in great measure he missed a lot that was profound in Plato's mind.

In spite of this what do we find? We find in effect Aristotle saying that if sensible objects imitate the Ideas in any way, then an internal principle is demanded. This Plato did not provide. The interior principle finds itself in the activity of the object and tends to unify in a perfect way all constituent parts of matter. Further nature is seen as an ascending scale of values, in each of which the essence tends in a mysterious way to approach pure Being or Thought. It would be incorrect to say that either Plato or Aristotle taught the whole truth, for they did not. On the other hand, it is not possible to consider one without the other. That which is good of Plato and that which is good of Aristotle must be merged in one stream of thought.

In the future, Neo-Platonism will endeavour to do this; their efforts will be repeated by philosophers of the Middle Ages and of modern times. If such a synthesis takes place however, it will be because of a Platonic content in Aristotle. To illustrate: Aristotle thought that Plato's idea of man was "dual." If he had, whilst thinking this, rejected a higher principle of thought in man and reduced the mind to pure matter, he would directly come into conflict with Plato. But he did not do this. Thus two elements are sustained; from Plato there is the concept that the individual Soul is more than the body and survives death individually. From Aristotle comes the idea that man is both soul and body.

Another instance of this is the idea of God prevailing with Aristotle, and that of the Good with Plato. It becomes quite evident upon consideration of this for one moment, that there was a basis for Christian teachings. And so it transpired.

191

Such examples as given above would only be useful in points of doctrine where one philosopher was partly right and partly wrong. When we come to read the logic of Aristotle this seems to present a tremendous advance on what Plato had provided. Moreover, it would seem to contain what was the content of logic in Platonic thought.

CHAPTER 34

ADVANCE

In 323 B.C., Alexander the Great died. Under him the Greek City State had been able to develop independently and this was the case also with his successors, with the disadvantage that those that followed Alexander fought among themselves, and this of its very nature could not have a lasting beneficial effect upon the States themselves. Alexander in some respects had a big mind for he thought not in terms of the City but of empire. Consequently, we now find Hellenistic culture rather than a national culture, particularly so since the result of Alexander's concepts brought about an opening up of the East. No longer did Athens, Corinth and Sparta stand alone as cultural centres, but gradually their influence and that of the east became merged, both finally owing allegiance to the Roman Empire.

The effect of this change was radical. The City State that Plato and Aristotle had known became part of a cosmopolitan organization made up of individuals. The result was to throw the individual much more upon his own resources, cut loose as he was from the old idea of the small State. Consequently, the society in which man now lived was much larger. In turn, this meant that various aspects of philosophy such as Physics and Metaphysics gave ground to what would provide for purely ethical material. This resulted in Metaphysical borrowings on no small scale from the older Schools. Philosophers before Socrates are consulted in this new trend; also there is a place now for the physics of Heraclitus and the Atomism of Democritus. The followers of Aristotle were not exempt from this; they too, consulted those thinkers before Socrates, the Stoic school taking from the Cynics and the Epicureans following the Cyrenaics in this way.

The men of the Roman Empire for the greater part were practical men. Great speculation had stopped short with the Greeks. The Roman idea was that character was all important. With this concept in mind, and the fact that traditions had gone with the Republic, it became increasingly necessary for a man to be able to find his way through life, following a uniform and straightforward line of action. The position here becomes interesting for this need gave rise to a new class of philosopher who helped man in his daily life, somewhat in the same way as the priest directs in the confessional in Christian times.

The outcome of this drift to the practical was the presentation of philosophy upon a popular basis, in a form that could be easily understood. It was taught in the Schools and for a while could have become a rival to the New Christian religion. On the face of it, possibly it would appear to satisfy the cravings of the human heart as religion can. If one did not believe in myths — and this was common — if it came to a question of life without religion at all, the choice was between mysticism from the East and philosophy. In this way, Stoicism and the ancient philosophy could, and were related. Plotinus took this a stage further. For the spirit of intellectual activity is so high with this thinker that it automatically tends to flow into religion and even ecstasy.

Fundamentally there is difference between ethics and religion. Ethics alone will lead to a spirit of independence whilst religion will lead to a dependence on God. In point of fact both these views aim at the same thing. The aim of the Greco-Roman citizen was to find a foundation that would suit him to follow, and upon which to build his new found life. In actual fact these two points of view readily mix as is found in Stoicism, and sometimes on a religious basis, whilst in Neo-Platonism we find an effort at a synthesis, with the religious aspect always paramount, but the ethical in full importance in its right place.

There were various stages of Greco-Roman philosophy, and they are as follows:

Firstly, one extending from the end of the fourth century B.C., to the middle of the first century B.C. Stoic and Epicurean philosophy was founded during this period. The aim of this was personal happiness. They reached back before Socrates for their doctrines. Opposite to these stands the Scepticism of Pyrrho. The movement between these streams of thought made for one sometimes choosing what was said by the other.

Secondly, this state of choice continued into the second period, which extended from the first century B.C. to the middle of the

194

third century A.D. The point to mention here is that more philosophical unity is attained. This unity runs as counterpart to the eclecticism or choice. Also there is a greater interest in the founders of the great philosophical systems. This latter would appear to belong mainly to scholars from Alexandria.

If science made its appearance at this time, it was not alone. Religious mysticism provided a great attraction. Scholars have drawn attention to the fact that these two, i.e. mysticism and science, dealt a death blow at speculation. This may or may not be true, as it is left to far more experienced writers than the present one to decide, but certainly this tendency would appear to grow in strength. As a result of contacts made with religion of the East, efforts were made to incorporate these eastern elements into speculative philosophy. It is true that Philo would seek to win over the Greeks by presenting argument in Greek dress.

The next period starts from the middle of the third century A.D., and goes through until the sixth century A.D., or in the case of Alexandria to the seventh century A.D. This is the era of Neo-Platonism, the idea of which was to make a complete synthesis of all philosophic doctrines, including Plato, Aristotle and those of the East. Its ultimate influence was extensive over a number of centuries. St. Augustine and the Pseudo-Dionysius were both its adherents.

During this epoch science greatly advanced. That is to say the sciences which are particular to something, or concern some particular reality. If philosophy and religion became united, the relationship between philosophy and science was less happy. These special sciences required special consideration. The circumstances which provided this intensive research reacted upon the sciences themselves. It is true that Aristotle's Lyceum had promoted research into science. But as a result of the researches now undertaken, centres of learning sprang up in the form of Institutes and Libraries, etc. Alexandria, Antioch and Pergamon were the centers where such developments took place. The library at Alexandria for example contained 42,800 works, whilst an even larger one at the palace contained 400,000 large papyrus rolls, and 90,000 smaller ones. As a matter of interest, Mark Antony presented Cleopatra with a library of some 200,000 rolls. This was the Pergamene library.

The possibility is that philosophy has not always treated the special sciences kindly. On the other hand, it provides a firm basis for further speculation which can rescue experiments from a purely worldly aspect. Throughout these observations the preservation of type, continuity of principle, power of assimilation, logical sequence, early anticipation, preservative additions, and chronic continuance of philosophy as an idea, are all acting together toward the furtherance of this distinctive and powerful discipline.

CHAPTER 35

THE STOICS

The Stoic School of Philosophy was founded by Zeno who lived from 336/5 B. C., when he was born at Citrum in Cyprus and died about 264/3 at Athens. He and his father apparently were both traders.

In 315 upon arrival at the capital, he read the Memorabilia of Xenophon, also Plato's Apology. These readings resulted in Zeno acquiring great admiration of Socrates. He followed a man one Crates the Cynic, because Zeno considered that this man most closely resembled Socrates. He also came into contact with Stilpo, though he listened to Xenophon and after the latter's death, he was drawn to other teachers. Finally, in perhaps 300 B. C., he started a School of his own. Tradition says he committed suicide. His writings left to us are fragmentary.

After Zeno, there was Cleanthes of Assos 331/30-233/2 and then Chrysippus in Cilicia 281/278-208/205 as successive heads of the school of philosophy. Chrysippus was taken to be the second founder on account of his close following of Stoic doctrine. He was a prolific writer by repute having written 705 books. In these compositions, the arguments were brilliant, but the general style did not measure up to the same standard.

Zeno had many pupils. Among them Diogenes of Seleucia came to Rome in 156/5 in company with other philosophers, their object being a form of public relations between Athens and Rome.

In Rome they gave talks which aroused admiration. Cato did not consider however, that philosophy mixed well with military powers, and he urged the Senate to remove them as soon as possible. Diogenes was succeeded by a native of Tarsus, a man called Antipater. What did the Stoics teach? Firstly, in the realm of logic they divided this discipline into Dialectic and Rhetoric. Sometimes Thirty Definitions were added, and also the Criteria of Truth. Aristotle had originally listed ten categories, but the Stoics reduced these to four viz. the substrate, essential constitution, accidental constitution, and the accidental relative constitution. Further, all propositions are simple unless they contain more than one proposition, if they do, then they are compound.

Plato had laid down a doctrine of transcendental universals which Aristotle had followed with concrete universals. Both these doctrines were discarded by the Stoics who satisfied themselves with particular knowledge. The particular only existed. As a result of these particulars the soul receives impressions and thus acquires knowledge. We find here the opposite to what Plato had taught, since he placed little faith in sense perception. On the basis of Stoic teaching if I see an animal resembling what I know to be a dog, then I see a dog, and not "dogness." The soul is empty before it knows, though knowledge of interior states were not ruled out. In all this perception, the material plays an important part. Then there is the memory which holds various perceptions in the form of recollection, in the absence of the material object.

This philosophy was a worldly philosophy; a philosophy that had to do with things rather than concepts or ideas. When it came to a question of the reason, it simply is a question of its development based on sense perception.

Truth was a particular object of interest with the Stoics. Again, however, it seems to have been reduced to a case of perception following on what a particular object represents. Consequently, truth and perception can be equated. This may be all very well, but there are occasions when the soul is capable of withholding assent to something that is obviously true from a point of view of perception. The Stoic answer to this objection is given by Sextus Empiricus when he says that truth has no hindrances. Truth can appear objectively, and also subjectively the latter affecting the soul's assent. But this is not a satisfactory explanation, for it leaves the question to a great extent unsolved.

When it came to a study of the Cosmos, the Stoics drew upon Heraclitus, Plato and Aristotle. From the former they took the idea of Fire as a primary substance, and somewhat intermixed the two latter philosophers with a theory of an ideal upon a material plane.

Reality is to these thinkers of two elements, active and passive. However, despite the fact that these are met with in Plato, with the Stoics there is a significant difference. The active principle is a material entity. The actual division between these two elements, i.e. active and passive is so slight, that it could be taken for one whole thing. Thus we arrive at monotheistic materialism.

The Stoics will say that matter does not possess qualities. At the same time, the eternal principle in things is God. Natural things in their behavior point to the fact that God exists and is the Orderer of the Universe. Again, man is possessed of self realization, and it would follow that the rest of the world would also be endowed because the part cannot be greater than the whole. God is Himself this Self-realization working for, and towards, all good.

In addition, God is the source from which lower things would come. The process is one of coming from God and returning to Him. So that everything in existence is the essence of God. There is some comparison between the world and God and the body and the soul. The same relationship exists between God and the world as exists between the soul and the body. In each case, there is a superior principle, the active forming principle of all other things. This lower stuff to which the active principle gives rise is in potency to many forms. Great is the emphasis laid on this procedure in the form of development. From small beginnings into individual and particular things, St. Augustine will use this idea and call it rationes seminales. As the world develops, fire becomes air, and thus will pass into water. Some of the water will change to earth, a second part will stay as water, whilst a third part becomes air, which once again returns to fire through rarefaction.

It is reasonable conjecture that Heraclitus did not forecast a universal conflagration. In spite of this, however, this doctrine was added by the Stoics, consequently we have the notion of chain destructions. The new creations will be a replica of the one that has gone before down to the individual particular. Nietzsche will adopt this idea in a much later time. But this notion did not allow for human freedom, and this in fact is a point of teaching. A substitute for Freedom is found in Fate. However, this concept does not differ greatly from that of God or Providence. Interiorly speaking, man is a free agent, and thus we can still speak of God's Will.

There remained the problem of evil to be explained. Chrysippus undertook an explanation by saying that the imperfection in individuals was the underlying factor of the whole. In an overall sense, in this way he would maintain that there was no evil.

Several more recent philosophies seem to have followed this trend, notably Leibniz and Spinoza. Chrysippus goes on to say that where there are two contraries, the existence of the one is impossible without the other, so, if one is taken away so is the other. This statement is found in Book One on Providence. To illustrate: A creature exists, and as it exists, it can feel pleasure. It is also true that it can feel pain. Not only this, but pain as a danger signal acts as a friend, warning of some disorder in the body. Again, if the pangs of hunger were never felt, we would not eat and thus become ill. But all this gives attention to physical evil. What is the attitude of the Stoics to moral evil?

They maintained that no action in itself was good or bad. But great emphasis was laid upon the intention of the person acting. Now this could mean any intention would in effect justify an otherwise good or bad act. For example, a person does not know it is wrong to steal, nevertheless, he steals money belonging to his neighbour. According to the Stoics, this act at best could only be materially evil, but it is impossible for it to be found evil on account of lack of knowledge of the person acting. Any act can be thought of as positive, and this is the reason the Stoics thought of no action *in itself* as evil. Let us take this a stage further. A mere *physical* act committed either in virtue or in sin does not change. But if the intention is considered apart from the act itself, then there is a case of moral responsibility. Now this last is not positive, for it indicates a privation of the Creator's original intention. In addition, it upsets the right order of the human will.

It is possible to have a right and a wrong intention. In the physical world, contraries work against one another. For example, honour is not appreciated without an understanding of dishonour. So it is in the moral order.

As far as it went, the Stoics were teaching truth, that is to say, if a person has a capacity for virtue, he also has for vice. Man has an extremely imperfect idea of the Supreme Good in this life, but his freedom is maintained. Again, it is better to have a freedom which implies a choice of vice, than have no freedom at all. But here we have reached the point of departure with the Stoics. For when they maintain that contraries always work against each other, they are mistaken. At most, we can only say that sin is a possible state, and not a necessary one. But it can easily remain possible indefinitely. Once again, there is a likeness between the physical and moral order. A bad thing will show a better one up in relief. The conclusion is that in the moral order, it is good for a person to be free. In this state, he *can* sin if he so desires. A better use of freedom, however, is the choice of right action.

The role of Providence is not clearly drawn. Is it responsible for minor mistakes or not? Anyhow, whatever befalls a person happens for the best. The idea of evil showing good up in relief recurs in Neo-Platonism, St. Augustine, Berkeley, Leibniz, a notion started by Chrysippus so many years before.

Concerning inanimate objects, Reason acts as a blind force. Plant life does not possess a soul, so here again Reason is a cohesive power. Animals have a soul and man is characterised by the faculty of reason. In this way, the human soul is noble above other things.

Chrysippus says that the centre of the soul is in the heart, but other Stoics placed it in the head. It did not seem possible that immortality on the part of the person would be achieved under Stoic teachings. They held that all Souls return to what was called the conflagration, except the souls of the specially wise. At the same time, devotion could and was shown to a Divine Principle in the hymn to Zeus. This was written by Cleanthes.

Nevertheless, this attachment to a greater Principle did not alter the fact that neither did the Stoics desert religion of a popular nature. Further, this philosophy was a satisfactory vehicle for divinations and oracles. This was because as a basic precept the Stoics had maintained a determinism. In this scheme, all parts are related.

But what of the ethics of the Stoics? These are well set out by a member of the latter Stoa who, in order to formulate the Stoic doctrine on this point, we can include here. This philosopher Seneca says that ethics are mainly concerned with behaviour of the human person. Happiness is the end of life and this is attained by virtue. This virtue must be practised, according to the nature or of the human will, working together with the Divine. Thus arises the famous Stoic expression "live according to nature." If a man follows the law of the universe, and his own nature, these are the same, as both are controlled by the same power.

Now, nature is not to be confused with instinctive urges that prompt people to follow their lower instincts. This is the meaning it had for the Cynics. But for our present consideration "nature" means a principle working in nature. A trully ethical end, therefore, is submission to the Divine Will by the human will.

Self preservation is the instinct most firmly rooted in the animal, and man in addition to this self preservation is endowed with reason. This could be equated as development of the human being. So with man, we find a natural element and also an element of virtue. This leads to a life that follows nature where nothing is done against the universal or order of reason.

To this argument an obvious objection arises. What is the use of letting a person follow nature if at the outset he cannot help doing so. The answer as far as the Stoics are concerned is that it is true that man will follow nature; but he can decide what act to perform or not to perform. Obviously this explanation relaxes somewhat the determinist element in Stoicism, but this much can be expected of any laws laid down by human beings. In a determinist philosophy, no action is strictly right or wrong. The reason is because lack of voluntary action does not allow for choice and ultimate responsibility. It was a Stoic concept that no action is wrong *in itself*. Consequently we find cannibalism, incest and homosexuality, being accepted as ordinary occurrences. This is clear from a statement by Cleanthes "if no evil prone, my will rebelled, I needs must follow still". Seneca wrote in the same fashion. However, this is not the complete picture. For we find a scale of values held by the Stoics which indicates that a man may climb to greater heights, whilst avoiding or assessing lower ones. Man's free nature cannot be denied, so deeply is it impressed upon the human soul.

Virtue contains a good in the full sense of the word. Something that is connected with neither vice nor virtue is accordingly neither good nor bad. Plato's idea of reward and punishment in the next life was thought to be ridiculous. The Stoic doctrine did allow for some things to be more preferred than others, while it is possible to be indifferent to others. These latter are in three groups (a) things in accord with nature, and thus having value; (b) against nature and with no value; (c) things which neither possess nor do not possess value. In this way, a scale of values was formed. What of pleasure? It accompanies certain activity, and is not an end in itself. One Stoic — Cleanthes — will say that pleasure is not in accord with nature.

The Stoics introduced Cardinal Virtues which are Moral Insight, Courage, Self-control or Temperance and justice. They are possessed as one, that is to say, altogether or not at all. Their root is Moral Insight for some, whilst for others it was mastery of self. There was general argument however in that they were connected through one subject, because the presence of the virtue means that all are present. Character would seem to be the emphasis of the Stoics, and this must be carried out in the right spirit. The Stoic idea was that the truly wise man is without passions. They went further than this by asserting man had complete control of his own life, which involved the choice of suicide, according to circumstances.

Now, it would seem that if one virtue were so linked with another, it would not leave much room for any grade or degree in virtue. Consequently, a person is either fully virtuous or not virtuous at all. The result of this teaching was that few attained virtue except in later life. The later Stoics modified these somewhat severe views however. For them, humanity patterned out into two huge camps, fools, and those progressing to wisdom.

Some affections and passions are irrational, for example, pleasure, sorrow, depression, desire and fear. When these affections occur, it is necessary to dispel them and become in a state of apathy. It became a question of self-mastery — all emotions that in their way enrich human nature if not carried to extreme were sublimated.

It is true to say that the Stoics inherited some Cynic characteristics, for instance, the idea of being independent of outside things, but in reality it passes beyond. Why is this? Because naturally man is meant to live in society as a regulation of reason and there is a simple law in this way for all men. So a cosmopolitan attitude is achieved. From this it emerges that man is a world citizen. As such, war is foolish, but at the same time, this puts us under an obligation to all men to forgive and to show mercy. Thus this merging into high spheres would be favoured by monism. But there is also the instinct to self love or self preservation starting from the individual and broadening out to embrace external things, family, friends, but weakening as it does so. This shows clearly a particular aim. It is to love those remote things with the ferocity with which we love ourselves.

CHAPTER 36

EPICURUS AND HIS SCHOOL

Epicurus is generally held to be the founder of Epicureanism. He was born at Samos in 342/1 B. C., where in his foundation years he listened first to Pamphilus who was a Platonist, and then later at Teos he heard Nausiphanes who taught the doctrine of Democritus. This latter thinker was very influential in forming the philosophical character and mind of Epicurus. At the age of eighteen, he did his military service in Athens and later studied at Colophon. Following this in 310, he taught at Mitylene, afterwards moving to Lampasius. Later still in 307/6, he opened a school in Athens. This school was started in the garden of Epicurus' home. It is evident that the manner of teaching remained very stable throughout, and in all probability, this was due to the influence of Epicurus himself. A unique feature was the learning by heart of doctrine in preference to written work on the part of pupils.

However, Epicurus himself wrote extensively, his output being approximately 300 books. Most of these are now lost. Three letters and various fragments only survive.

After Epicurus died, he was succeeded as Scholarch by Hermarchus, and after him came Polystratus. An ardent disciple of the new school was Metrodorus of Lampsacus. Cicero heard representatives of this school about 90 B.C. Another follower was a poet Lucretius Carus (91/51 B.C.) who wrote a poem on the new philosophy. This poem was called De Rerum Natura. Its idea was to free men from fear of the gods and death, and to bring them peace of mind.

The search for truth was of primary importance as far as Epicurus was concerned. For this reason, he did not give such weight to dialectic and logic as he gave to truth. He believed that logic had a place but this particular place was in the service of Physics. But again Physics served Ethics and so the latter discipline received more attention than the former one except truth.

Nowhere can be found a foundation in sense knowledge. He went on to point out that if one denied sensation, then one was deprived of any measure whatsoever.

The Epicureans held that certainty in astronomy was not possible, but when considering this view, we must not forget that the ancients lacked the modern scientific equipment of which we boast today.

So the first consideration is truth. The fundamental principle is Perception, the object of which is to attain what is clear. Perception occurs when images penetrate the sense organs. In this way, they never are false. Perception could be further subdivided into imaginative images; all perception coming about by virtue of sense images. It is possible for images to enter through the pores of the body as well as mentally, when this occurs they do not remain pure, and imaginative images will result. This in no way alters the fact that there is perception since both perceptions have arisen from exterior objects. Further, both perceptions as they stand are true. How then to account for error? It is a fault of judgement. The basis of this judgement is when the image possessed by us corresponds exactly with objective reality. How to be sure that this is accurate is difficult and this philosophy gives us no assistance in finding out.

What is a concept? After laying down Perception as the first principle, these thinkers advanced to describing as a second principle the concept. They said it was nothing more than an image retained by the mind. To illustrate: I have seen a horse. It makes a sense impression upon me which I retain. Afterwards, whenever I see a like animal, due to the retention of this image, I can recall a horse. Now, these concepts are always true, and it is only in the case of judgements that mistakes occur. If this concept has reference to future events, then we must appeal to experience as a guide.

A person's feelings are next considered as a measure for truth, and for behaviour. Pleasure leads to what we should do, whilst pain leads to what we should avoid.

In their survey of Physics, the Epicureans considered first a practical end. What does this mean? Principally in liberating man from fear of the gods and giving peace to the soul. Further, the object was to show that the gods did not interfere in human doings. If this were so, it was pointless for man to petition the gods. Epicurus went further than this. He went on to reject immortality, the point of which was to remove the fear of death. For according to the Epicureans, it was the fear of annihilation which causes the fear of death. Consequently, if that fear no longer exists, then there is no possible reason to fear death.

From this, Epicureanism moved to the adoption of the Atomist theory of Democritus; the reason was a practical one, as it served their particular end.

But we find ourselves going back still further. Nothing comes from nothing, and nothing passes into nothing. Had not the old Cosmologists of Greece said this? Most surely they had. That which does not exist cannot produce anything. If it were so, everything would produce everything. Again, if that which perished were destroyed completely, then other things that may follow them in existence could have no existence. The physical elements of the human body merely resolve themselves into other entities from whence they originally came. By a process of reduction, two elements are arrived at, viz. atoms and the void. The whole is a body, since our senses tell us that in every case our bodies exist, and the evidence of the senses cannot be untrue. Epicurus went on to say that this must be so, for if space were not a body, what material was there then for the senses to work on? Further, no attribute can be thought of which is not in some way an accident of some body.

The atoms are not of uniform size; they differ in form and weight. Apparently they came through the Void in the form of rain. This "raining" was not conceived as coming down straight.

Epicurus still had to explain the formation of the world. This he did by saying that the atoms in their downward path collided. But how to explain human freedom? The explanation was bound up with the atoms falling at an angle, thus forming new worlds as they went, and filling spaces which had hitherto been left unoccupied. The human soul is also made of atoms though of a finer quality than the others. There is a rational part of the soul situated around the heart which is characterized by joy and fear. Then he states that the irrational part of the soul is the principle of life. At death, the atoms separate, resulting in a loss of perception.

Thus once more we have a mechanical explanation of things. What the Stoics had held in theodicy would find little place with the Epicureans. The misery which attends on human nature at all levels connot be brought into line with the idea of a divine guidance. The gods are shown as being in a beautiful world of their own, and apparently the language used among them is Greek.

The gods in some ways resemble human beings. That is to say there are male and female forms. Also it appears that only the finest atoms were used in their composition. Epicurus needed the concept of gods for the idea of peace which he sought to convey to human beings. The question may arise if one cannot petition the gods in any way according to Epicurus, in what then does true piety consist? The answer is in the right use of reason and thought. Ultimately too, the wise man is not afraid to die, for he knows that death and its accompanying fear is due to fear of annihilation. But he does not fear annihilation, therefore, he does not fear death. As for the gods — they are unconcerned with human doings, and because of this they do not require any penance on the part of man.

The Epicurean teaching on ethics makes of pleasure a final aim in life. Everyone seeks pleasure and as a consequence of this, it is possible to live happily. But what exactly is meant by pleasure? Is it sensual pleasure, an absence of pain, an intellectual experience, or what is the definition of it? Again, could it be an instant experience, or something of a more permanent nature? In answer to this, we may say that Epicurus thought of pleasure mainly in an intellectual sense. Further, he considered it as something permanent. In itself, pleasure is not wrong. But at the same time, intense individual pleasure can produce a bad habit and consequent slavery to that habit. The result of this will be greater pain. Let us consider the question of pain. It may be very severe for the moment, but end up in producing health — as in the case of a severe operation. Thus, whilst in practice the effect of pleasure is good and that of pain is bad, the end must be thought of in either case in order to produce the maximum effect. By the process of reason, it is possible to endure even torture according to the Epicureans.

What is virtue in this philosophy? It is peace or directness of the soul, and it may be evaluated by its power to produce pleasure. Uplifting virtues bring more pleasure than do high living ambition, and so forth. Moderation, and a brightness of spirit are much preferable to these. If a man lives in justice, then he has no strife within him. Conversely, the unjust persons carry misery with them wherever they go. Probably, the Epicurean philosophy can be described as selfish. But the facts do not prove this, for it is simply the sound of their various doctrines. It was thought more meritorious to give than to receive. A person should cultivate friends in order to obtain peace of mind. Sometimes, one cannot make friends; in this case, it is better to try and live at peace with those about us. One is happiest if there is no fear from one's neighbours. It follows that confidence in one another must be a great virtue.

It is necessary for a person's life to be measured. That is to say, he must measure his actions to what is best, and not accept what appears advantageous at the outset. We also find that Epicurus makes a point of mentioning prudence as an outstanding asset, indeed as a virtue. He shows that prudence is the root of other virtues — a point that will be repeated by later thinkers — and he says unless one lives by it, it is not possible to live with honour. A definition of the virtuous man is interesting. He is not necessarily the one who enjoys pleasure, but he is the person who regulates his conduct in search of pleasure.

Along with all that has been said of this philosophy, it is possible to repeat that it might appear selfish when friendship is discussed. It seems that a friend does not exist except for some personal gain, but it must be remembered that a person loves a friend as he does himself. This surely is not uncontrolled selfishness. We must however, admit that there is an overall content of egoistic element in this teaching. Politics and peace of mind do not coincide; the politics disturbs the calm that would normally be had. This rule does not apply in the case of the man who goes in for politics for his own safety. Neither does it apply to the one person who is of such a nature that neither is it possible to live tranquilly outside this particular calling.

Two elements, those of pleasure and personal advantage stand out in the Epicurean teaching on law.

Now where does this philosophy draw for its ideas?

Leucippus and Democritus provides material for physics. The Stoics had gone to Heraclitus for their teaching on the world. From the point of view of ethics, however, the Epicureans and the Cyrenaics have much in common. But they do not agree exactly. For example, the idea of pleasure was dealt with positively by the latter, whilst a more negative approach was maintained by the Epicureans. The point of view on the mind and body also differed. The Cyrenaics considered bodily suffering as the worst, while on the other hand, the Epicurean theory of the intellect being capable of the greatest suffering was always maintained.

Despite these apparent differences, one was overshadowed by the other as the greater would overshadow the lesser. Epicureanism was on the scene, and took over Cyrenaicism.

At this point, we may recall our seven stages of development, viz. preservation of type, continuity of principle, power of assimilation, logical sequence, early anticipation, preservative additions, and chronic continuance. These, acting as one, have been faithfully followed throughout. They must be as a single intuition, though upon closer inspection, they reveal themselves as following each other in the order given. It will be upon this that we will base our conception of this development of philosophy, as these criteria apply in a universal sense.

CHAPTER 37

THE SCEPTICS AND OTHERS

We pass on now to the Sceptics who were founded by Pyrrho of Elis (360/270 B. C.). However, it must be noted that there are radical differences between this school and those which have gone before. Firstly, whereas the Stoics and Epicureans taught that knowledge will bring security and peace to the soul, the Sceptics denied all knowledge, and thus in a way became opposed to science.

Why this vast difference? The cause lies in the fact that Pyrrho had read of Democritus' ideas relating that it was not possible for human reason to grasp the interior qualities of a substance. Consequently, we know things as they appear to us as an individual. Different people will acquire different impressions; yet, none are wrong as far as perception goes. Under these circumstances, it will be very difficult to arrive at some norm of truth. What does the wise man do in such a case? He simply withholds any judgement at all. He will say nothing definite, but if pressed will introduce the notion of probability in his judgements. Thus decisive statements are not possible.

These concepts not unnaturally led to the most extraordinary complications. Nevertheless, it was what the adherents of this philosophy believed, and as such must be treated with charity and regard. In the practical sphere if I am a sceptic, I do not know if anything is right or wrong, beautiful or otherwise. I may *think* a certain thing possesses such attributes, but I can only advance a theory of probability.

According to the Sceptics, the path of action as outlined above is the path the wise man should take in acquiring peace of mind. By not entering into discussions of a decisive nature, inner peace will be maintained. The highest point here as stated above is one of probability.

We are told by Diogenes Laertius that Pyrrho spread his teaching by speech, and not by books. His follower Timon of Phlius is responsible for giving his views to the world. He composed some humorous verses, which were a parody on both Homer and Hesiod, and generally made fun of the Greek thinkers. He made exceptions of Xenophanes and Pyrrho. Timon, it seems, went further than Pyrrho had done, for he asserted that neither sense perception nor reason can be trusted. Once again in consequence of this, it is impossible to make any decisive judgement. If this is done, there will be no opportunity for the employment of specious theory, therefore the soul will remain in peace.

In later times, Cicero knew of Pyrrho, but it is doubtful if he knew of him as the founder of the Sceptic school. He preferred to look upon him as an upholder of morals, who spoke of the need of lack of consideration of externals. The question as to whether Pyrrho actually advanced the Sceptic cause is an open one. This is because there is nothing written to substantiate his theories apparently left to be passed on by tradition.

A school known as the Middle Academy followed a doctrine of Scepticism founded on Plato. Now, Plato was no Sceptic, but we find this teaching principally directed against the Stoics. The founder of the Middle Academy was Arcesilaus (about 315-241 B.C., the actual date is not certain). This thinker said he was certain of nothing, and followed the idea of not judging anything which had been taught by the Sceptics. Upon this basis, i.e., lack of precise judgement, he quoted Socrates in support of his claims, and from this, launched an attack upon the dogmatic position of the Stoics. We cannot prove anything to be false. Sense knowledge has no proof of validity, consequently, we may feel that our interior impressions equally lack decisive certitude.

Carneades of Cyrene (214/12-129/8 B.C.) founded yet a third school of philosophy which history has known as the new Academy. He followed Arcesilaus by holding that certitude is impossible in things. Apparently, if we ponder the matter, there is no sense perception which is not capable of being disproved, e.g. the influence of dreams and suchlike. Not only this, but it is evident that it is possible for people to suffer from delusions. Consequently, it does not seem that sense knowledge is reliable. Nor is it practical to appeal to reason as the Stoics do. For any concept as held must rely upon exterior objects. So we have a set of conclusions incapable of proof. This procedure can be carried to infinity. Now the Stoics will say that a universal order in things will prove a

Divine Being. But if first one *proves* this universal order, does it also prove the existence of God? But the Stoic doctrine can be carried further. They say it is rational. Very well. To be rational the thing must be animate. The latter is not proved. Thus ran the attack upon the Stoics. Again, if there is a first reason from which man's reason comes, how are we to prove that man's reason is not simply a notional phenomenon? The proof from design is well known, but it is not decisive. To design something, some power has to design; but again this is not proved.

In the face of this lack of proof, once again could not the universe be a natural production? If God is sensitive and can feel as the Stoics say, then it is possible for Him to suffer. They will say that God is brave or courageous. But what pains does He endure to substantiate this claim?

And what of Divine Providence? If Providence protects man, why does he fall into dangers? If reason is God's greatest gift to man, why is it that so many people use it to follow vice instead of virtue? If reason is what the Stoics claim, then it should not be simply "reason" but "right reason." Further, how can a competent thinker talk of neglect in God? It seems impossible that God should neglect things in His care.

The above may or may not be of interest to a general survey of this kind, but it does assist in showing, despite the contrary opinions, how the idea of philosophy remained firm and distinct. It retains what we have called elsewhere its chronic vigour.

But part of the blame for the present attack on Stoic doctrine lay at the door of the Stoics themselves, for they had adopted an atom theory which made everything, even God, material.

It is interesting to note that these thinkers were concerned with the explanation of pain and suffering. Certainly, we cannot explain this away to our complete satisfaction, but an explanation can be given in part and the fact that it *is* in part only will excuse the abandonment of any explanation at all. It is hoped to deal with this later on.

Eventually, the new Academy saw that it was impossible not to accept certitude of some description. To meet this need, they advanced their theories of probability, which meant that though I cannot be absolutely certain, I see a friend of mine in the distance, the fact that I should hear a voice, feel a handshake, and the like, should be sufficient to convince me of the probability of that particular person being present at a particular time.

But this school was not stable in its teaching. For Antiochus of Ascalon (d. 68 B.C.) led it back to dogma. Previously an agnostic Antiochus was heard by Cicero in 79/87. He (Antiochus) pointed out that if it is impossible to arrive at certainty, then all is doubtful. Now this is a contradiction, since the person who thinks must exist in order to think. It is impossible to think in any way at all, and not exist at the same time.

Antiochus was content in the assumption that his teaching was that of the great philosophers. Strictly speaking, he was an eclectic teaching Aristotle along with fragments from other thinkers, particularly the Stoics. This we see in his moral teachings. Cicero's opinion of him puts him as a Stoic more than a member of the Academy.

We next come to Terentius Varro (116/27 B.C.) who was a scholar and studied philosophy. For Varro, there is but one philosophy, and that is the one which propounds one God. God is the soul of the world, and acts as Governor by the use of reason; a great many age old myths should be discarded, for they do not give an accurate picture of the gods, and natural philosophers do not always agree. It is wrong to ignore the State's views on religion. Varro thinks that some of the concepts held at the moment could be re-thought philosophically to advantage.

Poseidonius influenced Varro in geography and culture generally, and these theories were passed on to Vitruvius and Pliny.

The Pythagoreans made much of number and mysticism and Varro adopted some of these views. Again, in later years, we will find Gellius, Macrobius and Martinus Capella thinking the same things. Varro is mentioned by St. Augustine in the City of God (chapter 2 Book VI). Augustine seemed to think he was outstanding among pagan scholars.

Finally there is another Roman eclectic and a very famous one, M. Tullius Cicero who was also a great thinker. He lived from January 3rd, 106, to December 7th, 43 B.C. His teachers in his youth were Phaedrus who taught Epicureanism, Philon of the Academy, Diodatus the Stoic, Antiochus of Ascalon and Zeno the Epicurean. In the light of the variety of teachers, Cicero had, it is not difficult to understand why he became an eclectic. His early and middle life were spent at Athens and Rhodes where his years were spent in an official capacity. But only in his closing years, that is to say, the last three years, did Cicero reconsider philosophy. He was very prolific as a writer during this time, writing fourteen full length philosophical works. One of these works, the Hortensius, will greatly influence St. Augustine. Unfortunately, it is now lost.

Cicero cannot claim unrivalled originality as can some other writers of note, but his Latin is beautiful and his style good. He found he could not rebut Sceptic doctrine, but although probably having a tendency to it, he wrote at length upon the force of conscience. He speaks of inner notions that we may have, and he does this in order to offset the probable dangers of Scepticism. These concepts, he says, are generated from nature.

He will agree that happiness should be the end of life, but this must be attained by virtue. At the same time, external goods as well seem to assist in this course for happiness. After some hesitation, Cicero points out that virtue must involve a mean. In general, he favours a practical approach rather than a speculative one.

Did God exist and if so can it be proved? Thus runs a question that fascinated Cicero and in his discussions upon it, he discarded the idea of anything mechanical, in the proof of God's existence.

The public religion should be kept intact, that is to say, purged from impurities, such as superstition and glorifying the immoral behavior of the gods. Belief in Providence is essential, and also the immortal character of the human soul.

One should be kind to one's neighbour. This concept Cicero took from the ninth letter of Plato.

CHAPTER 38

THE LATER STOICS

Some hundred to two hundred years before Christ, the Stoics garnered their philosophical material from here and from there. Mainly, they chose Platonic and Aristotelian doctrine. There were a number of reasons for this. They re-acted against the Academians and also from the fact that the Roman world was not interested in speculative philosophy, but only in its practical application. The men responsible for this Stoic eclecticism were Panaetius and Poseidonius.

The former was born 185/110-9 B.C. He resided in Rome for a while where he interested Scipio in Greek philosophy. Mucius Scaevola, the Roman historian, and the Greek historian Polybius were also influenced by him. Cicero used some of his material in his own work. In 129 B.C. Panaetius followed Antipater of Tarsus as Scholarch of Athens.

This new trend did not keep for long the set standard of Stoic doctrine. But it was not a radical change for certain Stoic principles were maintained, whilst others had to go. To illustrate: Panaetius retains the notion that the perfection of man is the perfection of his individual nature. On the other hand, he appears to forgo the idea of the possibility of being wise. In its place came the notion of proficiency. Further, we will learn that material goods are more important than has been thought hitherto, and the idea of an apathetic approach is gone. Consequently, the Stoic norm of behaviour is moderated, but now divination is gone. Astrology also found no place in this latest development. The immortality of the soul became doubtful. Popular theology was not applicable as far as Panaetius was concerned. His politics was largely influenced by Plato and Aristotle, though possibly his view was broader in scope than that of the two famous Greek philosophers.

Scaevola found three divisions in theology, and these he adopted from Panaetius. There is according to him firstly, poetic theology, which is false, philosophical theology which appeals to reason, but not for the masses, and thirdly, the theology of statesmen, where the traditional tract is found and it must be adopted for education.

Panaetius had a famous student whom we have already mentioned. This was Poseidonius of Apamaea (135/51 B. C.). He first met Panaetius at Athens after which Poseidonius travelled widely to Egypt and to Spain. He started a school at Rhodes in 97 B.C. In the year 78 B.C. Cicero paid a visit to him and Pompey the Roman general also visited him twice. No works of Poseidonius are in existence, and actually it is due to the research of scholars that we are now able to realise and appreciate his actual influence upon the philosophical world of this era. He appears as a student of history, geography, rationalist, and also as a mystic. Some have not hesitated to call him the greatest universal mind since Aristotle.

Poseidonius attempted to show that there was a connected unity in all nature. This order exists, we can assume, from the lowest mineral to God Himself. Obviously, the Divine is at the head of such a perfect arrangement and in this case, Divinity is depicted as activity acting with reason. Activity then permeates the world, the activity in question here proceeding from the sun. However, Poseidonius taught a contrary doctrine to his teacher Panaetius when he admitted of a conflagration in the world.

The idea of the world is a dual one. This trend was an influence from Plato. The two divisions that Poseidonius maintained were simply that the lower or material world is perishable whilst the supernatural or upper world is not. At the same time, the latter supports the former by the energy it gives to it. In a remarkable way, these two worlds are united in man who thus can appreciate the heavenly and the earthly horizons. Nor is this all. Since there are heavenly earthly elements in man, he is the highest of the earthly, whilst being the lowest in the spiritual order. By this notion of dualism which is met with here, the body is seen as a hindrance to the soul. Ideas of this sort were certainly inherited from Plato. Further, we understand that the soul may have pre-existence, and Poseidonius readmits immortality to the soul which had been denied by earlier Stoics. Now this would appear odd in view of the fact that he had advocated a world conflagration. Consequently, the immortality referred to is probably only proportional. There are grades in living things. This extends from a plant which is rudimentary to man who has the light of wisdom or is enabled to be given guidance and education.

We can say here that philosophy is definitely on the way to Neo-Platonism. Why is this? Let us see why.

In the first place, Poseidonius has taken a throwback to Heraclitus who found unity in difference. Poseidonius has done this by admitting unity in man. And we know that Neo-Platonism strove to unite those elements in one philosophy. Poseidonius is travelling along that same path.

Divine Providence would not see fit to prevent man from knowing of future events. In states of sleep or ecstasy, it is possible to achieve a link with the future, says Poseidonius. This then is the re-admittance of divination into Stoic doctrine.

In the realm of culture, it is the wise man who rules; he brings to others means for their betterment. An analogy might be made in the animal kingdom by saying it is the strongest beast that rules. Morality was followed by decadence, which resulted in the necessity of laws. The philosopher raised the standard of the common good, by applying himself to speculation, again for the benefit of all. We have said that Poseidonius had many intellectual interests. Wherever he gathered his material, he reduced it all to a concept of philosophy and it is in this, that his value as a philosopher lies as far as the development of philosophy is concerned.

In this transition period from Greek to Roman philosophy, we should mention Strato of Lampsacus who became head of the Peripatetic School at Athens. He held this position from approximately 287-269 B.C. He followed Democritus which would give him a monistic approach to philosophical problems. Again, we are presented with the idea that the world is contained of particles, above which there is emptiness. It is possible to divide these elements. The final qualities would seem to be the possession of warm and cold. It was natural for the formation of the world to come about, yet this formation could only be identified with God so far as God could be identified with nature. We may assume that on a universal basis, Strato followed Democritus, but this principle will not hold in particular things. His teachings will be heeded if we look forward to the period of Alexandrian studies. They followed him in medicine, astronomy and mechanics.

Strato thought it proper to equate human action with motion. Apparently the centre of the soul's activities is between the eyebrows. We can only know what has been previously a sense impression to us. The intellect takes a part in every perception.

But this is not following Aristotle, for Strato maintained throughout that there was no immortality of soul. He based this assumption on the fact that there is nothing beyond sense. Because of this, his notion of lack of immortality is quite logical, since thought can only survive in a spiritual form.

Strato had various successors, Lycon of Troas, Ariston of Chios and others, but the contribution they made to philosophy was negligible. Moreover, an electric element became apparent.

However, with the advent of Andronicus of Rhodes, things soon changed. Andronicus became the tenth Scholarch of Athens excluding Aristotle. He held this position from 70-60 B.C. He became Aristotle's first editor, and commented on the world himself, paying special attention to logic. Thus were started a line of commentators upon Aristotle ending with Alexander of Aphrodisias who gave lectures on philosophy from 198-211 A.D. This scholar was a fine thinker in many ways, but he did not hesitate to give his own views in opposition to Aristotle. His views ultimately led him to deny the soul's immortality. Why did Alexander fall into this trap? Mainly, it was due to his opposite views, coupled to remarks of Aristotle which were not sufficiently clarified.

The Posterior Analytics were dealt with well by Alexander, and they deal widely with logic. He points out that logic is deserving of as much attention as other parts of philosophy, despite the fact that it serves philosophy. To illustrate: man can become most like to God by contemplation. But this contemplation has to be shown by demonstration. This demonstration must therefore be held in high esteem for it throws light upon contemplation itself.

The physician Galen (129-199 A.D. approximately) and Aristocles of Messana taught of an active nous or mind which works throughout all nature.

The later Peripatetics could hardly deserve the name, and indeed gradually they became absorbed in Neo-Platonism. This represents the final effort of Greek philosophy to unite itself. Peripatetics after this time were either eclectics or commented on Aristotle.

A thinker named Themistius who was a pagan was born in 320 A.D. and died in 390 A.D. He taught at Constantinople and chose Aristotle as his master. He commented upon the philosopher's works and later on, however, became influenced by Plato.

CHAPTER 39

STOICS (CONTINUED)

Philosophy had to be practical to be of any use to the Roman Empire. It is not an idle boast to maintain that it did not fail in supplying this demand. The Stoics laid down sound practical principles which provided a firm basis for understanding the relationship of man to God and also to his fellowman. Choice or eclecticism however, was not absent from the Stoic deliberations. Science was not dis-regarded by the Stoics, and in the material left to us by Seneca, we gain a fair overall picture of the scientific advances which were made. We possess four of the eight books where Flavius Arrianus reported the lectures of Epictetus; in addition the meditations of Marcus Aurelius demonstrate the Stoic philosopher in a different sphere.

Annaeus Seneca of Cordoba was tutor to Nero. It was Nero's command that was responsible for Seneca committing suicide in 65 A.D. In all Seneca's writings, the practical is emphasized, there is little attention to the wherefore from a theological standpoint. Consequently, we do not find philosophy sought for its own sake, but as a means to something else, in this case a means to virtue.

It seems that philosophy studied for itself is a waste of time, only when a practical end is served is it useful. Physical theories do not go unheeded, but it is in bringing one's passions under control that we find man most like to God. Although Seneca does not think that philosophy should be studied for itself, he is not against the idea of the study of nature as an end. He speaks quite clearly of man as a combination of body and soul. Also he mentions the conflicts that such an arrangement must inevitably bring. However, evidence of Platonic thought cannot be ignored here. Virtue and happiness come from within, and no external thing whatever has the power to make man completely happy. It is certain that Seneca had the opportunity of seeing great wealth and fear of personal safety make psychological imprints on individual minds. Further, being at court he had unrivalled opportunities of seeing human nature in the grip of lust and debauchery of all descriptions.

It has been said by some writers that Seneca did not live up to his own moral teachings. But in the atmosphere in which he passed his life, it would be surprising if he did at all times maintain behaviour at the peak of moral perfection. A human being tends to become like his immediate surroundings. But this does not detract from the fact that he was utterly sincere. He knew of the force of temptation to lust, debauchery, avarice and so on, and he knew this from his own experiences and from observation. But such accurate knowledge as this lends force to a writer's words.

Seneca maintained that if a person is in control of reason, then that person can lead a good life if only he wills to do so. God will help such a person. If an effort is made to conquer the passions such a person would be better off than the ancients who were innocent from ignorance and absence of temptation.

The aim of this philosophy was to found moral ideals that were encouraging; where a person once having fallen to temptation fell yet again, and even so, would struggle to a better life. Naturally this would require the Stoic doctrine to be revised considerably. Not only this, but the transition from sin to virtue is not done at once. Because of this, we find three classes of what Seneca calls proficients. Firstly, there are those who have given up some of their sins, but not all. Secondly, there are those who wish to renounce their sins completely, but fall back occasionally. Thirdly, there is the group with sufficient will not to relapse, but who are still wanting confidence in themselves. They are the nearest to virtue and perfect wisdom.

Money and suchlike Seneca holds can be for good ends. If a wise man has money, he will always be master of it, and never the other way about. Advice is given on how to advance spiritually, the great thing here being self-examination daily, which Seneca himself practised. There is no point in this however, if no attempt is made to change oneself; further a change of place will not matter for wherever you are there is always the same bitter moral struggle within.

All men need each other's help. Thus there is a relationship between all men. Again, if anyone has been cruel or evil to us in any way, we must forgive him. He also advocates what amounts to active alms giving. At the same time, those who do evil should receive punishment. If we want to reform someone, punishment should be light. Never should it be carried out in rage, or an atmosphere of revenge.

A freed slave named Epictetus of Hierapolis next claims our attention. He was living from 50-138 A.D., and was freed by the Emperor Domitian, who expelled philosophers from Rome in 89 or 93 A.D. After this, Epictetus founded a school at Nicopolis in Epirus and spent the rest of his life there. Whilst at Nicopolis, he was heard by Flavius Arrianus who composed eight books on what he had heard. Of these, four are remaining.

Apparently, Epictetus had maintained that everyone could be happy as a gift of God. After all, self control and steadfast purpose are God's gifts. Is it true then, in the face of this, that Man's real nature is to commit sin? No, it is not; his real nature is to strive to do good and wish others well. All have sufficient moral interior sense to build up a good moral life when we praise people, praise is given to all classes, consequently all must possess these fundamental qualities.

Yet in spite of this, moral notions need strengthening, and for this purpose, instruction is necessary. True enough, these concepts are universal, but difficulty and weakness in their application will arise in particular cases. Education should aim at arming a person with practical knowledge and this it can do in two ways. First, to learn to apply universal principles to particular cases, and secondly, realizing that certain things are in our power to do, and others are not. A whole host of events would appear unavoidable, such as lack of wealth, or health, being out of favour with the Emperor, loss of friends, etc., but it is reassuring to know that these do not depend entirely upon the individual. But if these are beyond the will, judgements on various happenings are within it; further he can, by the advantage of education, bend his will to a right course.

What arises from this? Well, it is not enough for mc to merely *want* to be good, for that is simply wishing. I must *will* to be so, and with an iron will in order to offset temptations that will beset me. The human will is easily shaped however, and it must be remembered that the seeds of happiness come from within, as do the seeds of unhappiness.

Moral sins show a bad will. But this will can be overcome. How is this done? Simply by taking counsel with oneself, since no one has greater power of persuasion over the person than the person concerned.

Daily examination of conscience is excellent. Shun bad companions and places that can lead into sin. Nevertheless, if we do sin, we must struggle to raise ourselves afresh, keeping in our minds the ideal of a particular sage who happens to take our fancy. Always remember that God is always watching and our efforts must be directed to Him rather than to the wise man.

Again, we find a three stage advance in moral progress specified. First, all desire must be under reason, thus keeping emotions and feelings under control.

Second, a person must be trained properly to act as son, brother, or citizen.

Third, this stage is one of reflection by which the other two are fixed. This produces moral certainty.

A person has various duties to himself such as keeping clean which he must not neglect. Temperance, modesty, chastity are all upheld and the ways of adultery are subject to invective.

Money can be pursued, provided the end for which it is obtained is good. Epictetus says he would follow this sort of path himself. At the same time, it is easy to strive to acquire useless things, and it is then a person sees true foolishness.

Piety is a good thing. The main thing in piety is to have a proper opinion about the gods. Some will say for example, that a Divine Being does not exist. Others will not care if He exists or not. Again, there are people who staunchly maintain He does exist. This type will say sometimes that God only cares for heavenly things, whilst a fourth group will say that God exists and cares for everything both heavenly and earthly. A fifth type will not believe in God unless they can have complete knowledge.

Marriage is encouraged, though people who preach are exhorted to remain celibates. In this way, he is free to serve God in a more complete way. Obedience to the father is necessary, unless the latter directs to some obviously evil way. A person should be patriotic and take part in public life. War is not a good thing, and any ruler should show example to the nation he serves by his care for them.

To return a bad act for one done to us is not good. This conception bases itself upon the idea that the actual reason of other people's contempt of us is our lack of ability to do harm. But this is absurd. People despise their fellow men for the lack of goodness in them. There are, however, real occasions where punishment is merited, and in this, Epictetus does not differ from other Stoics.

Next, Epictetus deals with the Cynics whom he appears to have admired in some ways. He admired the manner in which they treated exterior things. This is logical for his own notion of happiness came from an inner disposition. So he says that if happiness is looked for in exterior things, unhappiness must result. Consequently, to acquire happiness, some mortification is necessary; otherwise unhappiness will be the result.

We pass on now to Marcus Aurelius, the Roman Emperor from 161-180. He composed a work of Meditations in Greek in twelve books. He held Epictetus in high regard, and Seneca, as well. Aurelius gave their thought a religious foundation. It is shown how close man can be to God under Divine Providence, and also the love necessary between all men. It is remarkable to think of a Roman Emperor talking in terms of compassion for the weakness of human nature. When, for example, one does us wrong, do we consider the viewpoint good or bad, that led to such an act? If our view is the same as the sinners, then we will surely understand. Further, a special gift is given man to be sorry for those who make mistakes. This arises from the fact that we are all related under God and such action was possibly not meant. Anyway, life is short, and no permanent injury is done. The organs of the body do not require payment for their action, a realization of their being is sufficient, and this clearly shows man is made to be kind.

Stoic materialism is lessened in this philosophy. It may be somewhat confusing as to why in the reign of one Emperor with such obvious Christian principles, the Christians themselves were persecuted. The answer lies in the fact that Aurelius upheld polytheism and he thought of a good citizen as one who maintains the State's laws. Marcus Aurelius divided man into three parts, memory, soul and mind. Two influences are clear here, that of Plato and that of Aristotle.

Mind is the greatest gift of God to man. It is indeed an echo of God Himself. It cannot be disregarded without disaster, the result being possible immorality as well as irreligion. To sum up: live with God and avoid wickedness.

Only a limited immortality was possible after death. The Emperor teaches that the soul is absorbed into Reason once again, and he compares this process to that of a river. But this does not alter the fate of the soul.

CHAPTER 40

CYNICISM AND OTHER DEVELOPMENTS

If we must seek a reason for Cynicism in philosophy, the answer is to be found in the moral disintegration of the Roman world. This is why a great increase in correspondence by such people as Diogenes and Crates is noted at this time. There are fifty-one letters by the former and thirty-six by the latter.

Again, such writers as Seneca, addressed himself to those at court almost exclusively. These members of the Roman court felt the grip of the fierce temptations of the flesh. Yet, at the same time, they suffered from satiety. Hence they were only too willing to listen to someone who could help them as indeed the case is today in many walks of life. But these upper classes were not the only people. There was the "man in the street" who was not influenced by Seneca, although Stoic philosophy had had some influence upon him. For the benefit of such people, the Cynics came into existence. These were men who might be styled as preachers. They were not as the rich classes, and they came to speak to the common man. One of them, Apollonius of Tyana was a mystic and he spoke of rivalry in Smyrna, the town being torn apart by political factors. He spoke again at Olympia to the crowd gathered there for the games. Another celebrated Cynic was Musonius who argued with the troops of Vespasian. He spoke of the horrors of war. Demetrius on another occasion defied the Emperor Nero, and was praised by Seneca for this action.

Naturally they had their detractors. One of these was Lucian who spoke of the Cynics' bad manners and obscenity in general. It is true that in the main Lucian treated the Cynics without sympathy; at the same time, he was not alone in his condemnation of them. He was followed by Martial, Petronius, Seneca, Epictetus, and Dion Chrysostom, the latter plainly stating that far from being philosophers, the Cynics held science in contempt. There was some truth in the assertion that the Cynics were egoistical. Demetrius who had spoken against Nero, thought nothing of insulting the Emperor Vespasian. The effect of this is very noticeable, as Nero and Vespasian were not alike in character. But the latter ignored Demetrius. However, these were not the only instances of Cynic bad behavior. When, for example, a Cynic named Proteus burnt himself to death to show his contempt for death, Lucian interpreted this action as a love of publicity. Vanity would hardly be the only motive prompting a man to take his own life.

But this philosophy does not lay itself open to overall condemnation, for it had its good adherents. Such a one was Demonax A.D. 50-150, who received overall praise for his good works. To illustrate: when the Athenians proposed gladiator shows in the city, Demonax suggested that they first remove the altar of Pity. The inference is obvious, i.e., a gladiator show and pity do not go together. In addition, he lived a simple life, but this did not prevent him being brought before the court on a charge of impiety. This was because he refused to sacrifice, saying that God does not need such things, and he also would not be initiated into the Eleusinian mysteries. He said if such things were for the common good, it was his duty to let people know; if they were against the common good, he must also be against them.

Another Cynic, Oenomaus of Gadara, refused to follow pagan fables dealing with the gods, and attacked divination and oracles. He claimed the latter were pure deception, for in any case, a normal person has free will and is responsible for his actions.

Probably, the most outstanding Cynic was Dion Chrysostom who was born about 40 A.D., and died in the reign of the Emperor Trajan. He was of aristocratic birth, his family coming from Prusa in Bithynia. He started his career as a rhetorician, he was later banished from Bithynia and Italy in 82 A.D. After this, he led a wandering life in extremely poor circumstances. It was during this time, that he became converted as a Cynic, and maintaining his rhetorical style, presented his orations in an attractive manner to the man in the street. His first principle was living in conformity with God's will, and with true virtue as its aim. He shows that a country person is freer than one who lives in a town, but the question presents itself, how can a town dweller live virtuously, when surrounded with so many temptations to luxury, or what is harmful to the soul or body? Apparently, even in those days, people had a wrong sense of values for Dion finds it necessary to warn them against this. Happiness is not in luxury, but in true piety. He gives examples of past empires — Alexander the

Great's among them. What are they now? Just a heap of bricks. When he arrived at Alexandria, he upbraids the people for their vices, and lust for sensation.

On the whole, Dion could be regarded as a Stoic; his social teachings were derived from that source. Thus, as God rules the world, so should an Emperor rule a State. Again, as there are many phenomena in the world, it can be seen that harmony exists between these agents. In like manner should the various States live in harmony with each other.

But Stoicism was not the only influence in Dion's life. He inherited from Poseidonius the idea of a theology in three parts, i.e., of philosophers, of poets and that of the State. Eventually, Dion became a favourite of the Emperor Trajan, who invited him to ride in the royal carriage. It is doubtful if Trajan would have understood everything Dion said, but this does him no injustice.

Before the court of Trajan, Dion gave many addresses. He pointed out that the good ruler looks after his people whilst the tyrant does not. A good ruler must be a religious man not open to flattery.

The fact that there is order in the universe provided Dion Chrysostom with a proof of God's existence. It is natural to wonder what He is like and the poets provide material for thought in this matter. The same task is approached by artists, sculptors and the like. These are not so successful, since you cannot adequately portray the nature of God out of stone or marble.

There was such a thing as Christianised Cynicism. Maximus of Alexandria arrived at Constantinople in 379 or 380 A.D. He became a friend of St. Gregory Nazianzen and was made Bishop in St. Gregory's absence. Thereafter, Maximus followed the Stoics, but without conciseness.

Repeatedly, it has been mentioned that various schools of philosophy became *eclectic* which means choosing. Accordingly, one such school was founded by Potamon of Alexandria in the reign of the Emperor Augustus. Its eclecticism ranged from the Stoics and Peripatetics to a commentary on Plato's Republic by Potamon himself.

The scope of this school increased with time however. We find Sextius including Pythagorean elements such as self examination and abstinence from flesh meat and then later again there is the doctrine of metempsychosis introduced by Sotion. The School

226

did not carry great influence except to mention Seneca as a pupil of Sotion.

Meantime, the Academy had fallen into Scepticism. It was Pyrrho wro revived it, and following him we have Aenesidemus of Knossos who can be regarded properly in the role of the real revivalist. He wrote eight books emphasizing how a practical line of thought should be followed. Pyrrho would have agreed with this, for he believed that Law, custom, tradition and the like can be adopted to practical purposes.

In his eight books, Aenesidemus laid out ten points in favour of the Sceptical position. This work was composed about 43 A.D.

First: Differences of things are simply different ideas of the same object.
Second: Differences in phenomena mean the same.
Third: The structures of the senses in each sense are different.
Fourth: The different perceptions of things are due to different states (e.g., age).
Fifth: Differences in perspective are deceptive.
Sixth: Objects as we see them are never in a pure State but mixed.
Seventh: Quality can offset perception.
Eighth: Relativity generally.
Ninth: Impressions are in proportion to perceptions.
Tenth: Morals, laws, myths, etc., imply differences.

Eventually, this list was reduced by Agrippa from ten to five points thus:

First: Variable views concern the same thing.
Second: The proof of anything is an infinite process.
Third: Objects appear differently to various people on account of various temperaments.
Fourth: Dogma is arbitrary in order to escape a regress into infinity.
Fifth: The necessity of including in the proof of anything the conclusion itself is tautologous.

The above were still further reduced to two:

First: Nothing can prove itself. Witnesses to a certain proof are necessary.
Second: It is not possible to render anything through anything else except if it be taken to infinity or involve a tautology.

It is worthwhile to note that these observations are based upon perception. But on the other hand, perception cannot err, and if there is error, this lies in the judgement.

Most of our material for the Sceptic doctrine comes from Sextus Empiricus (born A.D. 250). He maintained that it was impossible to prove anything by a syllogism. To illustrate: If I say "all men are mortal" I must employ induction to know that such a fact is so. How, if I move to the conclusion that "Socrates is mortal," is it impossible to know this without first knowing that all men are mortal? This idea will be revived by J. S. Mill in the nineteenth century. But his argument is only tenable if we substitute nominalism for Aristotle. Why is this? If by perception the essence of man is considered, then it must be taken in its universal context as including all men. Otherwise it is not universal. Consequently, the premise: "All men are mortal" takes its foundation from the universality of man's essence. Any conclusion contained in the major premise is implicit only, and the logical sequence enables the mind to move to an explicit consideration of fact.

It is true too, that the Sceptics argued against what constitutes a cause, but it must be remembered that all causes are relative, and this relation is contained within the mind. Further, a cause cannot be a simultaneous thing, and the effect can be either before or after.

Sceptic doctrine also sought to prove that God is either infinite or finite. If He were the first He would be unmoved, and so without a soul. On the other hand, if He were finite, He would be less than a complete unit. But it is shown that God is perfect. Neither were the Stoics clear upon the notion of Divine Providence. There is much suffering in the world which God could prevent if He so wished. As it continues, it is conceivable that God cannot prevent it. One cannot however, think along these lines and still have an adequate notion of God. Presuming that God could stop suffering through His power, one cannot explain why His help extends to some and not to others. Through this, we assume there is no Providence whatsoever.

Practical life demands that perception and thought be followed, as must be the satisfaction of instincts. To *look for* is the great thing in this life.

CHAPTER 41

A PYTHAGOREAN REVIVAL

In the first century B.C., there was a revival of Pythagorean philosophy. This is important for two reasons. First, because it assisted the religious life of the times and secondly because it is a decided step to what we know as Neo-Platonism. This revived Pythagorean philosophy came to be partly out of respect for Pythagoras but we have seen that at this stage, philosophy tended to be eclectic. So the new Pythagoreans became eclectic also. In addition to large slices of doctrine taken from Plato and Aristotle, emphasis was laid upon the relationship of the soul to the body. Indeed, colouring the whole of philosophy from Greek times to the present era, there is this interest on *how* the soul is connected to the body, as if in a tuneful harmony. Some early writers have actually spoken of the "harmony" of the body.

This revived philosophy was not united under one banner in absolute fashion, that is to say, each member was quite free to develop his own thought along those particular lines that suited his nature. Because they spoke of direct contact with the Deity, it is not surprising that this should give rise to reports of wonder workers from among them. Such a one was Apollonius of Tyana.

We are indebted to Sextus Empiricus for information concerning the new school. Everything they say starts from a point which generates a flow of lines which develop into surfaces, and from surfaces to three dimensional bodies. This is an older conception of Pythagoreanism based on the idea of one and the science of mathematics. But it can also be considered in another way. The development of surfaces can lay emphasis upon the plurality of such a system. This philosophy did eventually develop along these lines. We cannot look for originality in the new Pythagoreanism, only the idea of emanation is a bridge to Neo-Platonism.

This concept came about by the wish to keep God separate from the material world and thus maintain His supremacy. He is beyond all being. Probably, such an outlook was influenced by Judaeo-Alexandrian philosophy and various oriental factions as well. It is not over-stepping the mark to say that in germ it existed in Plato's mind. We find Apollonius of Tyana making a sharp definition between the first God and all other Gods. It is wrong he says to offer to the first God material sacrifice, since all material things are tainted with impurity. This God deserves nothing but the service of our highest faculty, i.e. the reason.

Next, there is Nicomachus of Gerasa (in Arabia) who was born about 140 A.D. He wrote a work on mathematics. He spoke of Ideas existing before the world; these ideas are numbers. Both these notions are from Plato. But these numbers are not existing in a world apart, but are in the Divine mind. Accordingly, they became types from which things in the world were patterned. This will be found in the thought of Philo and middle and late Platonism. We may see a link there with Christian times. The ideas of God's mind had come to be before Neo-Platonism which passed it on to the Christian Era. But other Platonic influences were at work elsewhere. Numenius of Apamea in Syria was well acquainted with the Jewish philosophy at Alexandria. He lived in the second century A.D. He held Plato in high esteem. He held to a Principle of Being. Such a power is also Pure Thought; for this reason it is not connected in any way with the world. But this is not all. He is also the Good. It would seem here that Numenius took Plato's form of the Good and Aristotle's concept of God for the same thing. But he follows Plato in the idea of the Demiurge forming the world. Numenius takes the world as created by the Demiurge from ideas and matter to be a third god.

This philosopher understands man as being in possession of two souls, one reasonable and the other unreasonable. It seems that the fact that a soul has to enter a body is something evil, and this idea will persist intermittently for many centuries. To summarise, the content of this philosophy: It is a synthesis of former thinkers with emphasis laid upon divine eminence.

There are two forms of literature in connexion with this new Pythagoreanism. The first is Hermetic Literature and the second Chaldaic Oracles. The first arose in the first century A.D. and there is some speculation as to whether it owes its origins to Egyptian writings. The Greeks found the God Thoth in Hermes. Consequently, they arrive at the name Hermes Trismegistos which comes from the Egyptian "great Thoth." But its Egyptian derivation is not all certain; there seems more probability it owed to Poseidonius. Its main point that salvation is possible through knowledge of God will eventually lead to Christian gnosticism. That is why it is included here, to make the historical sequence as complete as possible. The same central point of salvation was made in the Chaldic Oracles which were composed about 200 A.D.

At the beginning of the section, the name of Apollonius of Tyana was mentioned. A rhetorician named Philostratus wrote a life of Apollonius at the request of Julia Domna the second wife of Septimus Severus. By a somewhat devious way, Philostratus appears to have come by his material, but his overall intention is to represent Apollonius as a Sage. In addition, Philostratus appears to have knowledge of the Acts of the Apostles, the Gospels, and the Saints. He presents a Christ somewhat in Greek dress; but this is a fault of overemphasis. Despite the creditable points from this work, it is hard to discover Apollonius the man.

However, the work was well received, and it led to Apollonius being honoured in many ways. While he was thus honoured in Christian circles, this did not prevent pagan influences using his image to lessen the impact of Christianity. Hierocles, Governor of Lower Egypt, cited his "miracles" to offset the interest those of Christ had aroused. Further, it was made a point of pagan wisdom to show that Apollonius, although he was a "miracle" worker, was not thought of as God. Porphyry will also speak to Apollonius and so will St. Augustine.

This book, written in the year 200 A.D., was translated into Latin towards the end of the fourth century. The name of the translator was Virius Nicomachus Flavianus, a pagan; the work aroused considerable interest among Christians, and it was further revised by Sidonius Apollinaris.

CHAPTER 42

RENEWED PLATONISM

In the development of philosophy various tendencies have been associated with the overall philosophical idea. One is Scepticism, another is Dogmatism, on the part of the middle and new Academies. Nor must we be surprised at this. For one thing, the lectures of Plato were not in existence, and this led to an avid study of his more popular dialogues. Nevertheless, this left a gap in Platonic doctrine which the lectures should have filled. Consequently, Platonists took over forms of logic, upon which Plato himself had never held discussions. This logic was that of the Peripatetics, and provided the Platonists with a sound basis for further deliberations.

In addition, the religious need was felt just as strongly in this new Platonism, as it was in the new Pythagoreanism. The former had to go to the latter for help in formulating doctrine. Thus we will find a likeness between these two systems in some respects — for instance, in a belief in mysticism.

There was also an upsurge in the study of the Platonic dialogues, and commentaries were written upon them. This was the reason for the reverence shown to the memory of Plato, and to the man himself, at this period. Again, this tended to separate the Platonic system from all others. Indeed, there are to be found writings opposing those systems of philosophy which were not Platonic, such as the Peripatetics and the Stoics. Now, these two latter systems were opposites in character. So it was not possible for this middle Platonism as it is called, to be one unified body of thought. But middle Platonism is a mark of development, which would lead to Neo-Platonism where is found a true synthesis of thought between the teachings of Plato and Aristotle.

The two streams of thought at this period Peripatetic and Stoic, is found in Eudorus of Alexandria (app. 25 B. C.). He said that philosophy directed one to the use of the highest faculties, and that God is supreme. Socrates, Pythagoras and Plato had taught the same thing, and this shows a wide choice on the part of Eudorus. He agrees with the new Pythagoreans, also, in finding a three in one God. But this did not prevent him from writing a work against Aristotelian tendencies in philosophy. The next thinker, Plutarch of Chaeronea, was the author of a work on the lives of Greek and Roman thinkers, statesmen, and soldiers. He was born in approximately 45 A.D. and received his education in Athens. A Platonist Ammonius taught him mathematics. Often Plutarch paid visits to Rome where he knew a number of important people. The Emperor Trajan honoured him by giving him the rank of consul and later Plutarch became Archon Eponymos of Athens, and was for some years priest to the Delphic God, Apollo. He wrote quite a number of works including the lives referred to above, Moralia, and Commentaries on Plato. Also, there were books on psychology and astronomy, ethics and politics. He also included a survey of family life, pedagogy and religion. It is worthwhile to note that a number of works supposed to be by Plutarch are spurious, e.g., the Placita. What then was the content of this writer's thought? Firstly, it shows a tendency to eclecticism for he chose from most major schools of philosophy that had gone before him. Secondly, there is a decided effort to arrive at a purer conception of God. Consequently, emphasis is laid on prophecy and revelation which in its turn will help to give the idea of ecstacy to Plotinus. But this viewpoint caused him to deny God allowing evil in the world. This fact left Plutarch with the task of explaining the cause of evil. As an explanation, he gave the World-Soul which is thus compared as something imperfect to the perfect Goodness of God. But it seems at the point of creation that the World-Soul, now the principle of evil, was filled with reason which is derived from God. As it is now, the World-Soul is not entirely bereft of reason, so a dualism of good and bad is present.

Now, if God is so far above the world, it is understandable that lesser beings should be introduced under Him. This was not entirely new for Xenocrates and Poseidonius had introduced the idea of demons. These are as a bridge between God and Man. Some are closer to God, whilst others are akin to earth. The former are God's instruments of Providence. Plutarch did not believe in myths; he followed Poseidonius in a three-fold theology, which, at the same time, did not prevent him being sympathetic to the religion prevailing at the time. His point of view is that man worships God in many forms and under different names.

In psychology, Plutarch shows the influence myths had had upon the popular mind. He turns to the relationship between the Psyche and the Mind. As the Psyche is superior to the body, so the mind is superior to the Psyche. The passions are centred in the Psyche, so it is obvious that the mind, free from such burdens, should rule. Plutarch believed in immortality holding that there was happiness in the after life, where too, the companionship of friends once lost, is renewed. In his ethics, Plutarch maintains a golden mean principle. But he follows the Stoics in permitting suicide.

The world was created in time, and this world necessitates God being prior to the world. There will be found five elements and also five worlds.

In the second century A.D., a pupil of Gaius the Middle Platonist, distinguished the Father, God and the Mind and the Psyche. This philosopher's name was Albinus. He said that God the Father is unmoved, as Aristotle had taught. Nevertheless, He is not the mover of other things and so comes to be identified with a Supreme Being or God. This God works through the Mind or World Intellect. Between God and the world there are lesser gods or stars. An adoption of Plato's Ideas is used to explain the pattern of earthly things, and their relationship to Perfection. But the doctrine of Aristotle was not ignored either. For example, although the form of a thing is assumed to be a copy, the idea of God as unmoved, and not acting directly is Aristotelian. But when we come to examine the concept of God, Plato's doctrine is well in evidence. To illustrate: an Idea produces another idea and so on; but there is no indication where such a process would end. There is a gradual ascent to God through Beauty; this is yet again another Platonic concept. The influence of the Symposium can be seen here, as can the Timaeus, when Albinus speaks of the influence of the World-Soul.

The general worth of this thinker can be summed up in that he provided solid foundation for Neo-Platonism. He did this by fusing or attempting to write Plato's thought and that of Aristotle together. Once again to illustrate: The distinction between Father, God and the Mind, and Psyche will lead to the Neo-Platonic Being, Mind and Psyche. In psychology, and ethics, Albinus chose to follow Aristotle and the Stoics and probably, it would be hard to find a more perfect example of the complete eclectic.

Several other Middle Platonists follow Albinus. They are Apuleius (about 125 A.D.), Atticus, 176 A.D., Celsus and Maximus of Tyre, both about 180 A.D. Of these, Atticus remained more faithful to true Platonic doctrine, and probably this was the reason he wrote against Aristotle for the latter's not taking into account Divine Providence. Other points in Aristotle with which he disagreed were the eternity of the world, and not making clear his ideas on immortality. However, Atticus had absorbed a good deal of Stoic elements into his thinking, which would possibly account for this. We are of this opinion because of the stress laid upon Divine Immanence and the sufficiency of virtue which seem to some extent to oppose the Peripatetic idea that worldly goods are in a degree needed for human happiness. Overall, he maintained the Platonic Ideas making the Demiurge convertible with the Good. Matter was then the evil existent principle.

Celsus was opposed to Christianity. He wrote a work against it in 179 A.D., which was replied to by Origen. It is through this reply by Origen that we knew Celsus' work. God is completely above all things, and no material thing is the work of God. However, we have once again the concept of "Demons" to bridge the gap between God and the material universe.

Much the same line was followed by Maximus of Tyre. There is the transcendence of God upon which Maximus speaks very fully. He stresses that the ideal prayer to God is one of goodness, peace and hope.

CHAPTER 43

PHILOSOPHY, GREEKS AND JEWS

Philosophy, developing as it were through its particular modes, was bound in time to bring together two of the most famous nations of the ancient world. These were the Greeks and the Jews. The starting point of Greek philosophical influence was at Alexandria, but even if we look at Palestine itself, we will find traces of it reflected in a Jewish sect known as the Essenes. This sect was mentioned by Josephus in 160 B.C., and they show an influence both of the Orphics and the Pythagoreans. For example, they maintained a dualism of body and soul, believing also that the soul existed before its birth with the body. Fleshmeat was not acceptable, and neither was wine. When Antiochus Epiphanes tried to make all Jews in Palestine accept Greek thought and ways, it is noteworthy that he could rely upon certain support from within Palestine itself.

It was at Alexandria, however, that the real impact of the Greeks upon the Jews was felt. The Jews away from home seemed more ready to accept Greek thought, and we find this exemplified in Philo the Jew. It would almost seem that the Greeks and Jews together strove to unite Greek philosophy with Jewish theology. There were two reasons for this. Certain elements in Greek speculation would illustrate Jewish theology; secondly, portions of Greek thinking would harmonise with those of the Jews. Consequently, we find Jews claiming that the Greeks were dependent upon Jewish scripture for their inspiration. But this has no foundation in fact. Plato is the Greek philosopher concerned.

Thus we can turn to a consideration of Philo of Alexandria, who was born about 25 B.C., and died about 40 A.D. At the time of his death, he was Ambassador for the Alexandrian Jews to the Emperor Gaius.

The point of this thinker's philosophy will be to show that points of common truth are present in both Greek philosophy and the Jewish Scriptures. He pointed out, however, that when it is stated that God moves, this must not be understood in an absolute sense, because God is not a body, and we think of things moving as being corporal things only. Consequently, there is a "higher" and a "lower" meaning to Scripture, as is fitting to the understanding of various people.

It could be possible for this understanding to go beyond the limit of the Law, but if one is capable of the higher meaning of Scripture, then one is also discerning and, accordingly, will not fall into traps of this description. Philo gives his reasons for this. The soul is superior to the body, yet they are parts of man. Our sense of the allegorical is higher than the literal, accordingly, we should give due weight to both.

Jewish theology will teach that God is personal; but Greek thought will say He is Pure Being and Simple. It goes on to say that God does not occupy place, but contains all things within Himself. He is in every way transcendent, surpassing even the Good, and the Beautiful. Man advances in understanding God through science and this is a slow process. Further, man can never comprehend God, for to do this, he would have to be actually God. There are two ways of approaching God. One is through intuition, the other is ecstacy. Emphasis was certainly laid by Philo upon the Transcendence of God; but this much was asserted in the Jewish scriptures. But this drift led to the introduction of intermediaries between God and the World. It would seem the highest of these is the Nous or Mind, which Philo seems to rate as decidedly inferior to God. Even allowing for the fact that this teaching influenced the early Christians, there is a gulf separating it from orthodox Christian thought. The Word appears sometimes as almost an attribute of God, but this would do little to bridge the gap that this form of thinking would engender. Scholars have noted that Philo had three courses open to him. That of Monarchianism, that of Arianism, and lastly Athanasianism. His position was that he alternated between the first two, but never entertained the last, if we understand it as not to include reference to historic Man. All Ideas of Plato are contained in the Word. Therefore, the Word is the ideal world. This is agreement with the Neo-Pythagorean element which included Ideas in the World. The Logos had two forms of activity. The first was directed to the immaterial world of Ideas, and secondly that pertaining to the material world. We discover upon further analysis that these divisions are reflected in the human person. This is shown by the observation that there is reason as a faculty in the human being; from this flows the spoken word. So it seems that the Logos or Word is used by God to form the world.

In passages in the Old Testament, reference is made to the angel of God. Philo says that this is the Logos, or on occasions where other angels are referred to, he associates them with other powers. The Word is quite immaterial and yet quite a separate entity from God and quite certainly below Him in majesty. The Wisdom found in the Sapential books of the Bible were utilized by Plato. Into this, he also brought Platonic exemplars for instance, the Logos is the Word, the image of God, but at the same time, the exemplar of all creation. In summarised form, it would seem that the Logos stood at the apex of a gradual descent through him to all lesser creation. Certainly, He could be the aim of perfection; but He was still distinct from God. Regarding God as completely above creation in all things including His degree of perfection, this concept could be valid in Philo's eyes. It is through the Logos that God acts.

With respect to the other powers mentioned earlier, this thinker seemed to have some difficulty in deciding the actual position of the Logos to God. He seemed uncertain to attribute independence to Him, or consider Him as an attribute of God. This doubt saw its way through to the Platonic part of Plato's doctrine, where again he was uncertain whether to describe intermediary powers to God or to think of them as independent, that is, corresponding to the Ideas. If all these independent creations are seen in the Logos, that is well and good; but it does not solve the question of their status. Now, we can say that the Logos is an aspect of God. In this case, the powers will be qualified in a certain sense. On the other hand, we can conceive the Logos as independent of God. In this instance, we would have to think of the forces spoken of as nothing but minor powers. Philo never arrived at a satisfactory solution to this problem. But we can go so far as to assert that if we accept his teaching then we could never accept the Incarnation. Why? Because the position of God in this doctrine precludes all contact with matter, and by the Incarnation, God became a man. Christianity is content to leave the Incarnation as a mystery, and it does not adopt Philonic or Neo-Platonist approaches to it.

Philo would maintain that soul and body were to be thought of as one, whilst the sensual element in man is quite apart. This idea he derived from Plato. Following the Greek philosopher still further, he will say it is necessary for man to be freed of the influence of the senses. Virtue will bring happiness; as regards the passions, they will be subdued by apathy. This teaching takes a new trend when Philo says it is better to trust God than man. Science is good, but only up to a point. This point is reached when it is beneficial to the person's nature; beyond that, it is dangerous. The contemplation of God or ecstacy is ranked as the highest form of knowledge. This will be developed by the Neo-Platonists.

Philo in this way helped the Neo-Platonist cause; but it is doubtful if his influence on Christian thought was as strong as some have claimed it to be. However, he conceived the concept of God above all things, a scale of intermediaries, the soul inclining to God, and pointing to ecstacy as the State wherein the soul most fittingly achieves this inclination to perfection.

CHAPTER 44

PLOTINUS, PORPHYRY AND OTHERS

Two different accounts are given as to the birthplace of Plotinus. Eunapius says it was in Lycon, whilst Suidas states it as Lycopolis. Suffice it to say he was born in Egypt, approximately 203 or 204 A.D., although Porphyry will say it was in 205/6. Plotinus studied in Alexandria; while there, he heard a great many learned men. But they did not provide him with an adequate foundation upon which to build his thought. It was not until he heard Ammonius Saccas, that he felt he had found a teacher suited to his particular nature. He was then about twenty-eight years old. He stayed with Ammonius Saccas until 242 A.D., when he went on an expedition of the Emperor Gordian, the purpose of which was to study Persian philosophy. Unfortunately Gordian was killed in Mesopotamia and Plotinus went on to Rome where he arrived about the time he was forty. There he started a school and enjoyed the favour of the highest officials even to the Emperor Gallienus himself. It was at this time that Plotinus conceived the idea of founding an ideal city to be named Platonopolis in Champagne. The idea was to be a full realization of Plato's Republic. However, the plan fell through, the Emperor for some reason withholding his consent for the project.

At the age of sixty, Plotinus took Porphyry as a pupil. In later years, Porphyry will write a life of Plotinus and will arrange the writings of the master in some form of order. There are six books of nine chapters from which is derived the name Enneads. It is by this name that we know the works of Plotinus. Tradition says that Plotinus had a flowing style in his lectures. But his writings do not bear this out, and at the time they were written by Porphyry, Plotinus had very poor eyesight. Consequently, he could not correct mistakes in the original manuscript. As a result, Porphyry started with a great disadvantage, which has been reflected down the centuries in various editions of these works.

It would seem that Plotinus had a gentle disposition; whilst at Rome many questions were put before him, he acted as guide, and director to orphans. He made many friends, and no enemies, his nature showing a very affectionate streak. Rather nervous in bearing, he however, led a deep inner life, and Porphyry claims for him ecstatic union with God four times in six years.

In the year 269/70 A.D., due to long standing ill-health, Plotinus died. Porphyry was not with him at the time of his death, having gone to Sicily upon Plotinus' advice to recover from an acute attack of melancholia. The physician Eustochius was present however, to witness remarkable words from a dying pagan: "I was waiting for you, before that which is divine in me departs to unite itself with the Divine in the universe."

Plotinus never became a Christian. This probably would account for his silence upon the subject. However, he must have had some knowledge of it, for his own life was a model of spiritual and moral ideals. Through these self-same ideals, he passed on to St. Augustine of Hippo great inspirations.

What were the salient points in Plotinus' doctrine? First, the completely transcendent nature of God. Completely above all creation, God is thought of as the One. Being and essence are known to created things and to be possessed by them, but neither of these can be predicated of God. The Divine is more than all this. Many individual entities make up a multitude, but again this Principle is beyond them, and prior to them. But such a procedure in the eyes of Aristotle would lead to an infinite regress, and to ultimate absurdity, since by it we cannot arrive at a First Mover or necessary Being. There is another point also. If we assume that the One shares in every creature's individuality, then we arrive at the point where all things are identical, and distinction which is obvious must be explained. Under these circumstances, there is no explanation, except possibly to treat it in a form of phantasy of the mind. But it is just this rock of difficulty that ensures the One of Parmenides and the One of Plotinus going different ways. Plotinus was not holding to monism in the form of Parmenides. He was claiming God as One as the Neo-Pythagoreans and Middle Platonists had taught. It is important to realize this.

The position is then that God is transcendent and He is One. But because of this oneness, Plotinus would not admit of positive attributes in God. What does this mean? We cannot say God is this or that; if we do, we apply a limit to Him and make Him lesser than He is. It is permissible to say God is Good, provided "good" is not thought of as a quality possessed by God. To avoid this impasse God is more The Good than simply "good." This same idea will apply to our concepts of thought, will, and activity in relationship to God. But this view requires further explanation. It is clear that in the act of a person thinking, the thinker and the thing thought about are separated. Therefore, this will be contrary to the concept of One. If a person wills, the fact that they are willing something, the agent and that something are quite distinct. If a person acts, they perform an action but what they act upon to produce a difference is again quite distinct. The point of this argument is to show that according to Plotinus, God is above all distinctions whatsoever. He is completely self-identical, even to the point of lacking self-consciousness of Himself. We know that God is the One, and also that He is the Good. Nevertheless, Plotinus will assert that such descriptions are inadequate.

This reasoning gives rise to the objection that since God is so completely transcendent, how can the many finite things be accounted for? On the basis of what has been said, God would surely limit Himself, if He created finite things. Further, with the data at our disposal, we cannot say that God created the world. Why? Because when a thing is created, this involves activity. It has already been said that no activity can be ascribed to God; therefore we cannot say He created the world. Plotinus answers this objection by saying that things emanate from God, whilst remaining unmoved in Himself. By this idea, the complete freedom of the Divine Will is denied. We have to accept the alternative explanation that things proceed from God in the manner of the less perfect proceeding from the more perfect. In all nature, we find this principle evident, the first principle always remaining stable and unmoved.

The question that looms upon the horizon in consequence of this teaching is how far is pantheism related to Plotinus? Care is needed to answer this question. It is true he said that the world *proceeds* and creation from nothing is held to be wrong. For Plotinus however, the "ex nihilo" principle was wrong because he thought it would involve change in God. This would destroy the principle of something unmoved. It would also impair its transcendency. At the same time, he would wish to avoid a completely pantheistic approach or monism.

Accordingly, he adopted a middle course, avoiding purely

theistic creation on the one hand, and considering God and creature as one on the other.

We are told that the first to emanate from God is the Nous or mind. It is intuition and apprehension, having two objects the One and itself. The Ideas are contained in the Nous, both as universals and particulars. Plotinus adopts the teaching from Plato's Timaeus to explain this, where the Greek had spoken of the Demiurge. It is certain that the Ideas exist in the Nous; Plotinus experienced some opposition on this point from Longinus who would say that the Ideas and Nous are not One. Longinus appealed to Plato's Timaeus where the Ideas, the Demiurge are shown as apart. Porphyry held to the same ideas as Longinus, and it says much for the persuasive powers of Plotinus that he gave up this concept.

It is clear then that in Nous we first recognize distinction. The one itself is above such division. The point here is that elements of Plato and Aristotle are brought together. The Demiurge from Plato and the Mind from Aristotle are fused into the concept of Nous which is above time and therefore eternal as regards the soul. Its successive objects are many, e.g. man, horse, or some other particular. Nous, however, has all these objects realized within itself at once.

All this results in the development of the soul which corresponds to what Plato had depicted in the Timaeus. The function of the World-Soul is to form a bridge between the supernatural world and the sensual world. Consequently, it can look both ways, at once, i.e., upwards supernaturally and downwards to the sensual. Now Plato had shown only one World-Soul; Plotinus on the other hand holds there are two, one higher in a spiritual way, and consequently nearer to the Nous, and one lower which is more in contact with the material world. The former is apparently the true soul of phenomena in the universe, whilst the latter is described as nature. The Nous possesses the Ideas which are responsible for material creation. But the Ideas do not achieve direct working in the material world. Because of this, it was necessary for Plotinus to show where and in what manner the material creations were reflected. He did this by showing them to be the World-Soul. He also said that these reflections were contained within the Word, which is a throwback to Stoic teaching. But it was still necessary to adopt this to his doctrine of two

World-Souls. To achieve uniformity, he taught of a higher and of a lower soul.

The individual comes to be as a result of action of the World-Soul. In the person, two elements are found. One is higher and close to the Nous, the other is connected with the body. The soul existed before its union with the body. This union is taken to be a fall, but the higher part survives the death of the body, and according to this teaching does not remember its former life on earth. Individuals are bound together in the World-Soul, but this is not to say there is no immortality.

There is no point in saying that because a soul has at last reached its destination, it will cease to be. Not only will it survive, but it will also retain its individuality.

Beneath the soul in the order of creation, there is the material world. The path of light is one always radiating outwards from the centre to the outer rim. There is in this light a gradual tapering off until on the edge there is darkness which is actual matter.

The One creates matter, but matter is really only one entity in the process of emanation from the One. Consequently, matter being the lowest in this emanation, it can be regarded as opposite to the One. Where it combines with material being, it is not complete darkness. When it stands directly against the intelligible, it is quite obscure. In this way, Plotinus adopts the first principle from Aristotle, and the second from Plato. This will lead to the idea that there must be a substratum in objects of some sort, which is distinct from the things themselves. If abstraction is employed, it is clear we have the form of the thing and the underlying basis for that form. Matter then is made partly active by the form, which enables it to live apart from the total darkness of non-being. All phenomena then will find their meaning in intelligibles; as in nature, matter will correspond to a Supreme idea.

In cosmology, Plotinus adopts concepts from the Orphics and Neo-Pythagoreans who held matter as a principle of evil. In its lowest state, it is completely devoid of light and stands as an opposite to the Good. At this stage, it seems clear that Plotinus comes near to dualism; but matter is introduced as a privation and not something positive. It could be argued that in view of certain points in this teaching, Plotinus could easily depreciate the visible world. But in an overall sense, he does not do this, for he shows a harmony in the material world.

There are three parts to the individual soul. The first of these based on the Nous of Aristotle is quite pure and untouched by matter. The second stage is reached when the soul unites with matter and in a certain sense becomes contaminated. By uniting with matter however, a composite is formed. At all times, the intelligible must command the sensible. The third stage of the soul is complete union with God, the ascent to which must be started by an impulse of Eros. Again, we have elements from Plato and Aristotle, the impulse referred to being mentioned in the Symposium. Then by a process of catharsis or purification, the soul gradually ascends to a point where dualism is entirely absent, it is literally one with God and a state of ecstasy is reached. In this ecstasy which lies above discursive thought, the soul retains its individuality. Such a state is hard to describe. It is possible to achieve it in this life, but only fleetingly as when the soul is not hindered by the body. Man on this earth will lapse from this vision, but it is the life of the gods beyond all material pleasures.

Plotinus employs a giant form of synthesis throughout his whole system. In it, is found a mixture of logic, cosmology, psychology, metaphysics and ethics, bound up in one body of philosophy. But this is not all, for religion and mysticism also find a place, the latter showing how it is possible to achieve the highest degree of knowledge — that of God. As a result of Plotinus' personal view, which was that mysticism holds the highest place in philosophic attainments, it is safe to assume that in Neo-Platonism philosophy passes into religion.

In the future, Neo-Platonism will prove a rival to Christianity, but because of its complicated doctrines, it could never surpass the latter. Something that breathes of mystery always attracts, but this is not to be found in Neo-Platonism. This philosophy really appealed to the intellect, and would attract those striving for personal salvation, with the accent so much upon the personal as it was at this time. Christianity on the other hand could boast of a history and with this it combined speculative thought. Neo-Platonism lacked a history. Under the Christian banner, a person could act here in order to obtain eternity which would really make of every person a missioner if he acted properly. The natural instincts were not frowned upon, but consecrated to God. Despite this however, Neo-Platonism had a definite role to play in Christianity, one where the intellect showed Revealed Religion.

It is quite fitting therefore to show the greatest of respect and sympathy to Plotinus and the system he founded.

But what of those who followed Plotinus? The first of these was Amelius who spoke of three beings in the Nous. But by far the most important was Porphyry of Tyre (born 232/3 to approximately 301) who started to study with Plotinus in Rome in the year 262. He was a prolific writer; besides the life of Plotinus, his literary scope was very large, but probably the best known is the Isagoge or a form of introduction to the Categories of Aristotle. This work was tremendously influential among the Syrians, Arabs and Armenians right through to the Middle Ages. To summarise, he also tried to illustrate that there was complete agreement between Plato and Aristotle.

But this was not the only end for which Porphyry worked. He demonstrates the thought of Plotinus in a clear lucid fashion. Its end is salvation, the emphasis being laid upon the practical and the religious aspects. Always one must strive to turn from what is lower to what is higher. The first step to achieve this is to acquire a satisfactory social intercourse with one's neighbors. The next stage is one of catharsis or purification, the purpose of which is to reduce the emotions to a proportion. After this, the soul turns directly towards the Nous. The highest stage of perfection is found in the Nous itself. But the ascent just outlined is not attained for no expense. Porphyry advocates asceticism, celibacy, etc. to train the soul to this end.

For a balanced view, one cannot ignore the positive element in the philosophy of Porphyry. He held strong belief in this existence of demons, consequently, he would not condemn out of hand various superstitious practices. The result of this was that popular religion was upheld making of the pagan myths something of an allegory. What then is the important human factor in religion? It is deeds and not words. God rewards a person for the acts which constitute his life.

However, such accurate observations did not prevent Porphyry when in Sicily from writing fifteen books against Christianity. By the order of the Emperor Valentinian III, these works were burnt in the year 448 A.D. Theodosius III also took steps to destroy them. Consequently, it is not surprising that in recent years they are only known as fragments. Some Christian writers undertook to answer him in his allegations, among others, Methodius and Eusebius of Caesarea. St. Augustine did not think of Porphyry as a Christian, although Socrates the historian says that he abandoned it on account of bad treatment by some Christians at Caesarea in Palestine. It seems that it is uncertain and indeed possibly unsafe to conclude that Porphyry ever embraced Christianity. One good reason for this is that nowhere does he say himself that he became one. He even went so far as to attempt to prevent cultured people from joining the new faith. His arguments were to the effect that Christianity involved contradictions, that it lacked nobility and was illogical. The Bible came under special attack. Porphyry denied the authenticity of the Book of Daniel, and also the veracity of the authorship by Moses of the first five books of the Old Testament. Passing to the New Testament, he cast doubt by skilful argument on the Divinity of Christ.

CHAPTER 45

NEO-PLATONISM

Neo-Platonism spread to Syria and its main advocate there was Iamblichus who died in 330 A.D. This thinker had been a pupil of Porphyry and it can in all accuracy be said that Iamblichus exaggerated the doctrines handed down to him. This is very clearly seen in the way he deals with the hierarchy of being. His aim was to emphasise the complete separation of God from the material world. In doing this, he multiplied being between the material world and God at an alarming rate. Plotinus had said there is the One identified with the Good. But Iamblichus brought in another One over and above the Good, and therefore superior to the One who was identified with the Good. Neither did the multiplications end here; for he introduced a super terrestrial soul from which come two others. In addition to this, there are many angels and demons. As they stand, the order is to say the least, confused. To render them intelligible, he brought in a scheme of numbers which did not improve the situation. Over and above all this, he maintained innate human reason inclining towards the Good.

Religion and ethics are brought very close in Iamblichus' doctrine. Working upon the material Porphyry had left, he introduced theoretical virtues by which the soul is made capable of contemplating Nous. The soul can also identify itself with Nous, and then above this state it is possible to unite with the One in ecstacy. But for this state, to take place advanced purification is necessary of all miraculous and divinations etc. which play an important role in this philosophy. He also shows that a priestly class is superior to that of the philosopher.

Iamblichus had a pupil named Aedesius who founded the Pergamene school of philosophy. One of the aims of this school was the restoration of polytheism. A work was written by Sallustius called "On the Gods and the World" directed to promoting this idea. A rhetorician named Libonius one of the Emperor Julian's tutors wrote a work against Christianity. The Emperor Julian himself 322/363 A.D., was brought up a Christian, but fell into paganism. He advocated a polytheistic approach and for this purpose employed Neo-Platonist doctrines borrowed from Iamblichus. An example of this doctrine is the worship of the sun. The reason for this supposed worship is that in his opinion the sun is half way between intelligible and sensible matter.

Back in Athens, the interest in Neo-Platonism was in full swing. Plato and Aristotle were subjects of lively commentaries. One of these, on Aristotle's "De Anima", was written by Plutarch of Athens who was the son of Nestorius an Athenian Scholar. There were further works by Syrianus who followed Plutarch as head of the school of Athens. Syrianus however, did not believe in portraying uncompromising agreement between Plato and Aristotle. In his view, a study of Aristotle merely prepared one for a study of Plato, and great pains are taken to justify the position of Plato against Aristotle's attacks. After Syrianus, there was Dominus who was a Syrian of Jewish descent. The interest of this thinker was mathematics.

The most important person under this review at the moment is Proclus 410-485 A.D. He was born at Constantinople and became an Athenian Scholarch, a position he retained for many years. He had unbounded energy, and although much of his work is not now extant, we possess commentaries on the Timaeus, Republic, Parmenidea, Alcibiades I, and Cratylus. He possessed a very extensive knowledge of the philosophies of Plato and Aristotle and notwithstanding this, his other interests were very wide. He made a giant intellectual attempt to weld this depth of knowledge into a single system, the result of which was to earn for him the position of the greatest scholastic of ancient times. Subtlety and systematic form were brought to bear on the content of philosophy left behind by others. This would be a major event in the development of this science.

Proclus employed a three pronged development in the sphere of his philosophy. This was borrowed from Iamblichus, although in the present case its application went deeper than it had done previously. All things, we are told, are centred in the One. From the One comes all things from the highest to the lowest. Now, that which proceeds must be in some way like that from which it thus proceeded. At the same time, it will also be unlike that initial principle in some part of its essence. It follows from this that as the thing which is created or proceeds conforms to a First Principle, that Principle is thus capable of self communication. Consequently, there are now two notions of movements, one remaining in the agent, whilst the other is in the way of affecting exterior things. Now it is clear that since all things resemble the First Principle in some way, they must, in the degree to which they resemble it, incline towards it. But Proclus has observed a hierarchy of being. Because of this hierarchy, there is a turning back to the First Cause on the part of those that proceed. All this really involves a remaining in the principle, a proceeding and finally a turning back. This three pronged development already mentioned is regarded by Proclus as the basis for all proceeding things.

The first principle is considered as a First Cause from which all other things branch out. Because of the manner of emanations, some things are closer to and some further away from the First Cause. This idea of unity is always primary to anything multiple. This is clear if we realize that more than one is always preferable to unity, accidental goodness to Perfect Goodness, and so on. However, Perfect Goodness is above unity, causes and goodness, just as it is above being. The position now is that we are not in a position to say that the Perfect Good *is* anything; we can only say what it is *not*. This is because it is above all discursive thought. Proclus, like Iamblichus, multiplies the concept of Nous; Being, Life and Thought are the main divisions here, despite the fact that other divisions were introduced beyond these.

Next, Proclus considers the Soul which comes between the supersensible worlds. The latter is simply a copy of the former. The divine souls are Greek Gods, although they appear to be individually multiplied.

The object of the divine souls is to direct the world which is a living creature. Evil is impossible for it is absurd to attribute evil to a divine source. What then is it? It is an imperfection which is inseparable from the natures of the lower creatures.

In all this emanation the First Cause is unmoved. It brings things into existence, without itself being changed in any way. Its essence is always complete, consequently there is not disruption on the part of the producer. Now in this, Proclus follows Plotinus in avoiding a "creation from nothing" idea, and also true monism on the other hand.

In order that the Soul might be able to attain the One, it was necessary to attribute to it a power beyond that of thought. Proclus considered this as a principle of unity by which One and the Soul came together in ecstasy. As those who had taught before Porphyry, Proclus thought of the soul as a creation of light, as such it is halfway between two worlds, i.e. material and immaterial, and cannot die. There are three main stages in the ascent to the One, viz., Eros or love, Truth and Faith. Truth takes the soul beyond love, whilst Faith imposes a silence whereby it is possible to unite with the One. Proclus was succeeded by Marinus as head of the School. Marinus was a mathematician and very orthodox in his readings of Plato. He was succeeded by Isodorus.

Finally among the Athenian Scholarchs, there is Damascius to whom Marinus had taught mathematics. In his view since it was impossible for the relationship of the One to the mind to be understood, it seemed that the mind could not know truth. All phases in any language at all are inadequate, consequently, there is a gap between these and what is real. Damascius would not abandon speculation however, and upheld superstition.

An early commentator on Aristotle was Simplicius a follower of Damascius. He wrote commentaries on the Categories, Physics, De Caelo and De Anima. Particular interest is centred on the Physics fragment as it contains data of the pre Socratics.

As a consequence of the order issued by the Emperor Justinian which prevented the teaching of philosophy in Athens, Damascius and Simplicius went to Persia. This was in 529. However, they were disappointed with the general cultural level of the Persians and they returned to Athens in 533.

Throughout the later philosophical scene Alexandria had always something to offer, and at this stage this city provided a number of commentators on Plato and Aristotle. Among these were Hypatia who was murdered in 415 A.D. by a mob of fanatical Christians.

Asclepiodotus of Alexandria (5th century) studied science, medicine, mathematics and music. Ammonius, Ioannes Philoponus, Olympiodorus all followed each other in carrying the knowledge of Plato and Aristotle to the world.

Gradually the philosophic traits of Iamblichus and Proclus were weakened within the school at Alexandria. The result of this was that Christians and pagans could meet more with a general point of view. As a result Hellenic thought persisted in Constantinople. Stephanus of Alexandria was one of the first to teach the doctrine

251

of Plato and Aristotle at Constantinople. Neo-Platonism and Christianity were further linked by Hypatia's disciple Synesius becoming bishop of Ptolemais in 411 A.D. Ioannes Philoponus also became a Christian.

He wrote a work against Proclus' ideas of the eternity of the world. To strengthen his argument he cited extracts from Plato's Timaeus, where the idea of the creation in time is suggested. Philoponus also held that Plato got much of his knowledge from the Pentateuch and it is probable that this is the beginning of a tradition which has existed down the centuries linking Plato with the Bible, although it is a mistaken one.

Neo-Platonism also exerted an influence on various pagan thinkers. Among these is Hierocles of Alexandria who had a leaning towards Middle Platonism rather than Neo-Platonism. He is worthy of mention because he teaches of but one super terrestrial being the Demiurge, and also for positing creation out of nothing. This is despite the fact that he rejected creation in time. For Hierocles, Fate is something between Divine Providence and human freedom.

There is an element of speculation among the Neo-Platonists which can be associated with the later Western culture. This is in evidence by the commentaries on Plato and Aristotle which depict a high degree of learning. Once again, it is by these means that philosophy was taught to the Roman world, and finally passed to the Middle Ages. Among these later Neo-Platonists was Chalcidius who probably became a Christian. He translated Plato's Timaeus from Greek to Latin and wrote a commentary on it as well. Then Marius Victorinus who also became a Christian in later life translated Aristotle's Categories and De Interpretatione, Porphyry's Isogorge, and other works from Greek into Latin. He was responsible for commentaries on Cicero's Topics and De Inventiones, De Definitionibus and De Syllagismis Hypotheticus were original works of his. One of Marius Victorinus' main influences was upon St. Augustine.

Next, there is Vettius Agonius Praetextatus who died in 384 A.D., who translated Themistius' work on Aristotle's Posterior Analytics and Macrobius to whom can be attributed the Saturnalia and another commentary on Cicero, this time upon the Somnium Scipionis about 400 A.D. This commentary is of interest, for in addition to the Neo-Platonist themes employed, threads of a commentary that Porphyry had written upon Plato's Timaeus are interwoven also.

Turning then to the fifth century, we find Martianus Capella writing a work which still exists called De Nuptiius Mercurii et Philologiae. During the Middle Ages, this work acquired much importance. It is in the form of an Encyclopedia which treats of the liberal arts. Books three to nine concern the seven arts in themselves. The work achieved its importance in the Middle Ages for it supplied a basis for the education of the Trivium and Quadrivium.

But oustanding by far above the writers and thinkers of Neo-Platonism in its later stages is Boethius, who will be more fully treated in the Christian section of this work. Suffice it to say here that he was born in 480 A.D., and was executed in 524/5 supposedly for treason. He studied at Athens and whilst in prison wrote his famous De Consolatione Philosophiae. He wished to translate all the works of Aristotle from Greek into Latin but this project was never realized. Nevertheless, he translated the Categories, De Interpretatione, Topics, both Analytics and Sophistical arguments. It is possible that other translations can be attributed to him. Porphyry's Isogorge received yet another translation at his capable hands, it involved the famous problem of universals which saw the parting of the ways for Porphyry and Boethius.

Other commentaries followed. He also wrote several works on theology. In showing Boethius' work on commentary and translation, it does not double up on what will be said of him in the future. The object is to emphasise that as a translator and commentator, he was the main avenue down which the doctrine of Aristotle travelled to the West.

CHAPTER 46

RECOLLECTION

One thing has become very apparent as this survey has advanced. It is that each philosophy as it absorbs in sequence other ideas, modified although they may become, remains an intensely personal thing. Plato considered that truth in philosophy could not be communicated by books; he also taught that it was the personal, or soul contact, which gave one to another the content of ideas. Naturally a lot of ground covered here was originally couched in terms strange to us, and in conditions which would not put us at our ease today. It is mainly for this reason that we have tried to avoid as much as possible this particular course, and have resorted to a notion of development which is universal, whether we work in any science whatsoever, and in any time whatsoever. However, this will need some clarification. Development is a term which is used very loosely owing to defects of language. It can stand for a process or a result. Or something true or false. Or again, for something that is a development and nothing more, that is to say, an advance from the less perfect to the more perfect. This last is the most applicable here, for if we accept it as merely true or false, we are really accepting a notion of corruption or otherwise.

On the other hand, it is quite feasible to think of development as historical; being the gradual formation of opinion, concerning people, facts and events. Notions confined to a few, will spread to many, and gain general acclamation. Because of this, other authorities will cease to be. Truth is certainly the daughter of Time. This then is the development we have dealt with here; an approximation of facts and characters. It is obvious then that these remarks are not a digression; for philosophy is subject to movement as the day is subject to movement. If a thing exists in time, it must develop and human thought and enquiry has existed for a long time. We claim most humbly that the human intellect has developed for the glory of Almighty God.

We saw very simple beginnings to the process of organized human thought. On the shores of Asia Minor, we find men like Heraclitus or Parmenides finding a wealth of mental material which language at that time could not convey. This thought developed into the mighty systems of Plato and Aristotle; it furthered its advance under the Stoics. Then the noble character of Plotinus dominates the scene and this advances into Neo-Platonism where Greek thought struggles to unify itself. In all the history of human beings, there is nothing to compare with this. It is unique for its influences are felt to this day, to this very hour. In Sicily, the Greek temples are a source of admiration. The cathedrals in Gothic style erected in the Middle Ages, the works of painters such as Fra Angelico, Michelangelo, Rubens, or El Greco all bear testimony to a glorious heritage from ancient Greece. Do we today treasure the writings of Homer, Dante, or Shakespeare? If we do, and the modern world is proud of these treasures — then equal importance must be given to those who developed the intellect to a peak of perfection not since repeated. But it admittedly is not easy to plumb the depths of Greek thought. Mental effort and concentration are needed, but the reward of say, the study of Plato and Aristotle, far outstrips the initial outlay of mental power.

In a culture of any description, balance must be sought. Today, musical composers are made much of in their particular fields. If they are to be appreciated, then Greek drama, Greek architecture, Greek sculpture are always reminders of the greatness of the ancient Greek world. But these are not the only reminders, for we cannot know it in its fullness unless we realize the scope of Greek thought.

There is a particular thread running through the whole of Greek speculation. It is its pre-occupation with the One and the many. It is evident that many exist. But the task is to see the many as incorporated in the One, and to see them *as One*. This problem is very intense in the minds of those thinkers before Socrates who sought an explanation of the world. We find these thinkers seeking a purely material explanation. Sometimes the One is predominant, sometimes the many. Then the mechanical theories of Leucippus and Democritus involve the mind never rising above matter. This is probably due to the inadequacy of language, for the concept of mind above body is far clearer in Pythagoreanism.

Anaxagoras takes this idea further to consider the Mind or Nous as a separate entity.

When the Sophists came to grips with this problem, it seems that the aspect of the many is stressed. This would include the many ways of life and the opinion and so on. The next philosophical epoch, that of Socrates, put the emphasis upon unity. Here we have the idea that to form a judgement of any sort whatsoever, it is necessary to have some unity of thought upon which to base that judgement.

Plato saw the deeper and wider scope of such a problem. He expressed the content of it in diverse ways. The many created things existing, what experience really means are seen as products of a unified existence of Perfect Ideas. These ideas were capable of apprehension by the human mind, and they led to a wider sweep in the philosopher's vision, for now not only could he consider purely material beings, but heavenly ones as well. Now these immaterial creations are thought of as one large functioning unit, i.e. the perfect Exemplar or as the One. Older Cosmologists had conceived the idea of many entities. These were discarded by Plato, because he thought that it was impossible to penetrate material things by the power of concepts. Neither could conceptual thought grapple with the Infinite. Consequently, the world was ordered by the Mind or Soul. All this was very well and good as far as it went, but Plato could not adequately explain the chasm which existed between the Ideas of things and individual particulars. As a result what is left? Now there are two streams of thought, one representing Reality, and the other representing the particular material thing. In other words, we are left with a dualism, which Plato for all his brilliance in other fields failed to reconcile. We do not get an answer from Plato on how a tree can become a house or a table. Becoming in other words, is unexplainable.

We have to turn to Aristotle for an answer to these questions. The introduction of the doctrine of substantial form helped to solve the question of becoming. A sincere effort was made to form a synthesis of the One and the many, it was held that there were various creations within a species united together by the possession of a common form, this in no way incurring loss of individuality. Hylomorphism was the answer to the existence of things in the terrestrial world. But remarkable balance was maintained, with no leaning toward monism, that in turn would make it difficult to explain the many things in existence. An answer to existence was given, and at the same time an answer to why things become something else was provided. Aristotle also gave the ancient world the concept of the unmoved mover, which, whilst it served to explain why things moved, would also act as a unifying agent to material creation.

Now Plato had taught Exemplarism. Admittedly, the theory was not a perfect one, and Aristotle was not slow in pointing out where Plato had failed to justify his explanations. But he (Aristotle) did more than this. He rejected all exemplarism, yet insisted upon a final cause, with no worldly intermediary, the result being that again we are forced into dualism — this time between God and the independent world.

What happened after Aristotle? The Stoics will emphasize the One, the outcome of which is pantheism. On the contrary, the Epicureans will assert the power of the many, displaying a worldly science built really upon egoism. Gradually, however, we can see the converging of the elements of Pythagoreanism, Platonic, Aristotelian and Stoic elements fused in one philosophy, that of Neo-Platonism. This system showed the way to the solution of the age old problem of the many and the One. It said simply that the many must come from the One in some way. This would avoid Monism on the one hand and an independent world on the other. By introducing a scale of order in creation one above the other, these problems were avoided. But they gave rise to others. They spoke of "emanation" and steered a middle course between monism and the individual world. But what of creation out of nothing? This could not be satisfactorily answered by any Neo-Platonist or any other pagan philosophy, and we have to wait for the Christian era for any satisfactory solution.

But Greek philosophy can be viewed from another standpoint. In it we find genuine and sincere striving to know the final and real cause of the world. Now, intellectual effort of that description is very praiseworthy. Before Socrates, the "stuff" of the world was the consideration, and what is the permanent substratum which survives change? Plato to be consistent with his ideas must tend of an exemplary cause while asserting cause, mind and soul, broadening the material left by Anaxagoras. Aristotle was convinced that Plato ignored final causality, but in this he was wrong as exemplary causes are final causes also. Ideas and Ideals are convertible here. It is obvious that God acts for an end in the world, and Plato writes to this effect in the Timaeus. However, where Aristotle may have concluded that Plato ignored this fact of causes, may lie in the discrepancy shown in Plato's work between Exemplary and Efficient Cause. Neither does he show any imminent cause for terrestrial things, which Aristotle did do. Let us for a moment consider Aristotle's *final* Efficient and Exemplary Causes. God works as a Final Cause, but, owing to His changelessness, it is not clear how He can be at the same time an efficient cause of something. The fact that God is self sufficient would add to this difficulty. In other words, the philosopher failed to supply a final efficient cause. What were his probable views on this? Possibly, he thought that action by an Unmoved Mover is also a final efficient cause. This was all that was required, but this meant two things for Aristotle. It meant that the world was eternal and independent of God. It is absurd to think of an unmoved mover being responsible for the world's existence through the *unconscious* action of a final cause.

A necessary step was undoubtedly to form a synthesis of thought between Plato and Aristotle, and this was achieved by the Neo-Platonists. It is also true that Neo-Platonism as a philosophy was assisted by those small group of thinkers that immediately preceded it. But was this effort at unity successful? If we abide by the dictate of history, and the opinions of learned scholars, we must say that it was only partially so. Christianity on the other hand would successfully unite efficient, exemplary and final causes, in one all powerful God, the source of all creation.

In the consideration of Greek philosophy have we exhausted all the valid ways of examining it? The answer is no. There is the element of the individual, which we find in cosmology prior to Socrates. These thinkers thought of man as part of the world, and in the case of Heraclitus, we find him as the exponent of fire, whilst Leucippus thought of a human being in the terms of atoms. A step further will introduce us to the transmigration of souls apparent in Pythagorean philosophy. A step further again, and Empedocles will say that there is in the person some principle above matter, and it was this teaching that gave such splendid assistance to Plato, when he developed his philosophy. This angle of speculation is of a humanitarian nature, with the exception of Empedocles, levelling the person within the realm of matter. Socrates was interested in the person as a subject. Plato, however, depicted man as a creature with a will. He can be conscious of the values in life. Values that will enable him to lead either a good or bad life. He is shown also as an active member of a society. Plato wondered what is human nature like, what affects human behaviour, and consequently human society? In attempting to answer these questions, his researches were profound. But the outcome of this was to depict the human person as receiving reality from the immaterial world, and yet immersed in the fully material world below him.

It is true that Aristotle agreed with this idea of man as a form of half way Principle. Such also would be the opinion of Plato. Both these philosophers did not think of man as something final; over and above him there was a God who did not change, and contemplation of his Being represents the highest faculty in man. Psychology, behaviour and society were all dealt with by these thinkers. With Aristotle's work a curious position arises. In one phase, it was more human that that of Plato, in another less human. To illustrate: body and soul are closely unified with Aristotle, whilst basing our assumptions on an interpretation of De Anima, he does not identify an active intellect with all men, which would lead to a denial of the individual's immortality.

Despite these observations, Plato and Aristotle are two of the greatest thinkers the world has ever seen. Gradually man began to occupy the stage more and more, until we find in Roman times, human behaviour is the main point of issue. It led to the fine doctrines of the Stoa, Seneca, Marcus Aurelius and as an outstanding figure, Epictetus. To him, all men were brothers. The Stoics were concerned with moral behaviour, but it became clear that there is a great need in human nature for religion, which must be provided for. We find this idea developed in the notion of salvation, and finally in the teaching of Plotinus, when he envisaged an ecstatic union with the One. The Epicureans and Stoics will tend to a "levelling off" of the human person, but Neo-Platonism will strive to lead the soul straight to God.

But what of the science of knowledge or epistemology as it is called? Modern philosophy will claim that this branch of philosophy was a development of modern times, but this is not true in toto. The Middle Ages were interested in how a person knows, but even disregarding this, we can go to the ancients for vital points. On the other hand, it is true epistemology has made great strides in recent times, but this fact does not represent the whole picture.

In the case of the philosophers before Socrates, it was taken for granted that external things could be known. The Eleatic view of the problem was one of truth and one of opinion, though it is more than possible that they failed to realise the full complications of the question which they had opened up. This view is held here because of the Eleatic monism which denied sense experience. Such a position could eventually result in the undermining of metaphysics. Zeno, given as he was to great sweeps of dialectic, did not prevent the general trend of the Eleatics from being non-critical on the subject of knowledge.

With the Sophists relativity in thought made its appearance. Now this would involve implicit epistemology. Protagoras had said that man is the measure of all things. Very well, but in a wide sense what does this involve? It means he is the creator of his own independence, is foremost in ethics, and has complete access to metaphysical truth and makes his own moral values. What now was the relationship between Protagoras and theology? He mistrusted it. In addition, the Sophist view was that inquiry into the world was a waste of time. From this point on, if the Sophists had tried to show that human knowledge is derived from things, they would have entered the field of epistemology; in fact, however, their interest often strayed from philosophical paths. The importance of subject and object did not of necessity concern them. Therefore, the concept of knowledge did not develop and remained implicit.

The opposite was the case with Plato and Aristotle. The former had very clear ideas on what constituted knowledge, how it differed from opinion and imagination and so on. Moreover, he discussed reflective knowledge, and how mistakes can occur in the judgement — points not always recognized in dealing with this philosopher. We can take a step further, however, and class Plato as an epistemologist. Why? Because of his mighty concepts of an ascending scale of knowledge and their corresponding objects. Aristotle formulated a theory of abstraction, the mental image, and active and passive intellects.

When dealing with the Stagirite's philosophy on this subject, the two ways of looking at this question should be given due weight. They are "How do I know?" and "Can I know?" If we find an emphasis on the former in Aristotle's work, we will classify him as a psychologist. On the other hand, if we find emphasis upon the latter, we can consider him as an epistemologist. But the labels do not matter all that much; what is important is the fact that Aristotle considered the question of knowledge and advanced certain theories upon it.

Both Plato and Aristotle were quite decided in their views on knowledge. But at the same time Plato at least took for granted that it was possible for man to have knowledge at all. But in doing this, or in order to do it, he took from Heraclitus the fact of change, from the Sophists the relativity existing in sense, and from Pythagorean and Eleatic sources he accepted a rational element. If a mind is rational, it can then be superior to phenomena, and from Socrates, Plato took in germ, the idea of his metaphysics. Plato, like most Greeks at this time, was interested in Politics. For this reason, his ethics must submit to a change without value, and essences had to be recognized. But all this was certainly never questioned. He never queried what is technically called a priori elements in human knowledge. The same applies to Aristotle.

There is one main difference to note between the attitudes of Plato and Aristotle and modern epistemologists towards the problem of knowledge. In ancient times, the preoccupation seems to have been with *being;* nowadays it is with consciousness. This fact explains why the ancients, whilst remaining in a strict sense epistemologists, never questioned the ability of man to acquire the concepts of knowledge whereas today the great question is *"Can I know something?"*

Passing on to the Stoics and Epicureans actually they were compelled to take a stand on epistemology in order to support their philosophical ideas. Criticism was very severe, but as yet we have not arrived at the Kantian stage of a Critique of Pure Knowledge. The schools mentioned tried to find a dividing line between sense perception, imagination and hallucination.

Carneades in the New Academy will say there is no norm for truth, and it is not possible to acquire knowledge. Why make such a sweeping statement as this? Because he said that no sense perception is perfectly true and since intellectual knowledge is founded on sense, it is difficult to see, in the light of this, how it could be any more reliable than simple sense perception. Nor was this all, for the later Sceptics, worked out a dogmatic scheme for the relationship between sensation and judgement which process would turn them against the study of being qua "being." In short, epistemology did have a place in ancient thought, though

from a different standpoint to what it has nowadays, and a dogmatic approach is found to it above all others.

What was the attitude of ancient thinkers towards psychology?
Heraclitus related part of man to an ultimate Principle, whilst
Anaxagoras had been the first to use the concept of Nous or
Mind. However, the latter did not seem to be able to transfer the
idea of materialism purely by the power of speech. On the other
hand, Heraclitus had spoken of fire. Now, a human person according to Heraclitus was a purer form of this primary form of
fire. When we come to the Pythagoreans, they made a definite
distinction between soul and body. Metempsychosis was undoubtedly responsible for emphasis being put on this distinction,
for it led to the conclusion that there was no reason why a
particular soul should be involved with a particular body.

Let us see for a moment where the doctrine of Metempsychosis
can lead us. If I accept it, I must then accept the fact that memory
in the individual is not necessary in eternity. Nor is the fact that
I can reflect upon my actions necessary either. But if now I possess
both memory and reflection as integral parts of my soul, on the
basis of metempsychosis I can only go into eternity as an incomplete soul, since no explanation is given as to what happens to my
memory and reflection. Everything passes from something to something, and if the rest of me passes in this way, why does it not also
apply to the most important elements in my being?

It has been pointed out that the Pythagoreans had a great influence upon Plato. With this thinker, we find the soul as the principle of movement in man, also it is the field for the highest intellectual works. But it comes from "outside" and lives after the
body. According to Plato, the soul has parts. These parts are three
in number, the lowest part working on the body, the middle in
contact with reality, and the third with the supernatural. But Plato
was not interested in the soul, as a psychologist or biologist. His
interest in the soul was an ethical one. Always he was concerned
with an ethical standpoint, and this explains also his insistence
upon an adequate education. He maintained this view to the end
of his life. The importance here is to note that his emphasis was
ethical and not biological. Now let us turn to Aristotle.

The Stagirite opened his discussions upon the human soul after
the manner of Plato. That is to say, once again we find the insistence upon ethics. The highest part of man is the intellect which

is due to an exterior cause; it survives death and then we return once again to the accent placed on education for the soul's benefit. So far so good. But this is not the ultimate stamp that Aristotle placed on his psychology.

The characteristic here is one of biology. This view is taken as an overall view, and does not rest upon a cursory examination of any one particular work. Plato had treated the soul and the body as opposites. Aristotle with his doctrine of form gave the idea of something imminent, a particular body united to a particular soul. Certainly, the agent intellect survives death, but the whole conception would appear to be that the soul is dependent upon the body and when the latter dies, it affects the former. But the philosopher will not allow any idea of "making" by the Demiurge as Plato had done to explain where the soul came from in the first place. Memory, understanding, sensation, it is all a very empirical affair with Aristotle with consequent empirical explanations. It shows possibly that despite his attacks upon it, Aristotle was never perfectly free from the influence of his early Platonism. Also, a tension became apparent as time went on between this Platonism and his own ideas.

With the schools developing after Aristotle an important addition is seen. This is the advent of religion to the teaching on the soul. It culminated in Neo-Platonism, and through this doctrine can be seen the swing back to Platonism at the expense of Aristotle. This characteristic in philosophy was to persist for many centuries. Stoics and Epicureans were not in a position for a psychology that was a single study because their materialism demanded a certain approach and their ethics another approach. We must also admit that their studies in this respect were not as penetrating as they could have been. They did not worry about the nature or function of the soul, neither did they found a good psychology on an empirical basis. They were concerned with ethics and any psychology they may have developed was grafted upon ethical grounds. But all this was not without its side effects, for it focused attention on the religious, rather than the biological aspect of the soul. For ethical reasons the Epicureans denied the immortality of the soul, and held to its formation by the means of atoms. Now they did this not because they found out that the soul is made of atoms, but to coincide with their ethical beliefs. The psychology of the Epicureans fitted in much better with their ethics, than did the Stoic psychology and ethics. But Stoic psychology and Epicurean ethics were bound by a materialism which was hard to pierce.

But it does not matter in what era we find philosophy endeavouring to explain the psychical by material means — such an undertaking was always doomed to failure on account of faulty first principles, for it is not possible for the lesser to explain the greater. On the other hand, the psychical cannot be reduced to the material. Only in man are they intimately related while remaining distinct — indeed wondrous phenomena. Here we can enlist the services of both Plato and Aristotle for the former taught the distinction, whilst the latter emphasized their intimacy. If modern philosophy recognized this fact, it would avoid the pitfalls of idealism and suchlike.

It is necessary when treating of ethics to make a distinction between defined moral philosophy and ethical judgements made by particular persons. From the earliest times, the Greeks have made ethical judgements and the thought of the sages that followed from the Sophists to the Stoics simply reflected this trend in a greater or lesser degree, according to what was considered good morality at the prevailing time. But these moral judgements were dependent upon education, social life, tradition and so on. Clearly then, there must have been a difference in various countries when looking at the same moral problem.

In the face of this, two courses are open to philosophy. First, it can accept as natural behaviour the behaviour apparent in a certain community, and it can moreover assume that morality is relative because of these differences that are evident. There is no hard and fast rule. This was the Sophist approach.

Secondly, philosophy can lay emphasis upon the mistakes in moral attitude, at the same time holding to a firm and sure standard. Thus we have the approach of Plato and Aristotle. If mistakes occur in moral behaviour, it is due to error in the line of thought adopted. If a person pursues a purely self seeking path through life, this would seem to be a result of bad thinking on that person's part. But there are firm standards against which a person's behaviour may be measured, and Plato was quite decided about this.

This view is based on a concept of human nature, a line followed out by both Plato and Aristotle, and admitting of no variation. It is clear that man has certain powers or faculties which enable him to act virtuously. In this way, he can follow the good life. It is possible to form the ideal of man and also form an ideal of his moral activities. When these coincide there occurs the good man. Plato taught that God is always seeking to improve this ideal in human life. God and the ideal are never apart. He is always Reason and Divine Providence working for the good. He is the Creator of human reason, and indeed the Timaeus depicts Him as forming this specific attribute. What follows? If reason is formed by God, and is used by man, then he must be close to God; indeed he must be meant to work for God. Thus is his purpose in this life on earth. The standard is set up by God for man to work to, and this conflicts with Protagoras who taught the norm was set up by man. Obligation in a moral sense certainly is not brought out much, but it is impossible that the mental outlook that Plato would acquire from Socrates would obscure the concept of moral responsibility. Be that as it may, the Greek myths of reward and punishment dimly assisted to give a vague background of obligation. Plato did much to specify the content of the moral law, but did not carry this through to its conclusion.

It was left to Aristotle to develop the ideas of form. He did this very thoroughly and was very systematic in the process, but this resulted in the loss of Plato's transcendental values. Aristotle would encourage man to direct his energies to God, to that which was best. But it all seems a very empirical affair. This point is shown well, where in the Metaphysics, God is shown as being so far above the world, He does not work actively within it. If a man were to inquire of Aristotle what is the real obligation of living a life according to the Ethics what could the philosopher say? He could appeal to a right course of action, to the pursuit of happiness, and show that bad action would be the opposite of these. But he could not appeal to a transcendental reality, because in his system this reality was so far removed from the needs of everyday life.

But this was not entirely the case with later thinkers. All saw the necessity of an absolute norm of social behaviour; some like the Stoics would take it as based on Divine will, and upon reason which is in accordance with nature. All comes from God and returns to Him. Looking at the ethical standpoint from a purely worldly view made their doctrines hard to unify, but at least there was the fact that God's will was recognized. This could not be said of the Epicureans.

With Neo-Platonism the accent was on religion. Man's ethics was very much bound up with his struggle to get to God, but morals qua morals were simply a part of this journey. By acting in a moral way, a person is one with the required standard.

Again, those thinkers who were teaching this line of thought, saw it was necessary that the idea of God should predominate, and also that of Divine Providence. Now ethics had a sure foundation, for it takes its roots in being, and if a Supreme Being is made predominant the science of ethics can become a sure one, founded upon metaphysics.

But was not Greek philosophy a basis for Christianity? It most surely was, and this can be traced through right from the time of Heraclitus. This philosopher had conceived the idea of Reason in the world, operation as the Logos through the material element of Fire. This concept was taken up by the Stoics in later times. Then Anaxagoras talks of the Nous or Mind as a first principle. But it was Plato who was the first to formulate a natural theology. Before this there are but hints of God. The Pythagoreans formed a distinction of soul and body, but generally speaking in pre-Socratic times, the aim was to find an explanation of the world. Still, this line of reasoning could raise the question of a Supreme Being. But as we have pointed out it was to Plato with his doctrines of exemplarism and transcendence that Reason and Mind made an ever lasting mark on human thinking. Nor was this all. He taught man was immortal and rational, also the doctrine of retribution and psychology and asceticism. Plato went on to lay down a firm moral basis for behaviour, which owes a lot to Socrates, nevertheless, it provided the foundations for Christian ethics. To be specific, it is in the Laws that Plato points to the necessity of a mind, but probably, it is the overall ethics of the Greek philosopher's whole system which culminates in the idea of transcendency which to a great extent paved the way for the acceptance of Christian thought. Not only did Platonism provide the idea of transcendency, it also fostered actions of Providence, a right sense of values, immortality, etc. All these would assist Christianity in its march forward. It is a paradox, but a true one, that some of these principles were used by the adherents of Neo-Platonism to combat Christianity. Their argument was that the Incarnation is not in keeping with God's transcendental character. But eventually this objection fell to pieces, and one of the contributing factors to this was the philosophy of Plato replacing the material philosophies that had previously been followed. The spiritual element of Platonism helped to encourage Christianity, of that there can be little doubt.

On the other hand, it would be the height of foolishness to ignore the incomparable contribution that Aristotle made to Christianity. He was and is simply *the* philosopher. His natural theology as displayed in the Metaphysics with its superb scientific approach, became at the hands of St. Thomas Aquinas, the Christian natural theology. Observe however, that St. Thomas was never loath to adopt a principle that was apparent in Platonic thought if it assisted the search for truth.

Aristotle had become known to the Christian world through Arabian translations of his works. So naturally, this would lead to Arabian commentators. One of these, Averroës, concluded that the Greek philosopher had meant to infer that there was no personal immortality of the human soul. Apart from this in Aristotle, God is found as transcendence, Thought, an Absolute Final Cause. Later on the Platonic Ideas will be placed in the Mind of God, and in addition, we will be provided with an Efficient, Exemplary and Final Cause. All this will make the path of Christianity an easier one.

After Aristotle, various schools of thought had elements to offer the Christian faith. Amongst these were the Stoics with their noble concept of ethics, despite its overall tendency to become determinist. But from it one gains the impression of the brotherhood of man with God, self control and moral education by acceptance of the Divine Will. It was probably this insistence on brotherhood with God that gave to Christianity that impetus which Stoic philosophy by itself lacked. Now, Christianity had to teach masses of people moral behavior. Countless numbers of these people lacked the chance of a higher education. Consequently, the Christian faith had to build on sound principles apart from these it received by Revelation. The Stoic moral ethic provided part of this need, Christianity offered so much to the ordinary person and held out a reward in the after life in a manner beyond Stoic thinking.

In dealing with human nature, however, we must go beyond the stage of ethics. We must enter that field sacred to God and to many men, the field of religion. It is so obvious that man has a deep need of religion and Neo-Platonism had tried to satisfy the cravings of the human heart in this direction. As they tried to satisfy, so they drew more attention to this subject than normally would be the case. Consequently, Christian seed fell on fertile ground. The Church with its Sacraments overshadowed a philosophical system that appealed strongly to the intellect alone, and further Christianity was historical. It was historical in the sense that Our Lord was born, suffered, and died at a specific time, in a specific place. As such, it was opposite to a myth. This was a background beyond the scope of Neo-Platonism. On the other hand, Christianity offered salvation to all men, whatever their standing in life. Moreover, a system that was historical would appeal much more than a philosophy that displayed great facility in metaphysics. Neo-Platonism in one sense was bound with mystery; so was Christianity. The former may have wished to rival the Christian world. By so doing they barred many from entering Christianity. Notably Plotinus and Porphyry were two of these. But when we consider St. Augustine, we find his way to the Christian faith was shown him by Plotinus. Christianity was not a continuation of pagan teaching. Neither is it to be confused with a philosophical system. It is Revelation founded upon the Jews; *but* when the Christians began to think and ask questions, they found the ancients had left such a store of knowledge behind them as to attest to the everlasting glory of the human mind.

We have seen various opinions stated here where some historians of philosophy considered systems developing in a natural unruffled succession. As history, the fact of them following one another is true, but psychologically, this opens the door on many problems not dealt with to date by these writers. They did not allow for the divergent views in human thinking which are themselves the product of implicit and explicit reasoning.

Neither was any attempt made to show the difference between what is plainly a perversion or corruption and true development. With respect to implicit and explicit reasoning, they are not the same thing; thought is at once spontaneous and living. Now the growth of any dogma or doctrine is always implicit. It results from individual dispositions of the person who holds them, as we have indicated before in this work. These include birth, early parental, and early scholastic experiences, mental equipment, outlook and so on. It could almost be thought of as a moral issue. We have tried to demonstrate here how various persons, as the result of the above, conceived their ideas of their personal philosophy. Further, the needs of teaching, of conveying their thought to others would compel the thinkers dealt with here to necessarily formulate propositions and finally merge these into a system. Both Plato and Aristotle did this most effectively.

It may be that a particular thinker entertains personal opinions which in fact rebel against what is the true content at the deepest level of his being. In this case, the views held, philosophical or otherwise, will be the result of local environment. As the result of the conflict in such a person, the views will be insincere and probably unstable.

What of explicit reasoning? This could be described as a technical process of principle to conclusion, and a great mind does not act in this specific way, but the capacity for experience which it possesses, outweighs by far the power of conventional formulae. Such minds also we have met in these pages.

To our last points, we may say that a corruption can in reality be applied to that which is arranged. A material substance can be crushed but not corrupted. Corruption in itself is the breaking up of life, prior to its end. The body resolves itself into its component parts before this dissolution. The demolition is a reversal of all that has gone before it. Till this is reached, the body follows its own laws, with an aim and direction in its actions.

Now philosophy has always done this, indeed it is still doing it today. It is, in the question of philosophy, more the relation of one system to another which we have tried to show. These systems form one mighty organic whole. If philosophy were but a simple process of development it would hardly have parts. In that way, it could be said to be simple in the way that some have envisaged. But it has a multiplicity of parts, and this makes for its complexity. It is not suggested for one moment that they did not realize philosophy had parts. Purely as an historical fact have we tried to show that a *natural* development of *one* of these philosophies is not an adequate standpoint to treat of what actually did take place for all human thought is not uniform.

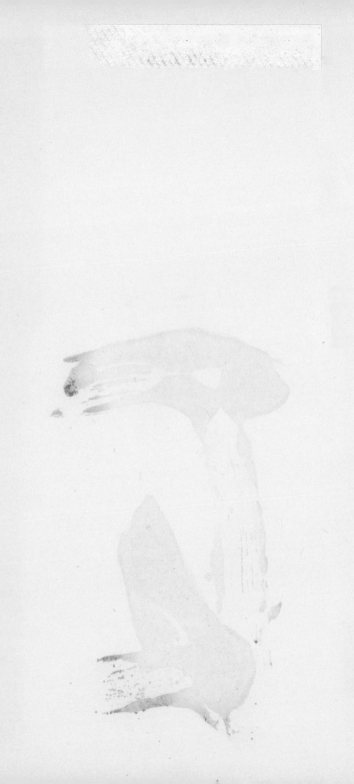